INSIGHT GUIDES

The world's largest collection of visual travel guides

Barcelona

Edited by Andrew Eames
Commissioning Editor in Spain: Don Murray
Managing Editor: Roger Williams

Editorial Director: Brian Bell

APA PUBLICATIONS
Part of the Langenscheidt Publishing Group

L

Eames

Thomson

Caldentey

Fernández-Armesto

INSIGHT GUIDES
Barcelona

CONTACTING THE EDITORS: Although every effort is made to provide accurate information in this publication, we live in a fast-changing world and would appreciate it if readers would call our attention to any errors or outdated information that may occur by writing to us at Apa Publications,
P.O. Box 7910, London SE1 8ZB, England.
Fax: (44) 171-620-1074.
e-mail: insight@apaguide.demon.co.uk.

First Edition 1990
Second Edition 1995
Second Edition (Updated) 1998

Distributed in the United States by
Langenscheidt Publishers Inc.
46–35 54th Road
Maspeth
NY 11378
Fax: (718) 784 0640

Distributed in the UK & Ireland by
GeoCenter International Ltd
The Viables Centre, Harrow Way
Basingstoke, Hampshire RG22 4BJ
Fax: (44) 1256-817988

Worldwide distribution enquiries:
APA Publications GmbH & Co. Verlag KG
(Singapore branch)
38 Joo Koon Road
Singapore 628990
Tel: 65-8651600
Fax: 65-8616438

Printed in Singapore by
Insight Print Services (Pte) Ltd
38 Joo Koon Road
Singapore 628990
Fax: 65-8616438

Barcelona is a city set for the 21st century. In recent years it has been dramatically remodelled, but it remains eternally stylish, keeping the best of its grand historic sites and matching them with consummate skill to designs for modern life. Duality is something the city thrives on: the streak of rational conservatism that Catalans call *seny* lives side by side with *rauxa*, irrational and creative dynamism.

The result is a city of enormous excitement, which lends itself well to the approach taken by the 190-title award-winning *Insight Guides* series created in 1970.

The books are carefully structured: the first section covers a destination's history, and then culture in a series of magazine-style essays. The main Places section provides a comprehensive run-down of the things worth seeing and doing, with a little bit of gossip thrown in for good measure. Finally, a fact-packed listings section contains all the information you'll need on travel, hotels, shops, restaurants and opening times. Complementing the text, remarkable photography sets out to communicate directly and provocatively life as it is lived by the locals.

Insight Guide: Barcelona is one of the eight books on Spain by the Insight team. The other titles are *Madrid, Southern Spain, Catalonia, Mallorca and the Balearics, Tenerife and the Western Canaries, Gran Canaria and the Eastern Canaries* and, covering the whole country, *Spain,* which won the prestigious Vega Inclan award.

The editor of *Insight Guide: Barcelona* was **Andrew Eames**. He first came across Insight Guides while working in South-east Asia as a young aspiring journalist. Since then, he has published his travel autobiography, *Crossing the Shadow Line,* and a travel book, *Four Scottish Journeys.* After editing this fully revised edition of *Insight Guide: Barcelona,* he says: "The city has changed so much in just a few years, mostly for the better. The modern architecture is definitely on the tourist route now, and the new waterfront has made a fundamental difference in the city's whole outlook."

Murray

Pascual

Semler

Working with Eames was **Don Murray**, a Canadian photojournalist who had contributed to *Insight Guide: Mallorca*. Murray started taking pictures while a pilot in the Canadian Air Force, turned his hobby into a profession by starting to write, and has had published seven books about the architecture of Mallorca. Murray ransacked the press corps of Barcelona for suitable writers for this book and saw the text through its translation stage; his pictures also feature in these pages. With the assistance of **Ana Pascual** he checked the accuracy and the Catalan content of the book. Pascual is a Mallorquine who went to university in Barcelona, from where she travelled extensively through Europe and North America. Back in Mallorca, she dedicates herself to research and journalism, sometimes in collaboration with Don Murray.

Carme Riera (who writes about the Catalan language) is one of the best-known Catalan writers. Her prize-winning novels have run through 30 editions, and have been translated into Castilian, German, Dutch, Greek, Russian, Czech and English. Riera teaches Spanish literature at Barcelona University.

Lluís Permanyer, who wrote the chapter on football, was a staff writer for the Barcelonan newspaper *La Vanguardia* and is considered to be the chronicler of the city. He has a law degree and has written 20 books, mostly art-orientated, and the libretto of an opera.

Like Permanyer, **Berta Caldentey** (chapters on Museums and Art and Inspiration) is also a born-and-bred Barcelonan who writes for newspapers and magazines, specialising in interviews with cultural celebrities and has worked for the publishers Circulo de Lectores.

For the past quarter of a century **Marcelo Aparicio** (chapters on the Plaça de Catalunya, the Gothic Quarter, the Jews, the Eixample and Shopping) has been dropping in and out of journalism, experimenting with a hippy life in Ibiza and running his own restaurant.

Xavier Martí was born in the Empúries region of Catalonia, which is much affected by the cold Tramuntana wind. He says he has had the writing bug since an early age, although he has tried to cure himself of it by small doses of contributions to most of Barcelona's newspapers, and in being involved with the launch of one. Martí wrote the chapters on the Ramblas, Montjuïc, the Waterfront and the Columbus Monument.

The history section of this book is the work of **Dr Felipe Fernández-Armesto**, fellow of St Antony's College, Oxford, and historian of three previous Insight Guides. Dr Fernández-Armesto worked on the Oxford University Press history of Spain, and since the first edition of this book was published, has written his own book on the city: *Barcelona: A Thousand Years of the City's Past*.

Three long-time resident foreigners in Barcelona were invaluable for their contributions. **George Semler** (chapters on Around Barcelona and on the Cosmopolitan City) is an American writer who has been living in the city for most of his working life. His children are multilingual in Catalan, Castilian and English. He has written a book on walks in the city and was a contributor to Insight Guide: Catalonia. **Geraldine Mitchell** (co-author of the chapters on the People) is an Irish journalist and some time resident of the city. **Judy Thomson**, who is by turns translator, public relations advisor and journalist, is a long-time resident of the *barri* Gòtic. She compiled the exhaustive Travel Tips section, wrote the chapters on the Olympics and New Look for the Nineties and keeps the book up to date.

Wassman

Martí

The photographs are primarily the work of **Bill Wassman**, an American with a real passion for Spain. **George Wright**, a British photographer who works extensively for UK colour magazines, produced some of the book's best portraits.

The translation work on the original Spanish texts was undertaken by **Nikki Cleugh**, the bilingual deputy editor on *Balearic Homes and Living*, published in Mallorca.

In London, Insight Guides' editorial centre, **Jill Anderson** skilfully marshalled the original text through a variety of Macintosh computers and the proof-reading and indexing for the previous revised edition were completed by **Jane Hutchings**.

CONTENTS

CONTENTS

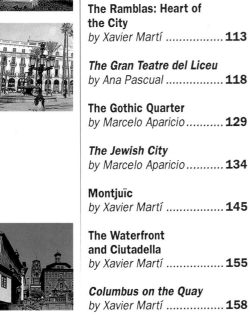

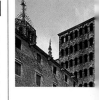

Barcelona is the heart, lungs and legs of Catalonia, which itself is the leading economic region of Spain. Covering 6.3 percent of the country's land mass and supporting 15.5 percent of the population, Catalonia produces 19.3 percent of the nation's gross domestic product. A remarkable 71 per cent of the region's people live in the greater metropolitan area of Barcelona itself (3.5 million in the metropolis, 1.6 million in the municipal area), jammed between the hills of Tibidabo, Montjuïc and the sea. Barcelona is the largest city on the Mediterranean seaboard.

Catalonia was once a state in its own right and many Barcelonans still believe that the region deserves more autonomy from the rest of Spain than it currently has. Certainly, Barcelona is like no other Spanish city. It has its own language and its own culture and customs. The Barcelonans are unlike most other Spaniards; they are more introverted, more work-motivated, more self-conscious, more difficult to get to know.

Perhaps because of the Catalans' own insistence on separateness, their city has had a turbulent past, caught between the various powers of Europe in its allegiances against Madrid. Its growth reflects the eras of its greatest successes, from the Roman walls, through the Gothic Quarter to the palaces of the 17th century, right up to the 19th-century Eixample. In its latest phase, the city reflects the work done for the 1992 Olympic Games, acknowledged around the world as a triumph for Barcelona. It transformed the waterfront, created whole new districts, and was a catalyst for a series of building works and changes to prepare the city for the 21st century.

The Catalan character has had to go underground so often that it expresses itself in surprising ways. The Eixample is studded with the extrovert work of modernist architects, of whom Gaudí was one; the Barcelona football club – a sort of unofficial army – has a vociferous following which sees goals as assertions of the Catalan identity. At times the club has been virtually shut down by central government, or forced to share its best players with Madrid.

All in all, it is a city with a lot to offer, and one which has repeatedly and insistently thrust itself to the forefront of European cities. In *Don Quixote*, Miguel de Cervantes wrote: "Barcelona: innately courteous, offering shelter to the travel-weary, hospitals for the poor, home for the brave, revenge for the offended, reciprocating friendship and unique in situation and beauty". This insistent city is worth getting to know.

Preceding pages: big dipper on Tibidabo hill; strange figure from the Wax Museum; the fishing port; windows on Gaudí's Casa Batlló; designer shop-window on Passeig de Gràcia. **Left**, downtown and the Sagrada Família seen from Montjuïc.

Barcelona has all the amenities of a great metropolis and all the self-consciousness of a capital city, but much of its dynamism has come from always having had something to prove, and its history is very largely one of achievements incubating in frustration.

Its citizen-historians have attributed to it a myth of ancient splendour which is unjustified by the facts. In the Middle Ages it was the centre of the greatest Mediterranean empire since Roman times, but never became a sovereign city in its own right, like Venice or Genoa. Until 1716 it was the capital of the nominally sovereign Catalan state and twice fought bloody wars against the rest of Spain to defend that status; but it never became a seat of government in modern times and, with the absorption of Catalonia into the Spanish monarchy, came to be ruled from a distance by its upstart rival, Madrid, an altogether younger city.

In the 19th century, it remained the centre of an increasingly vibrant Catalan national culture, which led to further conflicts – some of them bloody – over its constitutional relationship to the rest of Spain.

City of prodigies: The Barcelonans have never reconciled themselves to living in a provincial Spanish city and have always given themselves rival identities, be they Catalan, European or Mediterranean. In the past hundred years or so, Barcelona has been a "city of prodigies" (the title of Mendoza's book on the city which charts the period between the great exhibitions of 1888 and 1929), rising in economic stature to become the heart of the biggest conurbation of the Mediterranean coastline, and culturally acknowledged as one of the liveliest artistic centres in Europe.

But the rapidity and fragility of this rise, and its dependence on Barcelona's role as a Spanish city, making or purveying goods to a protected Spanish market, have been obscured by the myths of a long and glorious history of continuous greatness and of fidelity to Catalan tradition.

Roman rule: Although the Roman colony that preceded the modern city fed well off its "sea of oysters" and served rich men with such civilised amenities as porticoed baths and a forum with seven statues, it was always a small town of up to 25 to 30 acres (10 to 12 hectares) – to judge from the circuit of the walls, some of which are still standing. These

are dwarfed by those easily visited at nearby Tarragona and Empúries.

For Catalan historians, it used to be a point of honour to imagine antique greatness and "continuity" stretching back to the primeval forebears of modern Catalans. But, although the whole plain of Barcelona was well populated from neolithic times, and coins minted in the area prove the existence of a pre-Roman urban civilisation, no evidence of continuous settlement of the central site of historic Barcelona, on Mont Tàber, earlier than the 1st century AD has yet been found.

Pre-Roman Barkeno, a name found on

Left, 16th-century altar urn from Tarragona. **Right,** walls from the small Roman town still surround the Gothic Quarter.

early coins, may have been on the hill of Montjuïc, which the Romans inherited as a ritual centre: finds from here include an impressive Roman magistrate's seat, set ceremonially in the remains of some sort of stone enclosure.

Quiet years: For half a millennium after the end of Roman rule, Barcelona's history remains sparsely documented. Of the occupiers of those years – the Visigoths, the Moors, the Franks – only the first seem to have esteemed the city highly. According to the earliest historian of the Goths, pity for the inhabitants of Hispania, smarting under the blows of less romanised barbarians, moved

the Visigothic chief Athaulf to seize Barcelona "with his best men", leaving those "less adept in arms" to occupy the interior. This suggests that Barcelona was thought particularly desirable, or defensible, or both.

Narrators of the next century of Gothic history continue to associate Barcelona with politically important events: Athaulf was assassinated there, Amalaric was murdered in the city, and shortly after, in 540, Barcelona was the meeting-place of a synod.

Its modest growth during the Visigothic period can be detected in the excavations under the Palau Reial. Evidence here suggests that between the 4th and 6th centuries, the *intervallum* between the Roman building line and the ramparts was filled with new constructions. At the same time, streets were narrowed by building extensions. A building of noble dimensions appeared on part of the present palace site, which may have housed the royal assassination victims.

In this period the city was still without long-distance commerce and, for the Moors and Franks, seems to have been significant only as a frontier garrison or *ville-carrefour*.

Barcelona's potential for greatness only began to be realised when it was conquered, late in the 9th century, by the nascent Catalan state. This was a principality of regional importance, with its heartlands close by, its granary in the plain of Urgell and its defences in the mountains. Its warrior paladins adopted Barcelona as their favourite place of residence; they endowed it with religious foundations which stimulated urban growth; they kept – and sometimes spent – their treasure there; and as the state developed, they concentrated their court and counting-houses in Barcelona.

Wilfred the Hairy: Of the man acclaimed as the "founder" of the House of the Counts of Barcelona, little trace survives in the modern city: only the visitor brave enough to enter the dark alley of the Carrer d'Amargos, with its straggling balcony-plants and dangling laundry, will find the painted ceramic plaque proclaiming – almost certainly wrongly – that this was the limit of the palace of Count Wilfred the Hairy (who died in 898). The count, in a series of campaigns in the late 870s, united the hinterland of Barcelona with most of the other Frankish counties south of the Pyrenees.

By the early 10th century, Barcelona was already, in a sense, the "capital" of sovereign Catalonia. In about 911, Count Wilfred II chose a house of religion outside the walls for his mausoleum. His neglected grave, marked by an inscription discovered among rubble, deserved better treatment from the Barcelonans; for it was this sort of patronage, bestowing princely status on Barcelona, that began to turn the former hick-town into a medieval metropolis.

For the next 200 years, Barcelona's wealth

continued to come mostly from war and the agricultural produce of the plain. Its courtly status was its main source of urban character.

The first known boom happened in the late 10th century. Most historians have assumed that this must have been the result of commercially generated wealth; but there is no evidence to support that conjecture and it is at least as likely that the simple presence of the knights, the court and the growing colony of clergy were the sources of stimulation.

Early expansion: The growth of the cathedral chapter is the first clue to the city's growth: there were six canonries in 974, 17 by 1005. The canons were growing in soph-

prestige to attract a raid by al-Mansur, the predatory vizir of Córdoba. The raid inspired traditional lamentations, with lists of buildings destroyed and martyrdoms incurred; but, except for Sant Pere de les Puelles, which was burned with all its inmates, real losses seem to have been slight and, by encouraging rebuilding, al-Mansur may actually have stimulated the boom.

The Moorish threat did not long survive al-Mansur's death in 1002. By 1010 a raid on Córdoba by a large expedition of Catalans dramatically illustrated how the roles of victim and prey had been reversed. The empire of Córdoba was enfeebled by politics at the

istication as well as in numbers: retiring to houses of their own; acquiring a reputation for erudition; building up libraries – since disappeared – worthy, in one instance, of attracting a reader as famous for his learning as the future pope, Gerbert of Aurillac. They were not the only people building in the city, and the first satellite villages began to grow up outside the walls.

In 989 Barcelona was a target of sufficient

Left, Wilfred the Hairy, credited as the founder of modern Barcelona. **Above**, Roman remains in the Plaça Vila de Madrid.

centre and eroded by usurpations at the edges. In the 1030s it dissolved into small, competing successor-states. Like much of the rest of Christian Spain, Barcelona began to enjoy a bonanza on the proceeds of booty, tribute, ransom, payola and the wages of mercenaries.

An illumination in the *Liber Feudorum* (which can be seen by appointment in the Arxiu de la Corona d'Aragó, Carrer dels Comtes) shows Count Ramon Berenguer I counting out coins from a lapful of gold into his hand, for the price of the counties of Carcassonne and Béziers, which he bought.

The sort of expansion his forebears could contemplate only by conquest, he could undertake by purchase.

Golden age: By the 1070s, 95 percent of transactions in Barcelona were made in gold – a level never again attained in the city's history. Some of this money was invested in a maritime enterprise which for the next 500 years supplied the city's wealth and formed its character. In 1060, although Barcelona was already a "great town", according to the fastidious chronicler al-Bakri, the Barcelonans were still hiring their galleys from Moorish ports. By 1080 the counts possessed a fleet of their own, though it may not have been based in Barcelona.

Two charters of Ramon Berenguer III (who ruled 1082–1131) mention what sounds like substantial seaborne trade. In 1104 he granted a tenth of dues paid on "all goods that come in on any ship in all my honour"; in the following year four Jews were granted a monopoly of the shipping home of ransomed Moorish slaves. That some, at least, of this trade was going through Barcelona is suggested by the terms of privileges Ramon Berenguer granted to Genoa and Pisa in 1116, easing the tolls of goods beached in Barcelona.

Despite the deficiencies of its shoaly harbour, Barcelona was the point of departure for a fleet big enough to attempt the conquest of Mallorca – 500 vessels strong, according to the undoubtledly exaggerated report of the poet of the *Liber Maidiolichinus*, who accompanied the expedition and extolled its heroic failure in epic verse.

International commerce continued to develop gradually and in 1160 Benjamin of Tudela reported vessels of "Pisa, Genoa, Sicily, Greece, Alexandria and Asia" off the beach of Barcelona.

Architectural remains: Most of the buildings of this period were replaced in later eras of even greater prosperity: only Sant Pau del Camp, Santa Llucia and the Capella de Marcús remain. For a flavour of what Catalonia was like in the 11th and 12th centuries the visitor to Barcelona must go to the Museu de l'Art de Catalunya (MNAC), on Montjuïc, where the collection of murals transferred from rural churches shows the high quality of work that Catalan money could buy. The murals show the search for classical and Byzantine models by the artists: the wolf of Sant Joan de Boi bares predatory teeth as he starts around in a classical pose; the Seraphim of the apse with their feathery, eyed wings recall Byzantine mosaics.

In the streets, the explorer can match the map to documents that record the expansion of the 12th-century city. In 1160, Ramon Berenguer IV gave permission for a new public bath outside the city wall, where today the Carrer dels Banys Nous (literally "street of the new baths") curves in the spectral shadow of lost ramparts: the profits of this enterprise were to be divided equally between the count and the Jewish investor.

Merits of conquest: The winds and currents of the western Mediterranean meant that Barcelona had to solve its problem of access to the Balearic Islands, to become a great centre of long-distance commerce, rivalling Genoa and Pisa. An illumination in Barcelona University library shows a leading merchant of the city, entertaining the count-king "and the greater part of the nobles of Catalonia" in November or December 1228, and persuading them of the merits of conquering the islands.

In his extraordinary *Book of Deeds*, Jaume I (who reigned between 1213–76) identified his own motives for launching the conquest of the Balearics as essentially chivalric: there was more honour in conquering a single kingdom "in the midst of the sea, where God has been pleased to put it" than three on dry land. To chivalric and crusading satisfactions, the nobles who took part added substantial territorial rewards. The Barcelonans, however, and the other merchant-communities of the Catalan and Provençal worlds, needed little inducement. Their participation is explained by commercial motives: the anxiety to break the entrenched position of Moorish traders and their privileged partners from Genoa and Pisa.

Like so many imperial adventures, Barcelona's acquisition of a Mediterranean empire, beginning in the Balearics, marked the apogee of its achievement and sowed the seeds of its decline. The marks of both are everywhere in the old city today, in the form of great churches begun in the 13th or 14th centuries; in vast ritual and even industrial spaces that survive from that time; in building works slowed or halted in the 15th century and in decayed aristocratic streets of the late Middle Ages. The new walls of the reign of Jaume I enclosed an area more than 10 times greater than those they replaced.

The cathedral is the dominant monument of the 13th century: the cloister portal, with its obscure carving of harpies and wild men dragging a half-naked, pudge-faced warrior, contrasts with the elegant High Gothic of the west front and the interior.

The early 14th century, when the profits of magistrates, could dent the city's confidence or interrupt the building boom. Never was the city so spectacularly embellished as in the reign of Pere III (1336–87); he built the vaulted halls – more reminiscent of Italy than Spain – of the Saló de Cent (Plaça de Sant Jaume) and the Saló de Tinell, with its martial wall-paintings, in the palace of the Plaça del Rei. Pere III also rebuilt the shipyards on a larger scale, where galleys for the Mediterranean war effort had been built since the reign of Pere II (1276–85): the eight great bays of the Drassanes at the foot of the Ramblas can still be visited, and now house the Maritime Museum.

empire were perhaps at their height, was a time of frenzied building. The chapel of San Agata, in the count-kings' palace (the Palau Reial in the Plaça del Rei), was built by Jaume II (who died in 1327). The first stone of the church of El Pi was laid in 1322, that of Santa Maria del Mar, which still has its medieval glazing largely intact, in 1329.

Not even the Black Death – which killed half the city council and four of the five chief

Above, Ramon Berenguer, who presided over Barcelona's hyperactive trading period in the 12th century.

Private builders were also active. An example of late medieval urbanisation, the Carrer de Montcada, was driven through the old town in a broad, straight line and promptly colonised by the aristocracy: the modern visitor, seeking the street for the sake of the Picasso Museum, runs the risk of being more impressed by the medieval architecture of the street's palaces.

Price of conquest: The trading empire which paid for this was essentially a western Mediterranean affair. The deeds of Catalans in the east – of mercenaries in Thrace and Athens, of merchants in Alexandria and Constantinople – are justly renowned. But they took place in the wings of the main theatre. The conquest by Barcelona's count-kings, or their subjects, of Mallorca (1229), Ibiza (1235), Sicily (1282), Menorca (1287) and Sardinia (1324), and the territorial extension by a series of treaties from 1271 gave the count-kings something like a protectorate over a number of Maghribi ports: these were the landmarks of an empire of grain and gold, of silver and salt.

As the empire grew, its costs came to exceed its benefits. Mallorca proved a thankless daughter, sustaining a turbulent political relationship with the count-kings and using

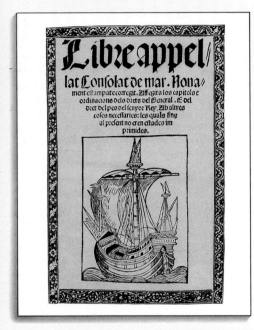

Catalan knowledge to set up shipping, arms and textile industries in competition with Barcelona's own. The ambition to control the western Mediterranean sea lanes caused wars with Genoa which were wasteful because Barcelona never had sufficient resources to exploit its victories. Above all, Sardinia was Barcelona's "Spanish ulcer"; the city seems largely to have borne the costs of conquest of the island by itself, with little support from the count-kings' other realms, while Sardinian resistance lasted, intermittently, for a hundred years, and exhausted the over-committed conquerors.

The empire which made a metropolis of Barcelona also sucked the rural life-blood out of Catalonia: as the centre of gravity of the count-kings' realms moved towards the city, the balance of population shifted. On the eve of the Black Death, Barcelona contained 20 percent of the population of Catalonia. The countryside could no longer keep the armies supplied with men or, perhaps, the city with food. In 1330 Barcelona experienced its first serious famine.

Never was a city more obviously the victim of its own success. Barcelona evinced the classic symptoms of the monster: corpulence induced by overfeeding, tentacles grown to uncontrollable lengths. Yet resolute civic spirit remains etched into the faces of the élite depicted, for instance, in Lluís Dalmau's *La Verge dels Consellers*, painted in 1443 to project a magnificent image of the city magistracy in the intimate company of heavenly protectors. Today the painting can be seen in the Museu de l'Art de Catalunya (MNAC) in the Palau Nacional on Montjuïc.

The passing of glory: Like the similar problem of the "decline" of Spain in the 17th century, that of the decline of Catalonia in the 15th has to be treated cautiously. Though it appears with hindsight that by the end of the century the gravity of power in the Iberian peninsula had shifted forever towards the centre, the experience in Catalonia seems too mottled with short-term checks, leaps and lurches to justify the use of a sweeping term like "decline", except in a relative sense: especially in the late 15th century, the neighbouring kingdoms of France and Castile were developing the means to mobilise unprecedented strength. Barcelona's 15th century, however, was at best an "era of difficulties" involving progressive exhaustion to ultimate prostration, redeemed only by the extraordinary mental resilience of an indomitably optimistic ruling class.

The city's predicament was a mixture of social violence, demographic stagnation and economic constraint. In the century after 1360, not a decade went by without a recurrence of plague, sometimes accompanied by famine; from 1426, the yield of the customs and wool tax plummeted and did not recover until the next century. Hearth-counts suggest a modest increase in population until the cataclysmic civil war of the 1460s: the count of 1500, showing 5,765 hearths, probably represents the lowest tally of households since the Black Death.

The protracted insecurity of this era of difficulties was bound to cause social tension. The first uncontrollable outburst was the pogrom of 1391, when the authorities were powerless to protect the Jews from massacre. In 1436 and 1437 popular agitations were effectively suppressed, but by the mid-century the failures of the city's natural rulers had attracted the sympathy of the city governor for a movement to democratise the

long run unseat the traditional ruling élite, but left it enfeebled and embittered against the count-king Joan II. His unpopularity grew as he tried to exploit Catalonia in what was felt to be a private attempt to meddle in Castile; he exacerbated his relations with his subjects by attempting to exclude his son and one of his daughters from succession to the throne. By appealing to popular elements in the towns and the peasants in the country, he alienated urban patricians and rural aristocrats alike.

Failed pretenders: As a result, no part of the realm entered the rebellion of 1462 more wholeheartedly than Barcelona; none suf-

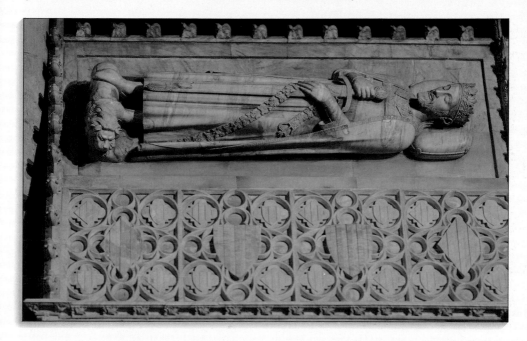

municipal institutions or – at least – to enlarge the élite. The name of the incumbent party, the *Biga*, probably signifies a large beam used in the construction of a building; that of the challengers, the *Busca*, a piece of tinder or bunch of kindling. The names evoke the natures of the parties: the solidity of the establishment, the incendiary menace of its opponents.

Their conflict in the 1450s did not in the

fered so much from the results. The insurgents' cause, never very promising, became desperate as each of the pretenders they put up to challenge the king died or dropped out in turn.

The siege that ended resistance in 1473, followed by punitive measures, left Barcelona devastated. "Today no trade at all is practised in this city," the *consellers* wrote. "Not a bolt of cloth is seen. The workers are unemployed and the men of property are deprived of their rents and goods... And of all our troubles, the worst is this: for we see our city turning into something no bigger than a village on the road to Vic."

Left, The *Llibre del Consolat de Mar*, a 13th-century compedium of maritime law, written in the reign of the conqueror-king Jaume I (above).

BARC

No visitor to Barcelona can fail to be struck by the relative dearth of great Renaissance and baroque buildings. There are examples of grandeur, but they are elusive: the Palau de la Generalitat hides its medieval core behind a Renaissance facade. Most of what survives in the city from the 16th and 17th centuries reflects private effort, rather than public wealth, and a history of slow recovery until 1640, before the terrible era of war and unrest which lasted until 1714.

Ports and palaces: In the 16th century, Barcelona kept closely enough in touch with fashion to earn praise from almost every visitor who left an account of the city. With the unremitting confidence that has characterised them in every age, the city fathers poured money into the creation of an artificial port in an attempt to recover lost trade: the task would remain incomplete for 300 years, but was never abandoned.

Private patrons like the Fivaller family could build splendid new palaces – theirs still stands in the Plaça de Sant Josep Oriol, where it now houses an Agricultural Association; and the Carrer Ample, a conspicuous straight gash across Anton van Wyngaerde's view of the town, was opened as a gesture to Renaissance town planning.

At the beginning of the century, Guicciardini commended the city for its beauty while lamenting the decline of its commerce; by the end, a measure of recovery can be detected in the terms of Lope de Vega's praise: "Just as a splendid facade enhances the value of a building, so great Barcelona stands at the entrance to Spain, like a portico framing a famous threshold."

Royal neglect: Barcelona's decline in the 16th century coincided with the progressive loss of the courtly status which, before the rise of the city's commercial importance, had been the foundation of its fortune. After

Preceding pages: Columbus presents the riches of his first voyage of discovery. Left, gold casket from the Museum of Catalan Art in the Palau Nacional. Right, the shield of a city-state.

the extinction of the ruling House of Barcelona in 1412, it had been governed by a series of kings whose main interests were in Castile or Naples and who spent ever less time in Barcelona. For a while from 1479 and continuously from 1516, her counts were also kings of Castile and were mainly concerned with the affairs of that larger and fiscally more productive country.

Yet the patriciate never lost their sense of ruling the capital of a sovereign principality

– or even a quasi-polis, a city with the potential, at least, to be a city-state like Genoa or Venice. From inside the Spanish monarchy, Barcelona affected the status of a foreign power and its representatives swaggered like the emissaries of foreign potentates.

When, for instance, a new viceroy of Catalonia was appointed in 1622, the congratulations of Barcelona were tendered by an ambassador, attended by 200 carriages, in what was rumoured to be the most magnificent procession ever seen in Madrid.

Twenty years earlier, the city's representative at court was honoured with so much pomp that "even the leading nobles of this court," he reported, "say that neither the nuncio of His Holiness himself, nor the envoy of the Emperor has ever been given such a reception... and the Castilians are all amazed that an ambassador who is a vassal of the king should be received with so much honour." A similar war of protocol was carried on inside the city, where leading magistrates demanded the right to remain hatted in the king's presence and disputed seats of honour in church with the viceroy's wife.

This was more than play-acting. The privileges (*privilegis*) and liberties (*furs*) which meant so much to Barcelona were never systematically codified and are difficult to define. The Castilian models, and the different nuances of Castilian thinking, which could not be translated into Catalan, tended to mislead policy makers in Madrid into misunderstandings about the sort of traditions they had to deal with in relations with Barcelona. In Castile, civic liberties normally rested in a charter granted by the king: they were a negotiable commodity, revered but not written in stone.

Private laws: Barcelona's identity, however, was bound up with the status in law of the principality of Catalonia as a distinct and equal partner in the Spanish monarchy. It had liberties not granted by the Prince as an act of grace, but governed by the *constitucions* – the statutes irrevocable except by the representative parliamentary assembly of Catalonia (the *corts*), which limited royal authority in the principality.

During the early 17th century, when the Spanish monarchy was tottering from the inevitable effects of immoderate greatness, the growing need for money and manpower made the Catalans fearful for their immunities. At a time when to be a very good Catalan was to be "jealous of the country's privileges", the implicit constitutional conflict between the interests of Spain and Catalonia was bound to be noticed in Barcelona, where all the institutions of the statehood of Catalonia, inherited from the Middle Ages, were concentrated, and where a large body of professional lawyers more or less lived by watching the *constitucions*.

The cost of the Thirty Years' War, and direct hostilities with France from 1635, brought the demands of the monarchy for money and men to a peak and the differences with the principality to a head. When Catalonia rose in revolt in 1640, and the rebels transferred their allegiance to Louis XIII of France, Barcelona was the head and heart of the rebellion.

Like the roughly contemporary rebellion in England, Catalonia's was reluctantly supported elsewhere. An anonymous but representative diarist in Barcelona squarely blamed the king's bad counsel for what he saw as "the greatest sorrow this Principality of Catalonia has suffered" which was "to have been obliged to rely upon a foreign prince, moved by necessity, and to have had no other recourse... May God and most holy Mary be pleased to return us to the grace of our father and lord, Felipe".

But, like the English war, the Catalan juggernaut rolled out of control. The élite of Barcelona had to share power with popular elements and 16 years of war devastated its land, depopulated its towns and despoiled its wealth. The siege of Barcelona in 1652 was one of the most desperate episodes of the war and it ended only when the citizens were "reduced to eating grass".

However, the successful army commander, Don Juan José of Austria, was the architect of a remarkable restoration of the broken city and of Catalonia's national pride. His very success raised the danger of another round of similar conflict.

In the second half of the 17th century, Barcelona had little respite. Civic-minded optimists like Feliu de la Penya had hardly begun to revive all things Catalan before the French wars of the 1680s and 1690s exposed her lands to more campaigns and the city to another siege.

Nationalist instincts: Then the War of the Spanish Succession plunged the entire monarchy into crisis. The Bourbon claimant, Felipe V, arrived in 1702, scattering rewards and promises with a lavish hand; but he was suspected of an arbitrary disposition and absolutist plans – an impression confirmed in Catalan eyes by his failure to invite the chief magistrates to cover their heads in his presence. His insensitive viceroy, Francisco

Fernández de Velasco, blundered into other infringements of the *constitucions*.

Despite the naturally peaceful inclinations of a mercantile élite, many of the leading members of Barcelonan society were willing to respond to Velasco's tactless rule with violence. Psychologically inclined to fight, they were also ideologically equipped to do so. It was an almost unquestioned assumption that Catalonia was a sovereign state with a right, in principle, to secede from a monarchy which had ambitions to control the whole country.

Catalans' reading of their own history represented theirs as a contractual monar-

chy, in which the contract between people and prince, once broken, could be repudiated. By the end of the war, when Barcelona was left to fight on alone, the inhabitants were inclined to blame the English for inveigling them into the fight with promises: the trick was performed, almost equally, with implicit threats. On 20 June 1705, when representatives of "the most Illustrious, Famous and Renowned Principality of Catalo-

Above, Felipe V, who made himself unpopular in Catalonia by refusing to respect the Catalan *constitucions* (statutes).

nia" signed a treaty with England in Genoa, the guns of British ships could be heard in local waters.

Catalans came to see the episode as a typical instance of England's habit of acquiring by bribery or intimidation an ally whom she would later abandon. From their point of view, the sixth clause of the treaty was the most important, by which England guaranteed that "now and in the future the Principality of Catalonia shall keep all the graces, privileges, laws and customs which severally and in common her people have enjoyed and do enjoy".

Defeat: In Barcelona it seems, appetite for war *vient en mangeant* (grew with eating), and the Barcelonans, after their shy start, became the most committed opponents of the Bourbon claimant, Felipe V. They joined the allied cause in a calculating spirit but clung on when all the other allies had withdrawn. They dared beyond hope, endured beyond reason and reaped the usual reward of that sort of heroism: defeat.

The previous recovery of 1652 was fatally misleading: it encouraged the Barcelonans to believe that their liberties could be ventured again and that a hopeless resistance would save them. The final siege lasted from August 1713 until November 1714, when the city capitulated (a date now celebrated by the Diada de Catalunya – Catalonia's national day).

The repression denounced by Catalan historians after Felipe's victory was really rather mild: clerics and generals were its only individually targeted victims. But the *constitucions* were abolished; Barcelona was reduced to the rank of a provincial city and subjected to the indignity of a permanent garrison – an army of occupation was billeted in what is now the Ciutadella Park.

Drive to be rich: Defeat turned the energies of the citizens to a mood of *enrichissez-vous*. Though the city was prostrate and revival slow, the 18th century as a whole was an era of forward-looking prosperity in which sustained economic growth began, thanks to new activities such as direct trade with the Americas and the beginnings of industrialisation based on imports of American cotton. Some of the palaces and villas of the Bourbon collaborators can still be seen: the finest of them, the Palau de Comillas, houses the Generalitat bookshop in the Ramblas; around the corner, the palace of the Comte de Fonallar enhances the commercial bustle of the popular shops in the Carrer de Portaferrissa.

The ensemble which has most to say about Barcelona's 18th century is the Barceloneta district, the first industrial suburb, begun in 1753 to house a population then beginning to burst out of the diminished city. The tight, neat grid of its streets, the contrast with the traditional cityscape of Barcelona, make it one of the earliest surviving examples of "enlightened" town planning in Europe.

In pre-industrial Barcelona manufacturing was a mainstay of the economy, but it was confined to the intimate society of the workshop and the master's home, regulated not by the impersonal market but by the powerful guilds. A visitor to the Museu de l'Història de la Ciutat in the Carrer del Veguer can see the sort of images which dominated the mental world of the guilds: their art reflected professional pride and devotion to their patron saints.

The book of privileges of the shoemakers is decorated with a huge but elegant gilt-bronze slipper with tapering toe; the silver-smiths' pattern books record, in meticulous detail, the masters' copyright to thousands of intricate designs. The market-gardeners' book of privileges, begun in 1453, is flanked by busts of their otherwise obscure patrons, saints Abdó and Senen, and the gaudily painted coffer in which their relics were preserved.

Prestigious guilds: Everywhere the images of saints are reminders that the guilds doubled as devotional confraternities. Evidence of their prestige and wealth can be found around the city today: the shoemakers' palatial hall, for instance, in the Plaça de Sant Felip Neri, decorated with the lion of St Mark, who converted the first Christian shoemaker; the graves of the masters in the cathedral cloister, bearing the same emblem; the sumptuous premises of the silk weavers' guild in the Via Laietana.

The beginnings of the transformation of Barcelona's economy to an industrial basis can be traced in the decline of the guilds. The 18th-century immigrants – most of them from communities in southern France, where languages similar to Catalan were spoken – "preferred factory life to subjection under the oligarchy of guild-masters".

The bridle-makers had 108 members in 1729, 47 in 1808 and 27 in 1814; the decline occurred during a period when the population of the city trebled and was at its most acute at a time of war and high demand for harnesses. In the textile industry, which was directly affected by reorganisation into factories, the decline was even more spectacular. By 1825, the cloth-dressers had only three members left, who had neither studios nor workshops and were too old to work.

In the last quarter of the 18th century a number of economic indicators seem to have accelerated. The rate of increase in wages between 1780 and 1797, for instance, was double that of Madrid. Manufacturers' profits, which had already doubled between 1720 and 1775, more than kept pace.

When an English traveller visited in 1786, he was particularly impressed by the Bernis factory, which employed 350 operatives making woollen cloth for America; the following year, the famous English economist and agrarian reformer, Arthur Young, could hear "the noise of business" everywhere. The Napoleonic wars and their aftermath interrupted progress. Amid post-war unemployment, after a terrible yellow fever epidemic in 1821, the city council of Barcelona lost its habitual optimism and publicly doubted whether the city would ever recover. In fact, though recovery was socially painful, it was complete: in 1836, the first steamship rolled off the slipway of Barceloneta; in 1848 Spain's first railway linked Barcelona to Mataró.

Social side-effects: Working-class degradation and unrest accompanied economic change. The pattern of life in Barcelona in on overcrowding in insanitary conditions.

Disorder incubated with disease and riots were a regular feature of the long, hot summer of 1854. With increasing frequency these took on revolutionary proportions. The rioters' targets gradually changed: there had been disturbances in the 18th century – in 1766, 1773 and 1789, when the targets had been grain speculators and the military service quotas. The insurgents of 1835 also attacked steam-powered factories, representatives of the government, and houses of religion; the disturbances of 1840–42 culminated in a political revolution by a coalition of the disaffected whose only rallying point

the mid-19th century was of fitful mass violence and intermittent plague.

Ildefons Cerdà (the urban planner who was to create the Eixample and transform Barcelona) surveyed the working-class way of life in the 1850s and found that a diet of bread and potatoes, enhanced with the odd sardine, was all an average family could afford. Observers blamed the cholera epidemic of 1854, which claimed 6,000 lives,

Left, the Ramblas, where the successful paraded their wealth. **Above**, workers from a textile factory, breeding grounds of discontent.

was the call for protective tariffs: it was suppressed by force.

In 1854 a series of strikes and Luddite outrages began in defiance of the spectacularly fast automation of the textile industry. The riots were soon deflected into political channels by the fall of a "progressive" ministry in Madrid; respectable radicals joined the mob in resistance. The barricades of Barcelona were reconquered in the bloodiest scenes the city had witnessed since 1714. A conservative observer noted with satisfaction: "The rebels were massacred as they were captured... The spectacle was magnificent."

The bloodshed of the mid-19th century was a shock to the sensibilities of the bourgeoisie; but the authorities' confidence that they would soon recover proved justified. The optimism of the burgeoning city was displayed in the competition, held in 1859, for a design for the expansion (*eixample*) of the city beyond the walls.

The public exhibition attracted huge crowds. Antoni Rovira i Trias submitted a popular plan, sympathetically integrating the old town; Ildefons Cerdà's proposal looked more rigidly modern. He made only minimal use of nodal *piazze* and masked the old town with a grid-plan of boulevards and public gardens. Political controversy, caused by the Madrid government's determination to impose Cerdà's solution, delayed work while the situation grew desperately urgent: in 1863, for instance, the rate of growth of the population of Barcelona was 27.4 percent, three times the Spanish national average.

The Spanish revolution of 1868, which swept the Bourbons from the throne, temporarily abated the differences between Barcelona and Madrid and in 1869 the laying out of the Eixample proceeded along the lines of the Cerdà plan.

Despite the delayed start and the slow initial growth, Barcelona's boom in the late 19th century was so rapid that the expectations of the plan were exceeded. In-filling robbed it of its best feature, the expansive parks and garden squares. The sudden grafting of a criss-cross of 19th-century branches on to the trunk of an ancient town created the view from Montjuïc – the image which defines the city's character, despite the subsequent (even greater) growth, to this day.

Political peace: The era of the Eixample was accompanied by relative social peace. The political energies of most of the Barcelonans were deflected into Catalanism, the movement for the recognition of Catalonia's distinctive institutions and the conservation of its language and cultural heritage. Bourgeois life moved out of the cafés on to pavement terraces and out of the house into the gas-lit streets that so dazzled Hans Christian Andersen when he visited in 1862.

One novelist called this the "gold fever era" when the industrialisation of Barcelona swallowed up huge amounts of capital, scattered among too many under-funded firms. The "gamblers' synagogue" – the unofficial

Bourse or stock exchange – began in 1858. Slack money and new money created a market for art and architecture that has given Barcelona the rather showy, experimental look that has characterised *le style barcelonais* ever since.

The symbol of this era of self-assurance was the Universal Exhibition of 1888. The idea originated with a Galician entrepreneur who had seen the Paris and Vienna exhibitions and it was taken up by Barcelona's Mayor Rius i Taulat after he came to office in city hall in 1885.

When he summoned the world to Barce-

Left, Catalanism and autonomy became heated national issues. **Right**, workers discussing strike action on the Ramblas.

lona on 13 June 1887, everything had still to be extemporised with less than a year to go. But not only did the citizens build on time the exhibition ground that cynics had deemed impossible, they also planted the Plaça de Colom with palms and drove the Rambla de Catalunya and the Paral.lel through suburbs where they had previously been stymied. The Hotel Internacional was built in only 60 days and its five floors proved unequal to the demand.

The exhibition opened 10 days late, but despite this it drew exhibitors from 20 countries and attracted well over 2 million visitors. It was an unprecedented occasion and it over a million people. Social conflict could hardly be avoided.

When the rail link was completed young French anarchists took the Barcelona Express and were shocked on arrival by the prostitutes: this was the character of the revolutionary anarchism that became the most potent force of Barcelona's political underworld: naïve and puritanical. In the 1890s, Barcelona was the "city of bombs", symbolised by Ramon Casas's restrained painting of the Corpus Christi procession that was attacked in 1896 (in the Museu d'Art Modern in Ciutadella Park).

In the early 1900s, while terrorism col-

inspired the young Josep Puig i Cadafalch (who would later become a major influence in the architecture, letters and politics of the city) with a vision of a great Barcelona. With the exhibition, the idea of Barcelona as a model of go-ahead hard work entered popular fiction.

Expansion and anarchy: But rapid growth never happens painlessly. In 1860, Barcelona had fewer than 200,000 inhabitants. By 1897, when the city limits were redefined to incorporate the towns of the immediate hinterland, the official figure was 383,908. By 1930, the conurbation contained well lapsed, the workers' movement was infused with anarchism. There was a general strike in 1901–02; the Setmana Tràgica of 1909, when a strangely self-disciplined mob systematically destroyed 70 buildings of religious orders while sparing other targets, was attributed to anarcho-syndicalism; the movement's spokesman, Francesc Ferrer, was executed for presumed complicity after a show trial which shocked the world.

Some of these tensions were reflected in the work of the modernist artists who gathered in the Quatre Gats café (today expensively restored in the Carrer Montsió). The most representative figure was Ramon Casas, whose father had made a fortune in the Indies and who, on his mother's side, was the heir to a textile mill. His inheritance thus combined two typical sources of the wealth of Barcelona in his day.

Horror painting genre: Casas's best works were problematical genre scenes, but his most memorable canvases, (many of which can be seen in the Museu d'Art Modern) are those in which the social commentary is most overt. *Barcelona 1902* is an extraordinarily dynamic composition, in which a mounted civil guard is about to trample a sprawling, dramatically foreshortened

mous crucifix; the penitents' black conical caps like pitchfork-prongs.

The public loved the engaging horror more than they feared the social import; horror-paintings in Barcelona were always popular and frequently connected with the traditions of public scourging – common until the early 19th century – and public execution, which continued until 1908.

A state of confusion existed throughout Spain in the first three decades of the 20th century. Eventually, in 1931, the Left won a resounding election victory and King Alfonso XIII was forced to leave Spain without formally abdicating. The Second Republic

worker in the foreground, while the crowd is cleared by the cavalry from a space which seems to grow before the onlooker's eyes. Casas's most famous work was *Garrote Vil,* of 1893, recording the public execution of a 19-year-old who had cut the throats of his victim and his own accomplice for a gold watch. Some aspects seem ironic: the clergy are a corpulent contingent, under an enor-

Left, demonstrators for independence in 1936, an idea that was vanquished by the 1936-39 Civil War. **Above**, a show of strength by victorious Nationalist troops in Plaça de Catalunya in 1939.

was proclaimed. To the Barcelonans' delight, the exiled socialist leader Francesc Macià returned from Paris to become president of the Barcelona Generalitat.

The Macià plan was an ambitious project to expand and develop the city, but its life was as shortlived as that of the Republic. The Right struck back, and the Civil War erupted before any major works could be completed.

In Barcelona the anarchist revolution of 1936 had made an enemy of anyone who wore a tie in the street. So when Franco's troops marched in with the slogan "Spain has arrived", a collaborationist bourgeoisie came out of the woodwork. Catalan culture went deeper underground than under the dictatorship of General Primo de Rivera. Josep Viladomat's monumental sculptured allegory, *La República*, found an ignominious refuge among the packing-cases of the municipal storehouse.

Immigrant flood: The big threat to Barcelona's identity under Franco came, however, not from repression but from economic growth. Three-quarters of a million immigrants, mostly from southern Spain, came to the city between 1950 and 1970, selling up their homes elsewhere to live in dreadful accommodation in the city. They were at-

tracted by the employment possibilities in Catalonia, which had firmly established itself as the economic powerhouse of the Spanish peninsula.

It was easy for Francoism to buy these people with job security and modest economic rewards, hard for Catalanism to win them with the blandishments of an alien tongue, an inhospitable culture and a mandarin creed. Yet when the exiled Catalan leader, Josep Taradellas, appeared after Franco's death on the balcony of the Generalitat in the Plaça de Sant Jaume, he found the immigrants willing to vote for autonomy.

His cry, *Jo soc aqui!* (Here I am at last!) contrasted with the "Spain has arrived" of the Francoists. A survey found that many *soi-disant* Andalucíans also considered themselves Catalans: but the main reason for favouring autonomy was rejection of Francoism, not Catalanist sentiment.

The dictatorship's other legacy was a proletariat with drawn fangs. Communists took the lead in organising a clandestine union movement from 1963: by the 1970s it was strong enough to attempt political strikes. But, as it grew in numbers, it became ideologically diluted. The union elections of 1975 put apolitical leaders in control of most branches, and "responsible" unionism has been dominant ever since. In partial consequence, investment has poured into what is now the biggest city of any along the Mediterranean coast.

Changing city: Walking in the streets today, one can stumble across contrasts which encapsulate the whole history of Barcelona, from country town to industrial wen. A *masia* – a farmhouse of the prosperous early-modern peasantry – still stands close to Sants railway station; another, rather grand, occupies the corner of the Passeig Maragall with the Carrer de Frederic Ramola. The remains of the villages of Santa Eulàlia de Vilapicina and Sant Martí dels Provençals survive among the tower blocks.

The latest changes in the cityscape, where recent works have opened up the seafront to diners and promenaders, have re-established a link with the more glorious maritime chapter of Barcelona's past.

This is, perhaps, more continuity than one might expect in such a brash and dynamic city. But Barcelona will cease to be Barcelona if the immigrants of the exclusively Spanish-speaking districts of the industrial *barris* remain unassimilated. Now that the Olympic Village has been handed over to the city and the harbour works are done, the Catalanisation of the masses is once again the administration's most urgent task.

<u>Left</u>, the bombing of Barcelona port during the Civil War by Italian aircraft loyal to Franco. <u>Right</u>, Francesc Macià, leader of the Generalitat during the short-lived Republic.

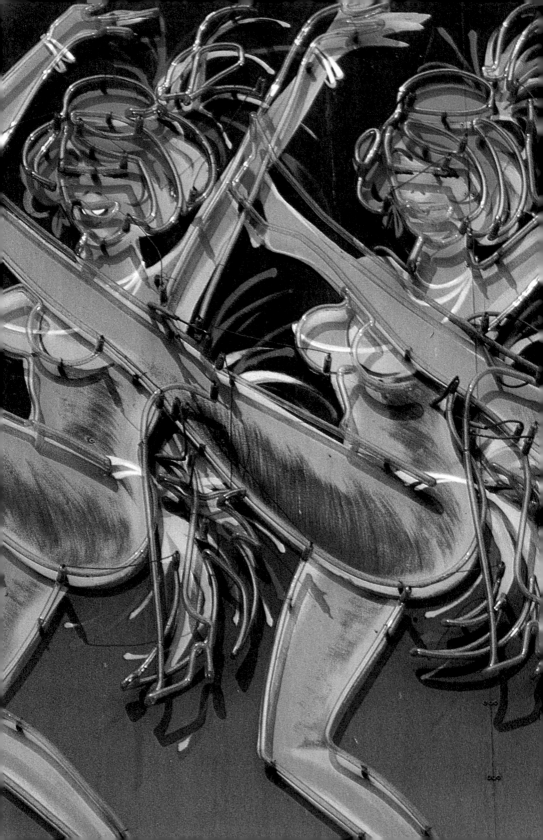

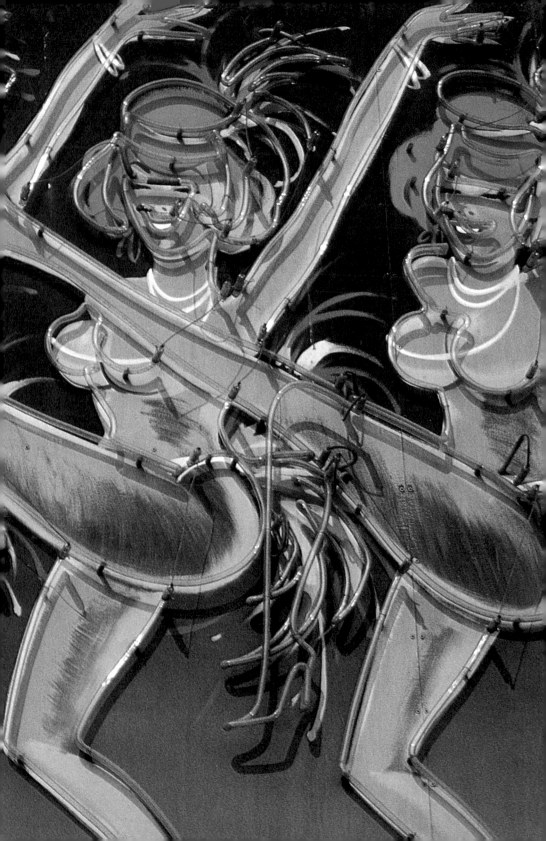

NEW LOOK FOR THE NINETIES

Since Barcelona hosted the Olympic Games in 1992, regarded as one of the most memorable Olympiads ever, the city authorities have made the most of their success.

In fact the city authorities made the most of the Games right from the beginning – for the good of Barcelona as much as for the good of sport. Much of today's Barcelona was shaped and structured for the Games, but the socialist City Council led by Pasqual Maragall, which played a critical role in obtaining the event and in its preparations, kept a political eye focused keenly on the future. As the citizens moaned about the dust and chaos churned up by the years of preparation, the City Council was quick to respond that it was the Barcelona of 1993 and beyond that was being built.

The Games were greeted as an opportunity for Barcelona to prove itself in the eyes of the world and to establish itself in a much more noticeable position on the map of Europe. As a public relations campaign it worked, judging by the 30 percent increase in visitors in the year following the Olympics. It was also a chance to catch up on time and funding lost over the Franco years, by modernising the structure and infrastructure of the city.

Event city: Barcelona has a history of propping itself up with international events. The 1888 Universal Exhibition was just such a pretext for frenzied activity to modernise the city, as was the 1929 Exhibition. With its complex about not being a capital, Barcelona is constantly trying to prove its importance both to Madrid, which holds Spain's purse-strings, and to the rest of Europe. History has shown that without a great occasion to cling on to, it tends to slip into decline.

The city was in need of attention. With 680 miles (1,100 km) of streets and an estimated 750,000 vehicles crammed within the natural boundaries formed by Montjuïc hill, the

Collserola range and the Mediterranean, traffic, noise and pollution had to be tackled. The population, which at the turn of the century was 537,354, had risen to 1.7 million by the late 1980s, making this one of the world's most densely-populated cities. Urban horrors had been committed during the dictatorship when profit came before the people's wellbeing; cheap housing was erected rapidly and with no sense of planning to cope with the flood of immigrants who came here

in search of work in the 1950s and 1960s.

For the Games, the city was restructured to accommodate the four nerve-centres: Montjuïc, Pedralbes-Diagonal, Vall d'Hebron and the Olympic Village. As they are strategically placed in four corners of the city, the road which was rapidly built to connect them and to rush athletes back and forth from village to event, is now an inner city ring-road. Known as Les Rondes, it is made up of the Ronda Litoral and the Ronda Dalt (the coastal road and the upper road).

For anyone who has ever experienced the notorious Friday night queue to leave the city

Preceding pages: neon in a Paral.lel Music Hall; supporters in full cry; opera fans. **Left**, keeping up with the Barcelona edition. **Right**, Pasqual Maragall, the city's long-serving mayor.

in the past, this ring-road is a shining example of the beneficial legacy of the Games. It was long overdue, but Barcelona needed the catalyst of the Olympics, and the accompanying funding, to bring it about. The statistics testify to the ring-road's success, claiming that traffic on the main routes through the city centre has been reduced by between 10 and 22 percent, while the speedier communication from suburb to industrial zone, or one corner of the city to another, has on average knocked 30 percent off journey times at the height of the working day.

Needless to say those founts of all city knowledge, the taxi drivers, tend to deny

attract foreign investment and international business. On the strength of what it has to offer, there is now feverish activity to sell the city as the capital of Southern Europe, and the best place to open an office covering Mediterranean markets.

In a survey on the best cities in Europe to set up a business, conducted among top executives, Barcelona ranked seventh, ahead of places like Munich, Berlin, Stockholm or Geneva. While the Spanish state is beset by political and economic problems, Barcelona has been recently named the European city (of 32 cities studied) with the greatest potential for growth over the next few years, with

these statistics, claiming the ring-road was built for the 1960s and will soon reach saturation point. As the volume of traffic in Barcelona continues to increase by nearly 2 percent a year, the taxi drivers may prove to have a point.

Capital of southern Europe: Such arguments will inevitably continue, but meanwhile post-Olympic Barcelona boasts to the world of its enormously improved road and rail network, its new international airport, state of the art telecommunications, innumerable hotel rooms, extensive office space, the latest congress facilities – all you could wish for to

an estimated increase of 3.4 percent a year.

As for the citizens of Barcelona, there is no shortage of internal PR to win over the cynics: they are constantly reminded by sophisticated publicity campaigns of what the new Barcelona should mean to them: new and improved housing in refurbished, better-equipped neighbourhoods, a new waterfront with nearly 5 miles (8 km) of beaches, new urban spaces, new sports and cultural facilities, improved public transport in and around the city, more efficient roads and so on.

And it seems to work. According to a recent UNESCO study financed by a Spanish bank, the people of Barcelona, along with Dubliners, are the Europeans who are most satisfied with the quality of life in their city.

Street critic: Evidently the study's authors avoided asking Señora Pili for her opinion; owner of a plant stall on La Rambla, she bends many an ear by railing against the excessive expenditure and bemoaning the increased rates she has to pay "to foot the bill of those Games". Her view of the newly-paved squares and the resurfaced roads with special kerbs for wheelchairs and prams does not encompass aesthetic or practical benefits; for her it smacks of someone in a high place having shares in the paving stone com-

Catalunya, designed by Ricardo Bofill in his all too recognisable neo-classical style, and a large Auditori Municipal, designed by Rafael Moneo, comprising two concert halls and other facilities. It does not have the charms of Domènech i Montaner's inimitable modernist Palau de la Musica, but its late 20th century acoustics will be more pleasing to the finely tuned ear.

At the end of 1995 the Museu d'Art Contemporani de Barcelona (MACBA) located in the district of El Raval in the old town, was finally opened. Designed by Richard Meier, it is a vital element in the Barcelona cultural scene, along with the

pany. Yet as if driven by some Olympic momentum new plans and building works keep appearing. The World Trade Center in the port, housing and long-awaited new cultural premises are being completed.

In a vast development area around the neglected Plaça de les Glòries, better known for its flea market Els Encants, there is a cultural complex called the Plaça de les Arts. It incorporates the Teatre Nacional de

Left, the Communist Party graphically endorses self-government on a Barcelona wall. **Above**, industry is at the heart of the local economy.

neighbouring CCCB (Centre de Cultura Contemporània de Barcelona).

Expansion points: On the commercial front, even more hotels and offices are being built. New shopping centres appear with alarming regularity. One of the most popular is L'Illa on the Diagonal. It is yet another concrete pile amid many in this expensive residential and commercial area, which has none of the charms of the elegant Eixample, but should nevertheless not be overlooked as one of the faces of contemporary Barcelona. At the other end of the Diagonal towards the sea, where the Eixample meets the former industrial district of Sant Martí, is Barcelona Glòries, the largest shopping and business centre of them all. And in the heart of the city, in Plaça Catalunya, El Triangle commercial centre is due to open in 1998, joining forces with a new Marks & Spencer and a refurbished El Corte Inglés department store.

Yet despite, rather than because of, all these claims to modernisation and improvement, Barcelona still remains today an attractive city to visit. At one time it looked as if the cleaning up in preparation for the Games was in danger of sanitising the city and washing away its charms. Superficially it may have been Europeanised by its face-

fronts are the well-preserved mirrored graphics of groceries that have not changed since the 19th century. If anything, the parade of characters on the Ramblas has become more eccentric and colourful than ever.

Always keenly aware of their individuality, the Catalans are showing no signs of relinquishing it. On the whole the city's renovations have been executed with vision and sensitivity; great respect has been shown for the original structures, exposing positive features in the architecture, or opening up areas so that one can better appreciate what was there before. The spectacular views across the port, for example, were obstructed

less commercial centres, but happily Barcelona's deeply engrained character, stemming from its Roman past through its Gothic glory to its industrial sweat and the weathering that comes from being a large Mediterranean port, is still there for all to enjoy.

More eccentric than ever: Despite the ubiquitous fast-food outlets, there are still old *bodegas* with nicotine-stained walls, where customers sit among the barrels eating the finest anchovies. The front line of elegant restaurants on the port is merely a distraction from the much better *paella* you will find in the streets behind. Amid the designer shop-

in the past by redundant industrial buildings. Now the port is a major feature of Barcelona.

The social benefits to the community of all the recent upheavals have been undeniable: the amount of public space made available in the city has increased by nearly 50 percent since 1975, the year Franco died. For the first time in many years the Catalans themselves have had the chance to manage their capital city in the way they choose. It's an opportunity they have certainly not wasted.

<u>Above,</u> Oriel Bohigas, architect of many Olympic changes in Barcelona.

THE OLYMPICS

On 17 December 1986, in Lausanne, the president of the International Olympic Committee, Switzerland, Juan Antonio Samaranch, proudly announced that the 25th Olympic Games would be held in his native Barcelona. This much anticipated news was greeted with jubilation in Spain, particularly by Barcelonans and Catalans. It was the fourth time the city had pitched for the Games and the canny Catalans were quick to recognise that it was a golden opportunity to attract long overdue investment in the city. Neglected infrastructure could be repaired, and it could become, some believed, a major city of the 21st century.

This vision took some battering in the following six years of upheaval, and there were serious doubts about whether too much was being being attempted in too short a time. But when the 25th Olympiad opened on 25 July 1992, the confident Catalans were proved right. The Games were a display of organisational skills: from the moment a burning arrow taken from the torch was unleashed to light up the Olympic flame in the renovated stadium on Montjuïc, to the departure of the last athlete from the reconstructed airport, everything went remarkably smoothly.

It was also, being Barcelona, something of a "designer Olympics". Everything looked good. Key elements in the infrastructure were designed by leading national and international architects – the Communications Tower on Collserola by Sir Norman Foster, the one on Montjuïc by Calatrava, the Palau Sant Jordi indoor stadium by Isozaki, the Vila Olímpica by the Barcelonan Mackay, Martorell, Bohigas and Puigdomenech.

From the starting blocks to the medal bearers' uniforms, designed by Barcelona's top fashion designer Toni Miró, the sporting events were meticulously staged for the maximum visual effect, with an eye on the 3½ million viewers around the world.

The 500,000 people who came to the city saw it spruced up with new roads, renovated plazas, freshly painted facades, urban sculptures and newly opened vistas. There were four centres of activity located in the four corners of the city, and 16 subsidiary centres, some outside the city. The key Olympic area in Barcelona itself was the hill of Montjuïc where the original stadium, built for the 1929 Universal Exhibition, was renovated to accommodate 70,000 spectators, and the Palau Sant Jordi indoor stadium, the INEF

Right: a burning arrow is fired to light the flame for the Barcelona Olympics.

(University of Physical Education) and the Picornell swimming pools were constructed. The hill was landscaped and a system of escalators was installed to make access easier. The Olympic Gallery in the stadium today recaptures the atmosphere and excitement of the Games through thousands of photographs, sound recordings and videos.

The other areas of Barcelona to benefit were around the football club on Diagonal, the Vall d'Hebron and, most spectacular of all, the Parc de Mar, built on 320 acres (130 hectares) of former industrial land by the sea. This incorporated the Olympic Village, which has now become a highly desirable area of seaside apartments, and the Olympic port, where dozens of new restaurants buzz every evening and at week-

ends. All four areas were linked up by a new ring road, the Cinturón.

Against this colourful background, amazing athletic feats were achieved. There were record numbers of world records (28), Olympic records (86), participating teams (172) and contestants (10,253). It was the first time countries of the former Soviet Union had participated, and South Africa turned up for the first time in 32 years.

The powerful Olympic spirit combined with the Mediterranean atmosphere to make a heady mix, and for 16 days and nights there was a sense of carnival in the streets. At the closing ceremony on 9 August it was an even prouder Samaranch who declared it had been one of the most successful Olympic Games ever. ∎

Did you hear the one about the drunken tourist who fell asleep one Saturday night on the cathedral steps? He couldn't get over the politeness and courtesy of the Barcelonans who, when he finally woke the next morning, were dancing on tip-toe all around him so as not to disturb him.

A likely story? For anyone who has seen Barcelonans of all ages dancing the *Sardana*, the Catalan national dance, in the cathedral square on a Sunday morning it is utterly plausible. The *Sardana* is polite, correct and very serious, more of a solemn ritual than a merry folk dance: its sober-faced participants link hands conspiratorially, and to the strains of a neat band of wind instruments, perform intricate footwork (on tip-toe) which defies imitation by hapless outsiders.

This highly symbolic dance says a great deal about Barcelonans: the unity, strength and intimacy of the circle, difficult to break into unless you know the steps; the solemnity and suppressed merriment; the established routine that is dutifully followed.

However, the Barcelonan cannot be summed up and pigeon-holed that easily. People from the rest of Spain tend to define the Barcelonan as cold and serious with an overbearing work ethic, but the enigma of the local character goes deeper than that.

Ask anyone arriving in the city while the Mercé is being celebrated (a whole week of festivities around the day of its patron saint on 24 September): the city bursts into a colourful explosion of parades of giants (*Gegants*) and mythical animals, brass bands and fantastical creatures on stilts; the sky is lit nightly by an extravaganza of fireworks. The serious Plaça Sant Jaume, the city's administrative centre, becomes the scene of high drama as *castellers*, awesome nine-storey human towers, compete in ever more daring feats; while at night it converts into an outdoor club with live music, as do other historic squares in the city; and the week culminates in a spell-binding, terrifying, paganistic ritual, the *correfoc*, guaranteed to break all European Union safety regulations, in which fire-breathing dragons chase reckless citizens around the streets. Outsiders witnessing these celebrations would define Barcelonans as wild, creative, fun-loving Mediterraneans.

Enigmatic city-dwellers: So who are the real Barcelonans? Like their city, they are full of

contrasts. They are urban creatures, slick in their city suits, but passionate about energetic weekends by the sea or in the mountains. They are capable of partying in designer bars until daylight, and still getting to the office at eight in the morning to put in a good day's work. They are adventurous travellers, visiting the remotest corners of the world, but always returning to the family fold. Of the people who moved out of the city in the past six years, only 2 percent settled abroad, whereas 74 percent never even got beyond Catalonia, mostly remaining within commuting distance of Barcelona. They abide

Preceding pages: Rosa Maria Malet, director of the Miró Foundation. Left, conductor Xavier Güell. Right, street musician.

by local traditions and convention, yet are refreshingly open to innovation and creativity. They would defend Barcelona to the end, but they are also constantly looking beyond it to new horizons and cultures, and will bend to positive outside influences.

Incomers: So much for the people whose families go back many generations, but a new breed of Barcelonan also exists. Known by the derogatory nickname of *xarnegos*, they are immigrants from other parts of Spain, driven out of Andalusia, Extremedura, Galicia and other less industrial regions by poverty and hunger. In 1900 the population in the city stood at 537,354 and by 1936 it

that these are former immigrants or their families, returning to their *pueblo*.

Taxi driver Juan Manuel is a typical example of this uneasy integration. He is from Albacete, 350 miles (560 km) southwest of Barcelona, and has been living in the Catalan capital since 1955. He drives a cab which, like its owner, has seen better days. He even has a Catalan wife. He doesn't beat about the bush when asked what he makes of the Barcelonans. "I can't stand them!" he spits. "They're cold, mean and tight-fisted. Invite them for a meal in your house and afterwards go for a coffee and brandy in the bar down the road: you can be sure they'll pay for their

had nearly doubled to just over a million, a quarter of whom were not native Barcelonans. Immigration reached massive proportions in the 1950s and 1960s; by the late 1960s the population had grown to 1.8 million.

The second and third generation *xarnegos* speak Catalan, and they inter-marry, but an uneasy wariness between these two breeds of Barcelonan may take years to remove and total integration may never be possible.

In the past decade emigration from Barcelona has exceeded immigration. Of the 24 percent who leave for other parts of Spain the largest amount go to Andalusia, suggesting

own drink and not even offer to get yours." Even his wife doesn't escape his harsh judgement. On the contrary: Juan Manuel apparently can't stand her either and resents her Catalan-ness.

"One Christmas she won a hamper at the textile factory where she worked. I could never understand what happened to those bottles of *cava* and the biscuits that were in it. Then one day I was looking for something in the back of a cupboard," says Juan Manuel, the bitterness growing in his voice, "and what do you think I found? I'm damned if she hadn't stashed the whole lot away!"

And there you have the core of an old platitude about the Barcelonan which is still tossed around today: he is stingy and unfriendly, puts his own interests first and is distrustful of outsiders.

"Of course there's another side to the coin," says Milagros Perez Oliva, who is not a Barcelonan but reckons that she knows how they tick after 10 years of living and working among them as a journalist. "They're workers, they like things to run efficiently and they aren't afraid of putting in the necessary effort to make it that way. If you have children and you and your spouse both work hard, it's difficult not to appear cold or un-

ence to business with other parts of Spain scarcely exists here.

The Catalans' work ethic – they've been referred to as the Protestants of southern Europe – is especially noticeable if you come to Barcelona after visiting the rest of Spain. It is perhaps less striking for someone who has flown in from Bonn or Tokyo. You can see it in the comparatively early closing of bars and restaurants ("early to bed, early to rise…"), shop opening hours which are the longest in Spain (just in case they missed a customer or two), and a respect for the clock which is bliss for anyone who has tried to make business appointments anywhere south

friendly to the outsider. But it doesn't mean you *are* that way. The Andaluz who spends his day in the bar is open and friendly, no doubt about that, but he doesn't get much done, does he?"

Passion for work: The most characteristic trait of the Barcelonans, and that of Catalans in general, is their passion for work, for economy, and, above all, for their famous *seny català* (prudence) in business. The *mañana* attitude so often referred to in refer-

of Madrid. In Barcelona, 10 o'clock means 10 o'clock, not half past 11.

But then Barcelona's background is purely mercantile, reaching back to the Phoenicians and Romans. Business has always been business; if you don't clinch the deal, your neighbour will – and that's no good for the bank balance. Barcelona has been built up through family enterprise, such as the legendary textile factories where offspring have always knuckled down to the job regardless of gender, with everyone feeling personally involved.

It is no coincidence that Catalonia and Japan are currently enjoying an entente. Japa-

Left, on the streets with a Catalan hat. **Above**, the top hat of authority.

COSMOPOLITAN CITY

Barcelona has always been a haven for foreigners. Greeks, Phoenicians, Carthaginians, were part of Barcelona's busy port life since well before the Roman conquest in 133 BC. Situated near the Crusade routes from western Europe, Barcelona continued to collect a foreign community during the Middle Ages, and when "infidels" (citizens of Muslim and Judaic faiths) were officially expelled from Spain in 1492, thousands of Barcelona residents became "new Christians".

George Orwell, in his Spanish Civil War memoir *Homage to Catalonia*, chronicled the

ideologically boiling Barcelona of 1936, filled with young foreigners from all over the world who had come to defend democracy in what had become a workers' city.

In the later years of Franco's rule, Barcelona became something of an ersatz Paris with its own Montmartre and Arc de Triomphe, or a Mediterranean Manhattan, with one foot in Europe and the other in the Hispanic world. Gabriel García Márquez, Mario Vargas Llosa and other international writers lived here during the 1960s and early 1970s in search of a combination of Europe, Spain and America: metropolitan energy and diversity at a survivable price and pace.

Since Franco's death, the foreign community has continued to grow, and is now estimated at 150,000. But figures differ wildly. The French colony, for example, is officially reported at 5,000, while the French Institute estimates 15,000 and long-time resident French citizens suggest 30,000 as being more realistic.

The German consulate reports 16,000 countrymen in the area, but German citizens are not required to register with consular authorities. The American colony, officially estimated at 5,000, is unofficially put at twice that figure. The British presence in Barcelona, estimated at 6,000, goes back to the beginning of the century and includes one of the founders of the local football club. The Italian colony, like the French, is large but linguistically and socially assimilated.

Barcelona's Lycée Français has long been one of the top preparatory schools, partly as an alternative to church and state-dominated education under Franco and partly as a result of the proximity of Catalan and French, linguistically more similar than Catalan and Spanish. The German School has flourished for decades, as have the Swiss, Italian, British and American Schools.

Foreigners come to Barcelona for a variety of reasons, all revolving around the basic formula of exciting, civilised living at unterrifying prices (although the latter is not quite so true now). Germans are frequently retired; French and Italians are usually married to Catalans; English, Irish and Americans are often teachers, writers and translators; Scandinavians may be entrepreneurs looking for a more rewarding tax structure.

The foreign business community is increasingly important in Barcelona as Spain's economy gains momentum. Foreign painters, sculptors, writers, actors, dancers, singers and artists are all attracted by the opportunity for personal and professional survival.

Barcelona is Spain, but it is partly removed from Celtiberia and the Hispanic world by its language and culture. It is mainstream Europe, yet part of the passionate Mediterranean. It is only a short flight from Rome, Zurich, Munich, Paris or London. Beaches as well as ski slopes are within easy reach. The city is bilingual in Catalan and Spanish, with French a closely related third language and English becoming a professionally necessary fourth.

Foreigners, all in all, do well here. Xenophilia, not xenophobia, is the rule, while passion, inspiration, civilisation, ambition and pleasure coexist peacefully in this ancient Catalan capital, a stone's throw from everywhere. ∎

nese investment has been substantial, from a Nissan car plant to the showpiece Hotel des Arts in the Olympic port, and many Catalan businesses are successful in Japan.

Apart from trade agreements, there is a cultural recognition which goes deeper than the yen. The Japanese flock to see the extravagant creativity of Gaudí, while the comic strip art of Japan is deeply admired by Barcelonans who have their own highly individual version of this art-form. Both nations share the paradoxical winning blend of the wild and the industrious.

The Barcelonans adhere fiercely to their traditions, but they are essentially a private mous identity as a separate people and – once – as a nation. The anti-central government sentiment is taken very seriously, although it is not without a touch of humour at times. Refer in passing to the city of Madrid and likely as not a Barcelonan will interject: "Someone told me that Madrid has once again become the capital of Spain."

Even during the repressive Franco regime, Barcelona retained its air of excitement and vitality. While the rest of Spain has changed enormously and extrovertedly since the death of the dictator, Barcelona's changes have not been so marked – the city is well used to centuries of changes of fortune, and

people. Their social life is wrapped in discretion and they rigorously respect the established social classes – although you are unlikely to find as much obsession with the aristocracy and with petty titles here as in other parts of the country.

An integral part of the Catalan temperament is the longstanding rivalry with Madrid. The history of Catalonia and the character of the Barcelonans are inextricably connected to the defence of their autono-

Left, eating out. **Above**, young and beautiful and up all hours of the night.

Franco's demise was just another of many.

Pitch battles: Football forms an important part of this urban duel. When the city's football team, the venerated "Barça", beats Madrid the work ethic is drowned in a delirium of nationalistic fervour because "our boys" have shown them once again. The red and gold of the Catalan colours combine with the blue and maroon ("*blau grana*") of the football club in a swirling mass down the Ramblas; woe betide the joker who says the word "Madrid" in anything above a whisper.

The *Ciutat Condal* (city state) has always been a promised land, for foreigners. During the 18th century the number of French immigrants was greater even than the number who arrived from Spain, and a Catalan-speaking Barcelonan is often as happy to converse with a foreigner in English or French as in Castilian. Today it is the South Americans who form the latest flourishing immigrant community, along with an influx of young northern Europeans, many of them artists and musicians who form a transient population, as life is not always as easy as expected. Many survive by teaching foreign languages and busking on the Ramblas.

The health and the use of the Catalan language has always been a key concern for

Barcelonans. All in all, some 6 million people worldwide speak Catalan as their mother tongue. There is a large Catalan media, including books, newspapers, television and radio stations, all centred on Barcelona. There have been times in the past when the language has been forced to go underground, particularly during the Franco regime. The Spanish Constitution of 1978 re-established Catalan as one of Spain's official languages.

In recent years the Generalitat's Department of Linguistic Policy has been particularly active in implementing Catalan, initially concentrating on the teaching of the language in schools, but new regulations introduced in 1997 have been described as "fundamentalist". Strict laws regarding the use of Catalan in commerce and other areas are quite alarming.

Personal freedom: The Barcelonans are far from being the staid, unimaginative and convention-bound people that one might imagine, given all that work weighing heavily on their minds. (Just look what they let Gaudí do.) There's room in the city for creativity and risk-taking without attracting social reprobation. "A sense of initiative is essential in order to get on probably because everyone is working so hard," says Montse, a partner in a group of graphic designers. "Barcelona has always been tolerant of difference and it's a place where women don't have to fight for their place. There's a wonderful freedom from silly conventions which allows you to go ahead and do your own thing if you want to."

Barcelona is probably the only place in Spain where you can declare yourself a vegetarian, an ecologist, a gay, a pacifist or even all four at once without provoking withering looks or worse.

Finally, good humour is an unexpected element of the Barcelonan character. However much part of a sales technique, it does a person good to be hailed as *reina* (queen) or *guapísima* (very pretty) – terms of endearment used on women of all ages, from eight to 80, in markets and bread shops especially. "But you're our customer," you will be told if you show gratitude for what could be mistaken for nascent friendship. Never mind: to be able to buy freshly cooked lentils or chick-peas from a smiling old man who's been up at 3.30am to start cooking them and who still has the vitality to crack a joke with you at midday is worth more than money.

In Barcelona on Midsummer's Eve (*Nit de San Joan* or St John's Day, 23–24 June), fire-crackers and fireworks never stop and bonfires are lit all over the city. The Barcelonans know that all work and no play would make them very dull indeed and that's something they have no desire to be.

Left, Bigas Luna, film director. **Right**, Ricardo Bofill, architect, at Gaudí's La Pedrera.

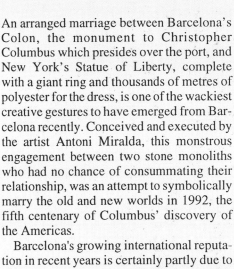

An arranged marriage between Barcelona's Colon, the monument to Christopher Columbus which presides over the port, and New York's Statue of Liberty, complete with a giant ring and thousands of metres of polyester for the dress, is one of the wackiest creative gestures to have emerged from Barcelona recently. Conceived and executed by the artist Antoni Miralda, this monstrous engagement between two stone monoliths who had no chance of consummating their relationship, was an attempt to symbolically marry the old and new worlds in 1992, the fifth centenary of Columbus' discovery of the Americas.

Barcelona's growing international reputation in recent years is certainly partly due to its creative genius. Whether it be founded on the turn-of-the-century Modernist architecture, the designer bars and discos of the late 1980s and early 1990s or flamboyant transatlantic marriages such as the one described above, Barcelona is now in bold print on the trendy tourist map. Its own incessant publicity campaign has helped, and the world media has responded. There was a time when it was impossible to pick up a magazine of general interest without finding an article on Barcelona and its creative inhabitants.

Creative games: The city's approach to the Olympic Games in 1992 endorsed this reputation: cuddly, grotesque Cobi, the Olympic mascot created by illustrator-cum-designer Javier Mariscal, was a far cry from the usual Disneyesque creature associated with Olympiads. The opening ceremony was a theatrical feast of creativity involving contemporary talent, culminating in a dramatically staged lighting of the Olympic flame by an archer. Many of the sporting events were presented with a cinematic artistry, notably the diving, with its breathtaking backdrop of the city below. Even the uniforms were designed by Antonio Miró, Barcelona's top fashion designer.

For the first time in the history of Barce-

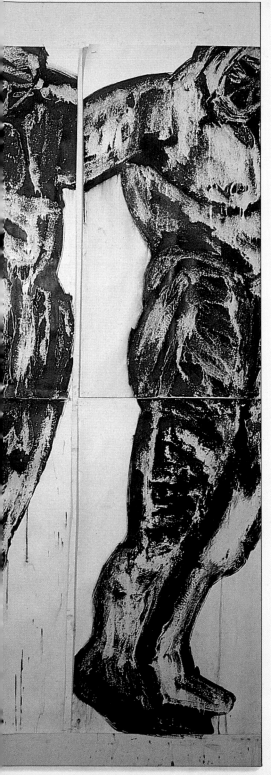

Left, Tomas Gomez, painter.

lona millions watched, but what they saw was a sense of creativity that had always been here. It seems to be endemic to the Catalan people, stemming from their fiercely individualistic spirit. It is another of those paradoxes: considered the most serious, hard-working people in Spain, they nevertheless continue to show the most creative flair. Recurring neglect from Madrid, or at worst full-scale repression, has only served to fuel that spirit. Where political independence is not possible, cultural independence is.

Under Franco, when the Catalan language was suppressed, a group of singer-songwriters emerged in the 1960s, who with their

middle class of Barcelona are remarkably open-minded when it comes to creativity. In fact they encourage it and patronise it, proud of its symbolic identity with Catalan individualism. The singular and daring architectural work of Gaudí and Domènech i Montaner would not have been seen in the central streets of the Eixample, if they had not been commissioned by rich and powerful industrialists like Eusebi Güell, Gaudí's main patron. Today the city council has proved to be an equally generous benefactor.

Barcelona has produced many leading artists over the past century, or been influential in the work of others, much of which can be

poetical protest songs known as the *nova cançó*, influenced a whole generation. Their protest was to sing in Catalan, to the extent that one of the main exponents, Joan Manuel Serrat, dared to refuse to perform Spain's Eurovision song contest entry in Castilian. He and other key figures, such as Raimon, Pi de la Serra and Lluis Llach, still compose and perform today.

Bourgeois but not boring: It is yet another Catalan enigma that much of the creative genius should have developed and survived thanks to the industrious private sector. Conventional and bourgeois they may be, but the

seen in the museums and galleries of the city. Picasso spent some of his formative years here at the turn of the century, a period well documented at the Museu Picasso. He was closely involved with a group of artists who used to meet in Els Quatre Gats café, notably Ramon Casas, Santiago Rusiñol and Miquel Utrillo who formed a movement of the same name. The café, in Carrer Montsió, is open as a bar and restaurant, but the atmosphere of the time is better captured in the evocative paintings and drawings of this group on display in the Museu D'Art Modern.

Born just off the Plaça Sant Jaume, Joan

Miró is one of Barcelona's most famous artists. The Fundació Miró on Montjuïc pays due homage to him and houses one of the largest collections of his work in the world. Of contemporary names, Barcelona's most internationally renowned and influential artist is Antoni Tàpies. His foundation to promote the study of modern art and culture is now housed in one of the city's first Modernist buildings, designed by Domènech i Montaner. Its interior has been redesigned as exhibition spaces, and it contains the most complete collection of Tàpies' own work.

Where to see it: It is hard to keep track of what's on and where: in a typical year in the

Gonzalo and the sculptors Susana Solana and Jaume Plensa. The more established galleries are congregated in the Passeig de Gràcia/Rambla de Catalunya area, particularly the street Consell de Cent, and in the Gothic quarter. A new generation of galleries, usually showing more avant-garde work, has grown up around the Born market and around the MACBA.

The opening of the Museu d'Art Contemporani (MACBA) completes the panorama of the century's art on view. It focuses on contemporary art since World War II, primarily Catalan, including the important Dau al Set group, but including Spanish and

early 1990s there were no fewer than 234 exhibitions in public spaces and 878 in private galleries. The Palau de la Virreina on the Ramblas is a good source of information.

Commercial art galleries abound in Barcelona, usually offering an opportunity to catch up with the city's new creative talent. Watch out in particular for the work of Miquel Barceló, Perico Pastor, Xavier Grau, J.M. Broto, Viladecans, Velilla and Albert

Far left, Miró's *Dona i Ocell* (woman and bird).
Left, *Núvol i Cadira* (cloud and chair) by Tàpies.
Above, metal beast on the Diagonal.

international works. In the midst of the medieval El Raval district just south of the Ramblas, this striking building designed by Richard Meier, together with the nearby Centre of Contemporary Culture (CCCB), is an exciting new element in Barcelona's creative scene.

Designer details: Just wandering around Barcelona, one is constantly reminded of its creative spirit manifested in its Modernist doorways, its art galleries, its street musicians and performers, its modern urban sculptures in the streets and squares and its designer bars and restaurants (and their lavatories), notably venues such as Nick Havanna, Tragaluz and Torres de Avila.

Venues like these are meeting points, neutral ground, where the city's intelligentsia congregate – particularly writers. Here, the barrier that divides Barcelona's literary world between those who write in Catalan and those who write in Castilian is overcome. Outside these premises they stick almost exclusively to their own linguistic group.

More literary works than ever are being published today and, strangely enough, it is the short story – that genre of writing always considered to be commercially unviable – that is finding greater acceptance among the

reading public. Maybe this has something to do with the unceasing labour carried out by publishing groups such as Anagrama or Quaderns Crema, a modest company that publishes in both languages and to whom we owe, among others, the discovery of the Catalan storyteller Quim Monzó.

Feel the pulse of the design-minded by visiting Vinçon, an emporium of interior and household design (at Passeig de Gràcia, 96) and BD Ediciones de Diseño (Mallorca, 291) where furniture designed by the grand old man Gaudí to the more contemporary Tusquets is for sale, in a house designed by

Domènech i Montaner. Go to any park, and you are bound to sit on a bench designed by one of the leading industrial designers; notice the street lamps in a renovated neighbourhood, the new plant pots, the ice-cream stalls or even the new paving, such as the hexagonal tiles in Passeig de Gràcia, designed in their time by one Antoni Gaudí.

Perhaps the most striking example of creativity as a way of life is the huge urban planning programme that has so radically changed the face of the city in recent years. Begun in the early 1980s in the first flush of the post-Franco socialist control of the town hall, it was further accelerated by the demands of the Olympic Games.

Sculpture opportunities: A particular phenomenon has been the creation of parks or urban spaces, their quality recognised by the Prince of Wales Award for Urban Design from Harvard in 1990. These new spaces have a social and aesthetic purpose in opening up dense, neglected inner-city areas and providing much needed community areas. Designed by Barcelona's leading architects, they have been duly dressed with modern sculptures by the likes of Chillida, Plensa, Anthony Caro, Ellsworth Kelly, Roy Lichtenstein and Beverly Pepper.

The latest idea to be born in Barcelona will, if successful, have far-reaching consequences. Known as Barcelona 2004, or the Universal Forum of Cultures, this ambitious plan is still at project stage but has the backing of UNESCO. The idea is for Barcelona to organise and host the first of a new kind of world event: a cultural forum that will go far beyond any World Exposition or Olympic games, bringing together the peoples of the world in a bid for culture, environmental harmony, and peace. An expected 25 million visitors over the five month duration will participate in conferences, exhibitions and shows in (what will be) this sustainable city. The rest of the world can participate through the Virtual Forum in cyberspace. There's really no stopping the tireless creative energy that flows through Barcelona.

<u>Left</u>, ancient and modern design in synthesis. <u>Right</u>, Barcelona is responsible for 80 percent of Spain's comic strip industry.

THE CATALAN LANGUAGE

In the modern world at least 6 million people use the Catalan language as their mother tongue. As well as being spoken in the city of Barcelona and the rest of northeast Spain, Catalan is also commonly used in the south of France, in Andorra, where it is the only official language, and, surprisingly, in the city of Alguer in Sardinia.

The Catalan-speaking area of Spain covers the four Catalan provinces of Barcelona, Tarragona, Lléida and Girona, the Balearic Islands (Mallorca, Menorca, Ibiza and Formentera), the community of València, which also includes Alicante and Castellón, and the three small border areas of Iecla, Jumella and Favanella, which lie within the province of Murcia. Within Catalonia the only exception is the mountainous Val d'Aran, where the people speak Arense, a language like Gascon.

Catalan is derived from Latin as used in the eastern part of the Pyrenees and shares characteristics with French, Italian and Castilian – particularly the dialects of Occitane and Aragón. To the linguist, modern Catalan seems a polyglot language, comprising something of everything on paper, but with a very individual sound when spoken.

The spread of the language outside Catalonia followed in the wake of the conquests of the kings of Catalunya and Aragón, particularly of Jaume I. In order to ensure his control of the land he distributed the new territory among his nobles on the condition that they repopulated it with Christian subjects. Consequently, after the conquest of Mallorca in 1229, the island was repopulated by Catalans, as was Ibiza in 1235. The differences in dialects that developed throughout both islands are the result of the differing origins of the new colonialists.

València, which was also conquered and repopulated by Jaume I between 1233 and 1238, was colonialised by Castilian-speak-

ing people from Aragón, but the Catalan language implanted itself only along the coast. Murcia too was conquered and colonised by Catalans. Ramon Muntaner, author of *Cronica*, one of the most brilliant works of Spanish medieval literature, refers to these Catalans, saying that they speak *del bell catalanesc del món* – the most beautiful Catalan in the world.

Literature: The first written words of Catalan appeared around the 9th century in Latin

texts. Although more extended texts have been found dating from the 11th century, it was not until the 12th century that the first complete manuscripts are found – translated fragments of *Forum Iudicorum* and *Homilies d'Organya*. Then, from the 13th century onwards, Catalan gradually began to replace Latin in legal and administrative documents.

It was a Mallorcan, Ramon Llull (1232–1315), who produced the first major work in Catalan: a vast encyclopedia of more than 200 volumes. The chroniclers of the time – Jaume I, Muntaner, Desclot and Pere III – all helped further to establish Catalan as a written language. The period from the end of the 14th century until the beginning of the 16th century was the Golden Century of Catalan literature, with the emergence of such names as Valencian-born Ausias March (1397–1459), who incorporated many of Petrarch's innovations in one of the best-ever examples of lyrical Catalan; or Joanot Martorell (1413–68), also from València, whose novel *Tirant lo blanc* was praised by Cervantes in *Don Quixote*.

With the coming to power of the House of Austria in 1516, the Castilianisation of Spain gained enormous strength, to the detriment of Catalan. At the end of the War of Succes-

sible without the triumph of the industrial revolution and the birth of a dynamic middle class. In the poem *La Pàtria*, written by Bonaventura Carles Aribau in 1833, a new period of language development began, albeit not without a certain amount of controversy. Some believed that the purest Catalan belonged to the year 1500, or even before, even though this would mean a massive use of archaic words and terminology which have long since fallen into disuse.

For others, the language should have been taken exclusively from that spoken at the day, even though it was replete with Castilianisations. From 1859, the celebration of *Els*

sion the Catalans were punished for having defended the Archduke Carlos against the pretensions of Felipe V and were made to accept the Castilian language. From this time literary works were scarce and relegated to a popular or religious standing.

Renaissance: But with the literary and social upheaval that resulted from the Romantic movement, the Catalans took a renewed interest in their medieval past and began the slow revitalisation of their language. In Catalonia "Romanticism" is known as the "Renaixença" (Renaissance).

The Renaixença would not have been pos-

Jocs Florals (the Floral Games, a poetry competition which derived from troubadour days with prizes of bouquets of flowers) acted as a spur to the updating of the written language, which still retained its medieval tendencies. The competition's motto, "Faith, Country and Love", was to be interpreted within the compositions entered.

In the end, cultural, economic and demographic factors finally decided the parameters of the written language, and it accepted the modernisations and Castilianisations which had crept into the spoken form. The unifying work of Pompeu Fabra (1868–

1948) set about establishing grammatical unity. Through the Institut d'Etudis Catalans a number of orthographic rules were drawn up in 1913. They were followed in 1917 by the *Diccionari Ortogràfic* and, finally, the *Diccionari General* in 1932.

Art movements: At the beginning of the 20th century Catalonia became involved with the literary movements of the day, first through the modernism movement and later with Noucentisme, a more conservative arts movement. Illustrious figures such as the writer Joan Maragall (1860–1911) and the painter Santiago Rusiñol (1861–1931) and Noucentistes such as poets Josep Carner

War (1936–39), the use of Catalan was forbidden and anyone heard speaking it in public could be fined. Towards the middle of the 1940s a certain tolerance had crept into this edict, but it was not until 1946 that magazines and books could once again be published in Catalan.

During this period many notable figures within the world of Catalan literature went into exile, from where they continued silently to "write [their] ill-treated language to save the word from such ignominy". The poem *Inici de Càntic en el Temple* by Salvador Espriu is representative of this period.

After the death of Franco, Josep Tarradel-

(1884–1970), Guerau de Liost (pseudonym of Jaume Bofill i Matas, 1878–1933) and Josep Maria Lopez Picó (1886–1959), along with essayist Eugeni d'Ors (1881–1954), all contributed to this period of prosperity. But it was not until the establishment of the Generalitat, in 1931, and the announcement of the short-lived "Estatut de Catalunya" in 1939, that Catalan achieved the rank of official language.

However, following the Spanish Civil

Left, independence stickers. **Above**, Jesus Ferrero, one of a new generation of writers.

las, the exiled president of the Generalitat, returned and the modern "Statute of Autonomy" was created. The Spanish constitution of 1978 re-established Catalan as one of the official languages in Spain.

Today, schools, universities, newspapers, magazines, books, theatre and television in Barcelona all operate in both languages. Most street names have been converted to Catalan, although some maps and even some Catalans continue to refer to places by their Castilian names. Moreover, Catalan was an official language of the 1992 Olympic Games.

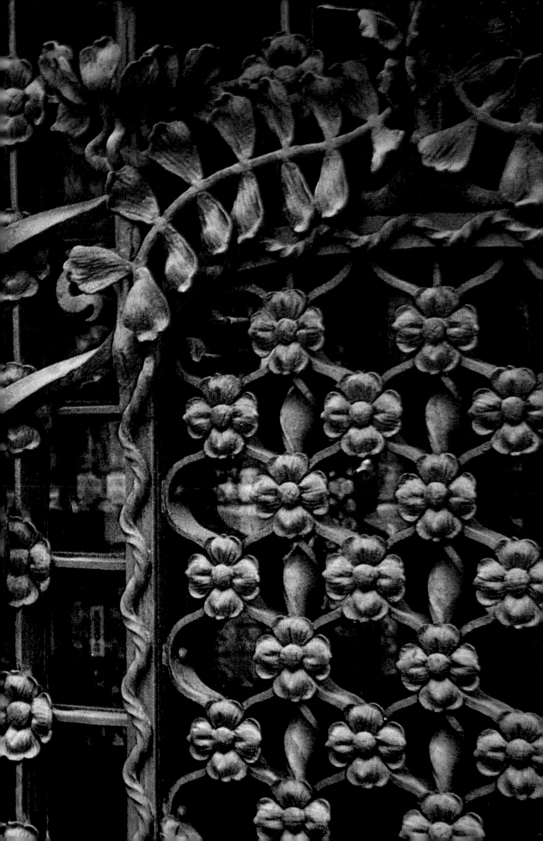

The French novelist Gustav Flaubert once stated that "bad taste is always the taste of the preceding epoch". In the years following its heyday, modernism in Barcelona was not only considered a style in bad taste, it was widely despised. The description "modernist" was intended to be deprecatory; it was used to ridicule anyone and anything which, in their turn, mocked what were considered to be traditional values. History, of course, was repeating itself: in earlier epochs, the words Gothic, baroque and Cubism were originally intended to be pejorative.

Shortly after the modernist era, the style was considered embarrassing by everyone, including many of the participating architects. In 1929, the year of the second World Fair, a guide was published called *The Art of Showing Barcelona,* explaining to any guide or citizen accompanying a tourist that he or she must explain "that the city had the *desgracia* (disgrace) of having a large part of the Eixample built in the modernist style".

Today it is no longer a disgrace: modernism is *the* architecture of Barcelona. Avoiding it would be tantamount to visiting Paris without seeing the Eiffel Tower.

Way of life: "Modernism" was the Catalan response to a variety of artistic currents running throughout Europe at the end of the 19th century. In Britain its equivalent was called "Modern Style". The Belgians named it the "Style 1900", while Germany, Austria and Italy knew it as "Jugend-stil", "Sezession-stil" and "Liberty". Since then it has become known almost universally by its French designation of "Art Nouveau".

But modernism in Catalonia, unlike its counterparts in the rest of Europe, became far more than a bizarre artistic style. It became a way of life. According to authors Cristina and Eduardo Mendoza, in their recent book *Barcelona Modernist,* "…the Barcelonans, and

especially the bourgeoisie, lived immersed in modernism: from the architecture of their houses to the most insignificant object; from the office in which (the man) passed the hours of his day to the café in which were held his *tertulias* (social chats); from his birth to his grave."

The fashion, which began as an anti-establishment art and ended up being the art of the establishment, was "too anarchic" to its many critics. It was an epoch preoccupied with the

decorative. Those most loyal to this new social wave were architects and decorators, a group which included furniture makers, makers of mosaics, ceramicists, jewellers and ironworkers. The least faithful to the trend were painters and writers. Today the most obvious remnants of this period, which ended in the mid-1920s, are the myriad houses scattered through the Eixample.

"When one contemplates a building, a sculpture, or a painting, that which is most noticeable is its decorative content," wrote A. Cirici Pellicer, one of the first of modernism's academics. For the modernists them-

Preceding pages: extreme decoration is the common thread to all modernist works. **Left**, breath-catching detail in Montaner's Palau de la Música Catalana. **Right**, modernist delicacies.

selves, decoration of even the smallest detail became an obsession. The complexity of the detail of the facades is quite stunning, particularly on buildings such as the Palau de la Música Catalana, by Lluís Domènech i Montaner, which is considered to be the most remarkable of the modernist buildings.

Most visitors will see modernism from the outside, unaware that the interior continues the ornamental theme. The Palau de la Música is evidence of this. With gigantic winged Pegasuses "flying" from the upper balcony columns, a stained-glass ceiling which will leave the visitor with a stiff neck, and a long roll-call of sculptures and ceram-

end of the Middle Ages (thus Catalan Gothic architecture, of which there are numerous fine examples in the Gothic Quarter). Neo-Gothic design was a reminder to the scholars and the public that their predecessors had been among the most daring in Europe.

But alongside this hearkening back to the past, a period of cultural and political nationalism had begun to develop within Catalonia. Wealthy flag-waving patrons such as Eusebi Güell and the Marquès de Comillas wanted to show their commitment to a new order of Catalan originality; a second "golden age". They invested huge sums to patronise the unknown talents of architects

ics dedicated to musical muses, it is hard to imagine that first-timers could concentrate on the concert for which they have paid. An itinerary has been set up, *La Ruta del Modernisme*, allowing visitors to see the interiors of many buildings (details at the centre in Casa Lleó Morera).

Origins: Catalonian modernism was the sum of a series of reflections of foreign currents in art and design. At the time, local students of architecture were taught from a strongly neo-Gothic standpoint which emphasised the importance of Catalan power and ingenuity during its "golden age" at the

such as Gaudí and Domènech i Montaner.

The movement took its roots in medievalism, a Gothic return to the Middle Ages, and in pre-Raphaelite ingenuity called primitivism. Into the pot was thrown a bit of Moorish orientalism, which had been in fashion in Catalonia since the middle of the 19th century. Neo-*mudéjar* decorative trends and techniques can be seen in many of the earliest examples, including what is considered to be the first modernist building, Casa Viçens (Carrer de les Carolines, 18–24). The brick-and-tile building, which Antoni Gaudí completed in 1878, shows strong Moorish influence which was soon to evaporate from the movement because of its obvious association with the rest of Spain and its contradiction of the very *raison d'être* of Catalan modernism's spirit of "rebellion".

William Morris, the English pre-Raphaelite artist and writer, who was instrumental in Britain in reviving traditional artisan skills in his Arts and Crafts movement, was also admired by Catalan modernists.

Big names: But while there was a synthesis of ideas among Catalan modernists, the three big names, Lluís Domènech i Montaner, Josep Puig i Cadafalch and Antoni Gaudí, were extremely diverse in their interpreta-

ered a modernist. According to Mendoza: "his genius permitted him to live in a world populated exclusively with his own fantasies. His life and his works coincided with the general characteristics of a period which, in its fervour for renovation, was fertile ground for his immeasurable creativity."

The three architects and their individual and conflicting interpretations of the modernist theme come together in the so-called "Mansana de la Discòrdia" (the Block of Discord) on the Passeig de Gràcia between Carrer d'Aragó and Carrer Consell de Cent. Almost side by side stand what are among the best works of the three most celebrated

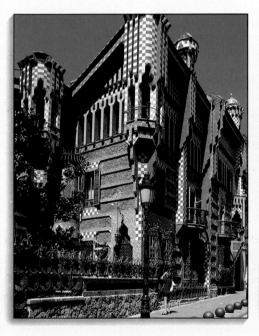

tions of the style. While second-generation Puig i Cadafalch worked in both neo-Gothic and modernism, his mentor at the Escola Superior d'Arquitectura de la Llotja, Domènech i Montaner, was busy expressing the "theory of organic rationality" in which every element must be self explanatory. And Gaudí? Well, Gaudí was just being himself.

In reality, the best known of them all, Antoni Gaudí i Cornet, can't even be consid-

exponents of modernism. On the southern corner is Lluís Domènech i Montaner's Casa Lleó Morera, two entrances further north is the Casa Amatller by Josep Puig i Cadafalch, and next door to that is one of Gaudí's best-known buildings, Casa Batlló.

Style samples: The most original of the three is Gaudí's. Since he "ignored that which didn't pertain to his own work", his work is unique and quite free from previous and contemporary influences. It is marked by his distinctive sinuous expressionist shapes and judicious use of ceramics. It is obvious from its shape, both inside and out,

Left, La Pedrera by Gaudí. **Above**, Casa Viçens, Gaudí's first work. **Right**, inside Montaner's Casa Lleó Morera.

that the author never had to think of mundane practicalities such as "where the desk was going to fit". The lack of attention to practicalities explains why some modernist buildings are not easily rented out or sold.

Next door the colourful geometric facade of the much younger Puig i Cadafalch competes very well for attention. First planned when the architect was only 21, Casa Amatller was finally completed 10 years later, in 1900. Both the facade and the interior demonstrate the architect's combination of neo-Gothic and modernist influences. The majestic entranceway is heavily Gothic while passageways within are evidently neo-

mudéjar. The first-floor library is impressive for its stained glass and the enormous fireplace covered with mythical figures.

The final building is Montaner's Casa Lleó Morera. The facade, which shows definite similarities to its big brother the Palau de la Música in its overpowering attention to detail, has been partially disfigured by the shop at street level. The interior, some of which is in the Museu d'Art Modern, also has many similarities to the Palau in its stained glass and use of mosaics and tiling.

Career credits: Gaudí, whose bizarre creations led people erroneously to suppose that

he inspired the pejorative word "gaudy", is the creator of the best-known of Barcelona's long list of modernist buildings. Headed by the Temple of the Sagrada Família, the list runs through such landmarks as the Park Güell and La Pedrera (both declared of world interest by UNESCO), Palau Güell, the pavilions of Finca Güell, Torre Bellesguard and the Col.legi de les Teresianes.

The list of modernist buildings attributed to Domènech i Montaner is just as long, if not as familiar to the visitor, as that of Gaudí. Following William Morris's lead, the architect, who became director of the Escola Superior d'Arquitectura de la Llotja, often worked with teams, installing a group of architects, ceramicists, sculptors, and glass and iron makers in a community workshop. Beginning with the site of the Museu Zoològic, a castle-shaped building within the confines of the Parc de la Ciutadella, his personal catalogue includes the Palau de la Música Catalana, Casa Fustes, Hotel España, La Rotonda and the monumental Hospital de la Santa Creu i de Sant Pau, an obligatory stop not far from the Sagrada Família (*see next chapter*).

The works of Josep Puig i Cadafalch are less impressive only because modernism had come and almost gone before he reached the height of his productivity as an architect. As well as Casa Amatller, he created such important buildings as the Casa Terrades (or Casa de les Punxes) and the Casa Macaya, culture centre of the "la Caixa" Foundation.

Other talented architects failed to achieve big-name status. Casa Comalat, for example, by Salvador Valeri i Pupurull, is two buildings in one. The floral building on the Diagonal (number 442) is difficult to reconcile with the tiled facade facing Carrer de Corsega (number 316), but these are two sides of the same building.

Other important names include Josep Jujol, who, as well as being the architect of Casa Planells, also on the Diagonal (number 332), created the serpentine ceramic bench in Gaudí's Park Güell, a feature often mistakenly attributed to Gaudí.

Left, chimney detail in Casa Amatller. **Right**, the disturbing nocturnal face of Casa Batlló.

THE SAGA OF THE SAGRADA FAMÍLIA

Antoni Gaudí's fame has spread beyond Catalonia and books dedicated to his life and work have been translated into every major language. To the Japanese, for example, Gaudí is more than a Catalan architect; he is a reason for visiting Spain. One Japanese tourist was so captivated by the project that he stayed on as a member of the workforce.

Antoni Gaudí i Cornet was born in the Catalonian town of Reus on 25 June 1852, the son of a coppersmith. Two years after graduating from the Escola Superior d'Arquitectura de la Llotja in 1878, he finished his first architectural work: a house built for Manuel Viçens on Carrer de Carolinas. But it wasn't until he met Eusebi Güell, a wealthy industrialist who wanted to establish a unique identity for Catalonia, that his talents as a creator were to be realised.

The Sagrada Família, Gaudí's most famous work, was actually begun in 1882 as a neo-Gothic structure under the direction of the architect Francesc P. Villar. Gaudí took over the project nine years later, changing the temple's very style.

Well before Gaudí's death in 1926, he realised that the work which had filled the last years of his life, the Temple of the Sagrada Família, would not be finished in his lifetime. He admitted "It is not possible for one generation to erect the entire temple; let us then leave such a forceful example of our passing that the coming generations will feel the urge to do as much or more."

Because of his obsession with the "temple", Gaudí had become a virtual recluse. He died unrecognised in a hospital bed, two days after being crushed by the wheels of a tram. At the time of his death, at 74, only one of the planned towers had been finished; another three stood shrouded in scaffolding. Fittingly, his body is entombed in the crypt of his most famous work.

Piecemeal progress: During the Civil War the anti-Church sentiment which resulted in

Left, the Sagrada Família as it stands today. **Right**, a model of what it should finally look like.

the pillaging of nearly all of the major churches in Barcelona left only two religious structures untouched – the Cathedral of Barcelona and the Sagrada Família. Except for those years, the construction work has continued – at times sporadically, at times with great urgency – under the auspices of members of Gaudí's original team.

The project has never been without its detractors. George Orwell, for example, is quoted as describing the Sagrada as "one of

the most hideous buildings in the world", and its four towers as "four crenellated spires exactly the shape of hock bottles". Many believe the temple should be left as an unfinished monument to its famous creator. Why, they ask, is the work of one of the greatest 20th-century architects being finished in a style which often has little to do with his life, his time and his ideas? The debate has kept Gaudí's name alive all over the world.

Yet Gaudí was far from being rigid in his ideas; he bequeathed to his disciples complete liberty to carry on in whatever manner they deemed suitable for their time. Today the work progresses under the control of co-ordinating architect Jordi Bonet Armengol, son of one of the maestro's long-standing aides. Although the younger Bonet hadn't been born when Gaudí met his untimely death, he recalls growing up playing among the piles of rocks that have always dotted the construction site.

Gaudí steered away from the common solutions of academic architecture. He chose instead the complex geometry of nature. "Originality is to return to the origins," he is quoted as saying. While others were busy hiding chimneys, he would put them in the centre of the facade. While others were look-

ceptual and engineering investigation by the team of architects. Once each step has been approved, draughtsmen draw up plans of each piece using the models designed and built by Gaudí, many of which were smashed in the Civil War and have had to be pieced together from mountains of fragments. As much as 15 percent of the work has had to be designed anew on the drawing boards of the five resident architects on the project, helped by computers in the architecture department of Barcelona university.

Models are built under the auspices of Jordi Cusso, who began working on the facades as an apprentice in 1967. If the

ing for the "non-colour" of classical archae-ology, he used what he called *el revestim-iento cerámico* (ceramic decoration).

Team work: Although he was a "genius out of context", Gaudí was content to share with others some of the responsibilities in the building of the Sagrada Família. His col-laborators included Francesc Berenguer, Josep Maria Jujol and Joan Rubio i Bellver, who was both his disciple and his student.

Because of the complexity of Gaudí's work – architecturally, symbolically and philosophically – every stage of the temple's construction is preceded by involved con-

shapes are geometric, the prototypes are nor-mally built from plaster; if they are sculp-tures, they are modelled in plasticine. Jordi Cusso admits that at times he has nightmares about the gigantic jigsaw puzzle upon which he is working.

The Sagrada Família has three facades: the Pasión (Passion) on Carrer de Sardenya, the Nacimiento (Nativity) on Carrer de Marina and the Gloria (Glory) on Carrer de Mal-lorca. The first two, with their soaring tiled towers, have been instrumental in spreading the temple's fame throughout the world. The third, which was originally planned as the principal entranceway and is orientated towards the midday sun, is slowly beginning to take form, and with time will become as eye-catching as the others.

Price of liberty: Apart from the continuing debate about the temple's completion, a recent focus of controversy has been the work of local artist Josep M. Subirachs. Given "total liberty" by Bonet, he has designed a series of *avant-garde* sculptures for the Pasión facade (also known as the *Fachada del Dolor* or pain) which to most casual onlookers seem strongly out of character. The project, which is a series of sculpted scenes from the life of Christ, begins at the

cos of the eastern facade, are a joy to behold in themselves and in their fidelity to Gaudí's original work.

The work is financed primarily through donations and bequests. Another small but significant source is ticket sales to visitors. The 30-strong workforce have made great advances recently on the central nave which is nearly covered, but the Sagrada is still only 40 percent completed.

New tower: Work is also being considered on the almost forgotten central tower, planned to soar 200 ft (60 metres) above the existing towers, which themselves reach 450 ft (120 metres). Although a final decision on

bottom left of the facade with the Last Supper, follows an S-shaped path towards the Crucifixion at the apex and finishes at the upper right with Christ's burial.

On the other hand the restoration and continuation of the sculptures on the opposite side of the temple – the Nacimiento facade – are being undertaken by a Japanese sculptor, Etsuro Sotoo. The statues, newer than the surrounding background of the three porti-

Left, Jordi Cusso working on a new model. **Above**, Jordi Bonet Armengol, co-ordinating architect on the project.

its viability will take years to be reached, early experimentation with the plan has already required 50 workmen to pour up to 1,000 tonnes of cement a day into subfloor pylons which need to reach a weight of 8,000 metric tonnes to sustain the central tower in earthquakes and 100mph (160kph) winds.

With the aid of modern material such as reinforced concrete, subcontracting to outside workshops and using computers to solve problems, some of Gaudí's original ideas, once discarded on the grounds of impossibility, are being re-examined. But the eventual shape still remains uncertain.

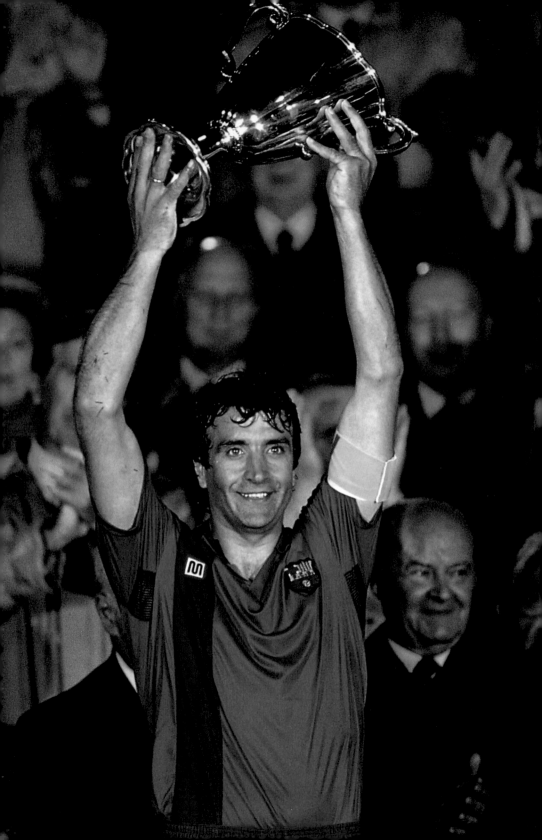

Barcelona Football Club, known throughout the sporting world as Barça, was founded in 1899 by Hans Gamper, a Swiss living in Barcelona. It is one of the oldest clubs in Europe. In a long and chequered history it has played a surprising political role, championing Catalan nationalism and liberty; it is the city's army, opera and ballet all in one and all Barcelona celebrates with its victories and weeps with its defeats.

The team lost no time in becoming well established. By 1922 it already had its own stadium, recognised at the time as one of the best in Spain and abroad, and it signed up two of the most sought-after and mythical players of the time: forward Samitier and goalkeeper Zamora.

Even at this stage matches between Barça and rival teams, such as the club Español (founded in 1903, also in Barcelona), and the Madrid team, were studded with incidents. At times the rivalry was so heated that the public was not permitted to attend.

Suppression: In 1925 a band from a British warship played the Royal march *Himno de la España Monárquica* just before the game. Even before the band had completed the opening bars the public started jeering and whistling – a spontaneous reaction against the Spanish monarchy that had accommodated the dictatorship of General Primo de Rivera. Rivera's policy had been to suppress not only personal freedom but cultural events and, more important still for the fans of Barça, the Catalan national spirit. After the incident the government ordered the Barcelona football ground to be closed.

Needless to say, popular dissatisfaction reached even higher levels during the long dictatorship of General Francisco Franco. The year 1939 saw a Franco loyalist nominated as the club's president and up until the 1950s the board of directors was kept under control by the obligatory presence at meetings of a Falangist and a member of the armed forces. However, even though the vast majority of the club's presidents and governors were no less than government vigilantes, they all became ardent followers of Barça's fortunes in football.

In 1941 a serious incident occurred during the cup match between Barcelona and Madrid. It had been ordained, before the match, that Madrid should win. As a gesture of the absurdity of the fixture, Barcelona allowed

them to win by 11 goals to one. The Barça goal-keeper was suspended for life for waving his cap on high each time he allowed the Madrid team to score.

Star sharing: Barça's fortunes really improved with the signing of the player Kubala in 1951. So powerful was the team becoming that the government ordered the removal of the equally skilful Di Stefano, also a new signing. The club's president Martí Carreto was threatened to such an extent that he eventually had to agree to share Kubala (known as the *Saeta Rubia* – the "blond arrow") with the Madrid team. The pact had

Preceding pages: even monks can't resist a game. **Left**, yet another victory for Barça. **Right**, Kubala, the "blond arrow" of the 1950s.

the player alternating between the two teams – an absurd situation almost unparalleled in world football.

Martí Carreto came under intense pressure at the time. He was ordered to the capital Madrid by the president of the Spanish Football Federation and told that the financial operation carried out to pay for Di Stefano's transfer was in fact illegal. The Federation's president – with the National Sports Delegate General Moscardó phoning every few minutes to increase the pressure – also threatened Carreto with reprisals against his textile industry. In the end the entire board of directors of Barça resigned in protest at the

ing the last years of the Franco regime). It has played a key role in Catalanising the enormous numbers of immigrants who have flooded into the city over the years. It is also, literally, more than just a football club, maintaining nine other sports sections, of which the most noteworthy are the basketball, hockey (on roller skates) and handball teams (one of whose star players is Urdangarín, the Infanta Cristina's husband).

But Barça has always been more than just a club in the way it has extended its activities beyond purely sporting events. During the last years of the dictator the club came to symbolise freedom. For decades thousands

forcible removal of the great Di Stefano.

Cradle to grave: The unusually high number of Barça members – 108,000 – is proof enough of the club's popularity. It is the world's largest organisation where memberships pass from father to son and where newborn babies are made members only hours after birth. No fewer than 80,000 of the members have permanent seats in the impressive Camp Nou stadium, which after a recent minor extension is the largest in Europe with a seating capacity of 120,000.

Barça has also been "more than just a club" (a slogan which became popular dur-

of members and fans frantically waved the blue and garnet flag of Barça as a substitute for the Catalan flag, which in those days was forbidden by Franco. A victory over Real Madrid was equivalent to a victory over the oppressive central government which had tyrannised the capital of Catalonia since 1939. As long as General Franco lived, "no other major political victory of any importance was possible".

In this spontaneous fashion Barça became the focal point for Catalan nationalism, and the nationalists could use the matches to maintain the fervour of their nation with much less risk than if they had organised a rally or demonstration.

Barça's political role reflects the importance of sports in general as a way of helping countries to make their mark at an international level. Members of the Welsh rugby team regularly put their small country – and its champions of nationalism – on the European map; the former East Germany overcame its political stigma by winning Olympic medals, and more than one Third World country has made its mark through the achievements and triumphs of its athletes.

The re-establishment of democracy has not lessened the strength of support for Barça.

justified why they are consistently considered one of the best teams in the world. Despite more than 15 trophies in the past ten years, the club remains very demanding on its players. Great players have come and gone, some of them succumbing to the pressures. Those who do make it are guaranteed a place of honour in Barça's enviable history. Cruyff – also a legendary player for the club in the 1970s, Venables and Robson are just three examples of great managers who have successfully made their way into the club. With players such as Maradona, Schuster, Lineker, Stoichkov, Romario or Ronaldo wearing the famous Barça colours

Indeed, the enormous social and financial back-up of Catalan society provides the basis for its power. The recent creation of a foundation, for example, enables Barcelona to remain a football club, whereas other Spanish clubs have inevitably begun the transformation into limited companies.

Superiority and strength: Recent history is also a true reflection of the club's enormity and insatiable appetite for victory. Both at national and international level, Barça has

in the last few years, the main objective now will be to maintain the same standard. The future looks promising with the 100th anniversary in 1999, and an exciting mixture of homegrown talent and world class foreigners on the field.

Demand for tickets is quite high, but there is usually availability if you apply long enough in advance. Obtaining tickets for major matches though, such as fixtures against Real Madrid, is impossible.

The club's museum is one of the most visited in the city and is an obligatory attraction for football fans from all over the world.

Left, fan club paraphernalia. **Above**, fan-filled taxi with Catalan and Barça flags.

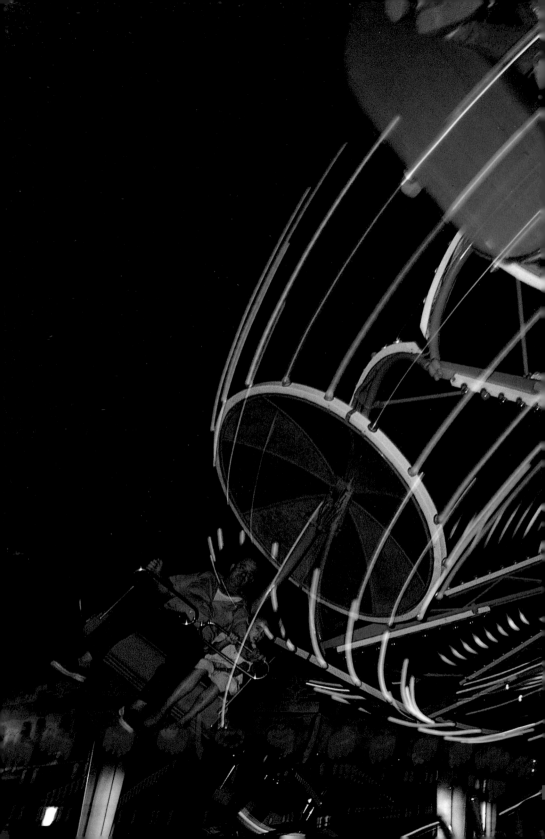

Barcelona divides neatly and conveniently into chunks of city from different periods. The old city is "old" only in the sense that it predates the city's expansion at the end of the 19th century. It is clearly identifiable from any map as the area where the streets are not regimented and symmetrical, and down its spine runs the Ramblas, the nerve centre of Barcelona.

Encapsulated within the old city is an even older one, known today as the Gothic Quarter, surrounded by Roman walls and comprising most of Barcelona's best-known historical landmarks. Within this narrow-streeted quarter are the Cathedral, the town hall, the mansions of medieval merchants (now museums and galleries) and the bishops' palaces.

The new city that burst out of the old walls is called the Eixample, and even Barcelonans will admit that its grid-like streets are monotonous in layout. But the overall monotony is broken by the best restaurants, art galleries, parks and above all the best examples of modernism, that eclectic style of architecture which isn't really a style at all, but a collection of a wide range of styles amalgamated into one. Be prepared, though, to travel some distance, as the Eixample is huge and the best modernist buildings are widely scattered.

Barcelona is squeezed between a semi-circle of hills and the sea. The hills are significant landmarks in themselves. Montjuïc was transformed for the 1992 Olympic Games with a crown of superb sports facilities; it offers the best views of the city and of the harbour, which is crossed by a cable car from the hill to Barceloneta, the fishermen's quarter. The waterfront has been cleaned up and remodelled, with elegant promenades appearing where once tumbledown warehousing separated the city from the sea. The new seafront promenade now rivals the Ramblas as a venue for evening strollers, and reaches right out to the Olympic Village and Port, a whole new district in itself.

Preceding pages: Magic Fountains below the Palau Nacional; detail from Güell park; fairgound attraction on Montjuïc. **Left**, the city from Tibidabo.

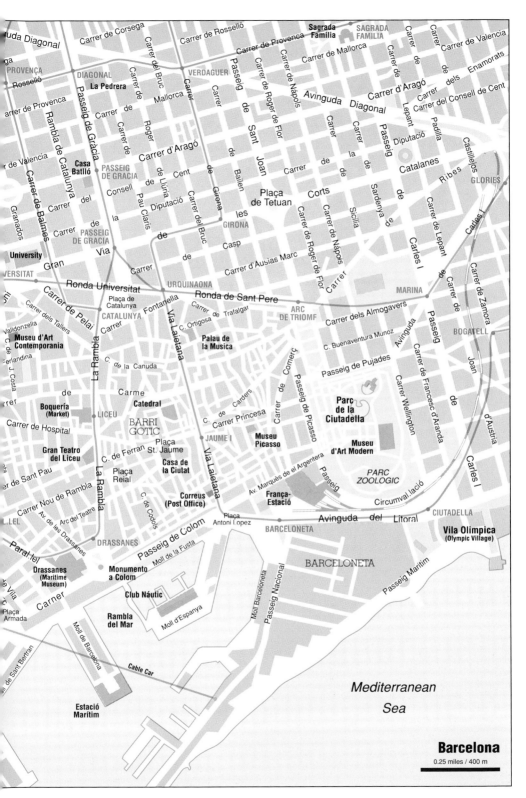

Carrer de Corsega
Carrer de Rosselló
Carrer de Provença
Sagrada Família
SAGRADA FAMILIA
Carrer de Valencia
Avinguda Diagonal
PROVENÇA
DIAGONAL
La Pedrera
VERDAGUER
Carrer de Mallorca
Carrer d'Aragó
Carrer del Consell de Cent
Carrer dels Enamorats
Rosselló
arrer de Provenca
Passeig de Gràcia
Carrer del Bruc
Carrer de Mallorca
Passeig
Carrer de Nàpols
Avinguda Diagonal
Carrer de Roger de Flor
Carrer de Lepant
Padilla
Casillejos
GLORIES
Rambla de Catalunya
Carrer de
Carrer de
Roger
de Sant Joan
de Bailen
Passeig de Sant Joan
Diputació
Sardenya
Catalanes
Ribes
de Valencia
Casa Batlló
PASSEIG DE GRACIA
Carrer d'Aragó
de Llúria
Cent
Carrer
de
la
de
Sicilia
Corts
Plaça de Tetuan
Carrer de Balmes
Carrer
del
Pau Claris
Consell
Diputació
Carrer del Bruc
de Girona
les
GIRONA
Carrer de Nàpols
Carrer de Roger de Flor
Carrer de Lepant
Carles I
Granados
Carrer
de
PASSEIG DE GRACIA
la
de
Casp
Carrer de
University
Via
de
Carrer d'Ausiàs Marc
MARINA
Carrer de Zamora
Gran
Carrer
VERSITAT
Ronda Universitat
URQUINAONA
Ronda de Sant Pere
BOGATELL
Carrer de Pelai
Plaça de Catalunya
Fontanella
Carrer de Trafalgar
ARC DE TRIOMF
Carrer dels Almogàvers
Passeig
Carrer de
Joan
Carrer dels Tallers
CATALUNYA
Carrer
C. Ortigosa
C. de la Canuda
Via Laietana
Palau de la Musica
C. Buenaventura Munoz
Passeig de Pujades
Carrer de Francesc d'Aranda
de
Valldonzella
Museu d'Art Contemporania
erlandina
C. de J. Costa
rer
Carme
Catedral
Carrer de Comerç
Passeig de Picasso
Parc de la Ciutadella
Carrer de Wellington
d'Àustria
Boquería (Market)
LICEU
BARRI GOTIC
C. de Carders
Carrer Princesa
Museu Picasso
Carles I
Carrer de Hospital
Gran Teatro del Liceu
C. de Ferran
Plaça St. Jaume
JAUME I
Museu d'Art Modern
PARC ZOOLOGIC
de Sant Pau
Plaça Reial
Casa de la Ciutat
Av. Marquès de el Argentera
Passeig
Circumval.lació
CIUTADELLA
La Rambla
Correus (Post Office)
França-Estació
Carrer Nou de Rambla
C. de Codols
Plaça Antoni López
Avinguda del Litoral
Vila Olimpica (Olympic Village)
L.LEL
Av. de les Drassanes
Arc del Teatre
Plaça
BARCELONETA
Paral·lel
DRASSANES
Passeig de Colom
Moll de la Fusta
BARCELONETA
le Vila
Drassanes (Maritime Museum)
Monumento a Colom
Moll Barceloneta
Passeig Nacional
Passeig Marítim
Carner
Club Náutic
Moll d'Espanya
Plaça Armada
Rambla del Mar
Moll de Barcelona
Cable Car
Mediterranean Sea
Estació Marítim

Barcelona

0.25 miles / 400 m

	1	2	3	4	5

A

L1 Metro Line 1 ☒ Renfe (Main Line)
L2 Metro Line 2 ○ Station interchange
L3 Metro Line 3 ☒ Station for the Port
L4 Metro Line 4 ═ Tramvia Blau (Tram)
L5 Metro Line 5 ✚ Funicular
◆ Station ⚑ Telefèric (cable car)
▶ Terminus

B

Ferrocarrils de la
Generalitat de Catalunya
(Suburban Line)

Riu Llobregat

C

L3 Zona Universitaria

Palau Reial

Maria Cristina

L5 Cornellà

Sant   Can   Can   Pubilla
Ildefons Boixeres Vidalet Cases

Gavarra

Collblanc

Les Corts

D

Can Serra

Florida

Badal

Plaça del Centre

Torrassa

Hospital
Clinic

Rbla.
Just Oliveras

Santa Eulàlia

Plaça de Sants

Entença

Sants Estació

Mercat
Nou

Av. Carrilet

L'Hospitalet

Tarragona

Bellvitge

Hostafrancs

Espanya   Rocafort   Urgell

E

L1
Feixa Llarga

Poble Sec

F

Parc de Montjuïc

Paral·le

Castell

Mirador

G

North

102

	1	2	3	4	5

THE PLAÇA DE CATALUNYA

The Plaça de Catalunya is the hub of Barcelona in terms of transport and city communications, as well as the link to the airport. But it is also the centre of the city in a much wider sense: in the middle of the square itself paving stones are arranged into the shape of a star which, they say, is also the centre of the capital of Catalonia.

If you have a point to make, you do it in the Plaça de Catalunya. But, unless you have arranged a rendezvous here, this is not really a square for lingering long: the banks that line the square don't make it particularly people-friendly. Fortunately the amount of traffic circling the square has been reduced by new city ring roads and increasing pedestrianisation.

Where old meets new: Catalunya is the pivotal point of the old and new cities. To the north and west of the square is the regimented Eixample, with its broad avenues, business quarters, elegant shopping and modernist architecture. To the east is the Gothic Quarter, a maze of dark, ancient streets whose walls exude ancient history. The Ramblas, the spinal chord of the city, leads its flood of humanity down from the Plaça to the southeast, changing character several times before it reaches the recently revived port area. Further south still, the Olympic hill of Montjuïc dominates both port and town.

When the medieval wall of Barcelona was demolished back in 1859 and work on the Eixample began, the Plaça was a large field outside the city, traversed by a mountain stream (the stream bed was later to form the foundations of the Ramblas) and connected to the inner city by means of an entrance called the Portal dels Orbs. The entrance was later renamed the Portal de l'Angel because,

Right, a paving-stone star marks the centre of the Catalan capital.

so the story goes, when Sant Ferrer crossed through this doorway with his followers, he was greeted by an angel.

The Plaça as it stands today had a difficult birth. The 19th-century Plan Cerdà, a project for the redevelopment of Barcelona, called for the creation of a square a little further inland, at the junction of the Passeig de Gràcia, the Gran Via de les Corts Catalanes and Carrer de Consell de Cent. Another rival project presented by Antoni Rovira i Trías proposed an enormous plaza 2,600 by 1,300 ft (800 by 400 metres) to be called the "Forum Isabel II". Yet another plan for a plaza similar to that which we know today was designed in 1868 by Miquel Garriga.

While the authorities were endeavouring to reach an agreement – planning permission was hard to get even then – the owners of the corresponding plots of land got fed up with waiting and began to build. In 1902, Lord Mayor Ledesma ordered the demolition of all these buildings but it was another quarter of a century before the Plaça took on its current manifestation. Based on a design by Francesc Nebot, the square was opened by King Alfonso XII in 1927.

A series of statues was added to the furniture of the square: of particular note are two in front of the dominant buildings to the west: *La Diosa* by the great Catalan sculptor Josep Clará (there is a museum with a permanent exhibition of his works towards Tididabo) and *El Pastor Tocando el Caramillo* (shepherd playing the flute) by Pau Gargallo. Unfortunately, traffic pollution has eaten into their finer details. Recently added to the south corner is *Monument a Macià* by Josep Subirachs, which looks rather like an inverted flight of steps.

Tea and politics: The buildings which surround the square combine nostalgia with business. The corner of **Carrer de Rivadeneyra** (now dominated by the Hard Rock Café and Marks & Spencer), for example, was the site of the almost mythical Maison Dorée café. Such was the character of this establishment that,

Goddess in the square.

when it finally closed its doors in 1918, another café of the same name opened at number 6. "It was never the same," wrote Lluís Permanyer, city historian, who relates that it was in this establishment that a tradition of "five o'clock tea" was introduced to Barcelona.

Another meeting point of intellectuals was the old Hotel Colón, which has since become the headquarters of the Banco Español de Crédito (*Banesto*). Older generations of Republicans remember when the facade of the hotel was covered in portraits during the Civil War. With giant posters of Marx, Lenin and Stalin, there was no mistaking that this was the headquarters of the Unified Socialist Party of Catalonia (PSUC), then the leading socialist group.

In the late 1960s, a student demonstration gave new meaning to that generation's slogan "Imagination is Power". A rebel with a sense of humour placed several boxes of washing powder in one of the fountains. A few hours later the cardboard boxes disintegrated and both the fountain and the police force attending the demonstration were awash in soapsuds.

Place to demonstrate: Sooner or later all those who have something to say, be it in protest, acclamation or celebration, find their way to the Plaça de Catalunya. Among such demonstrations and just causes, one in particular will remain a memorable event: the Diada de Catalunya, which celebrates regional nationalism (actually the defeat of Catalan forces after the siege of 1714). The Diada held on 11 September 1978 was possibly one of the most massive popular demonstrations to be seen in the Plaça de Catalunya or, indeed, in Spain in recent years.

The Plaça has not escaped the radical changes which have swept through the city. A new stretch of promenade has established the final link between the Ramblas and the Rambla de Catalunya, and the monumental department store El Corte Inglés, has a new facade, although it continues to bear a resem-

Below, pavement painting. Right, shepherd playing the flute by Pau Gargallo.

blance to a prison. The store is so named ("The English Cut") because its distant origins lie in a humble Madrid tailor's shop. And on the southern side is El Triangle, a large commercial and business centre with shops, offices and cinemas, which opened in 1998. Its Café Zurich will be a far cry from the traditional meeting place that was demolished to make way for this development, but in this prime position looking down La Rambla no doubt it will mature into a new landmark.

Four corners: From the northern corner the **Ronda de Sant Pere** is a wide avenue of manorial residences, where once the great textile families were located. From the same corner the **Passeig de Gràcia**, a handsome avenue lined with the city's most elegant boutiques, heads west, through select bookshops and famous art galleries, into the **Eixample**, a region of rigid avenues with glimpses of Barcelona's best modernist buildings in the distance.

The plaça is a starting point for either

version of **Las Ramblas**, the lower part of which starts with the **Rambla de Canaletas**, or the upper section, the **Rambla de Catalunya**, which runs parallel with Passeig de Gràcia. The latter properly begins where a statue of a thoughtful bull (perhaps contemplating his breed's banishment from the city – no bullfighting here except for tourists) marks the beginning of a largely traffic-free avenue; art galleries, book-shops, and cinemas adjoin bars specialising in hot chocolate and pastries.

Where **Carrer Pelai** meets the plaça subways lead down to the immense Metro station, which also houses the Catalunya railway (FGC).

Moving further around the plaça, the pedestrianised **Avinguda del Portal de l'Angel** is at its finest at Christmas time when the glittering shop window displays vie with one another to create the greatest impact.

Opposite, beneath the plaça, is the useful and efficient Tourist Information Centre. Apart from the elegant **Gas building**, the Portal de l'Angel is a busy shopping street. Along the way are vendors with popcorn, sweetmeats and, throughout the festive season, roasted chestnuts. This avenue leads eventually into the heart of the *barri* **Gòtic** (Gothic Quarter).

Just before the Quarter begins is the **Plaça Nova**, the venue for gruesome public hangings and executions in the Middle Ages. In 1989–90 it was again the scene of controversy, when workmen making an underground car park stumbled upon Roman remains. The work has now been completed, with the key finds taking their place in the city museums. Meanwhile visitors can now benefit from an unhindered view of the **cathedral**, as well as the Picasso doodles that adorn the concrete facades of the **Col.legi d'Arquitectes** (actually executed by Norwegian artist Carl Neijar from Picasso originals). The Plaça Nova has become a venue for Sardana dances on Sunday lunchtimes and an antique market on Thursdays.

Meeting place for excursions into the city (left) or just for talking (right).

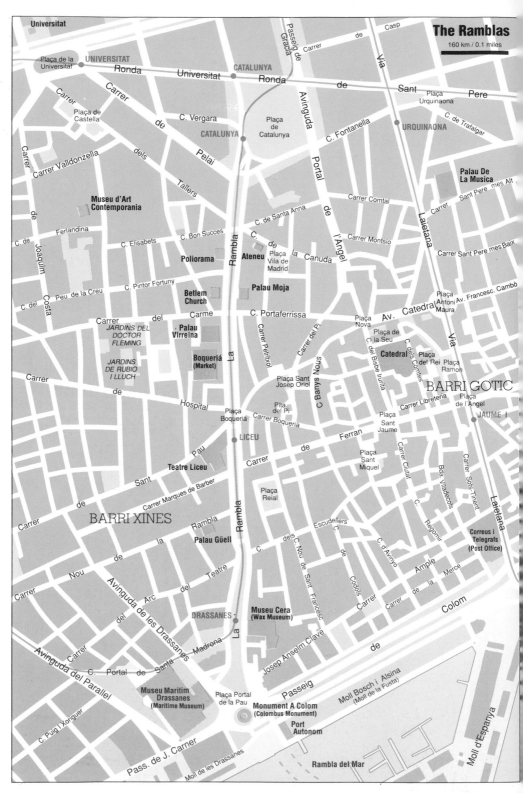

The Ramblas

160 km / 0.1 miles

Universitat

Plaça de la Universitat

UNIVERSITAT

Ronda Universitat CATALUNYA Ronda de Sant Pere

Carrer Carrer

Plaça de Castella

C. Vergara

Plaça de Catalunya

Passeig de Gràcia

Carrer de Casp

Via

Plaça Urquinaona

URQUINAONA

C. de Trafalgar

Pelai

CATALUNYA

Plaça de Catalunya

Avinguda

C. Fontanella

Palau De La Musica

Carrer Valldonzella

dels

Tallers

Portal

Carrer Comtal

Carrer Sant Pere mes Alt

Laietana

Museu d'Art Contemporania

C. de Santa Anna

de

Carrer

Carrer Sant Pere mes Baix

Ferlandina

C. Elisabets

C. Bon Succes

C. de Santa Anna

l'Àngel

Carrer Montsio

C. de Joaquim

C. de Costa

Poliorama

Ateneu

Plaça Vila de Madrid

de la Canuda

Plaça Antoni Maura

Av. Francesc. Cambó

C. del Costa

Peu de la Creu

C. Pintor Fortuny

Betlem Church

Palau Moja

Rambla

C.

Plaça Nova

Av. Catedral

Via

Carrer del

Carme

C. Portaferrissa

Plaça del Pi

Plaça de la Seu

Plaça del Rei

Plaça Ramon

JARDINS DEL DOCTOR FLEMING

Palau Virreina

Carrer Petritxol

C del Bisbe Irurita

Catedral

Plaça dels Comtes

JARDINS DE RUBIO I LLUCH

Boqueria (Market)

La

Plaça Sant Josep Oriol

C Banys Nous

Carrer Llibreteria

BARRI GOTIC

Plaça de l'Àngel

Carrer

de

Hospital

Plaça Boqueria

Plta. del Pi

Carrer Boqueria

Plaça Sant Jaume

JAUME I

LICEU

de

Ferran

Plaça Sant Miquel

Pau

Carrer

Plaça Sant Ciutat

Bda. Viladecols

Teatre Liceu

Sant

Carrer Marques de Barber

Plaça Reial

Carrer Ciutat

Carrer Sots-Tinent

BARRI XINES

Rambla

Escudellers

C.

Regomir

Laietana

de

Rambla

Palau Güell

la

Teatre

dels

C. Nou de Sant Francesc

de

Còdols

C. d'Avinyo

Ample

Correus i Telegrafs (Post Office)

Merce

Nou

Avinguda de les Drassanes

Arc

del

Carrer

de la

Colom

Carrer

de

DRASSANES

Museu Cera (Wax Museum)

Carrer

Carrer

Avinguda del Parallel

C. Portal de Santa Madrona

Josep Anselm Clave

de

Museu Maritim Drassanes (Maritime Museum)

Plaça Portal de la Pau

Monument A Colom (Colombus Monument)

Passeig

Moll Bosch i Alsina (Moll de la Fusta)

Moll d'Espanya

C. Puig i Xoriguer

Port Autonom

Pass. de J. Carner

Moll de les Drassanes

Rambla del Mar

112

THE RAMBLAS: HEART OF THE CITY

It has often been said that nowhere else in the world does 5,000 ft (1,500 metres) of asphalt reflect so well both the lifestyle and the pulse of a city as does the **Ramblas** in Barcelona.

This avenue, or collection of avenues head-to-head, is a perennial attraction for visitors and locals, year in, year out. Yet the Ramblas is constantly changing, not only with the seasons but with every passing hour, by day and by night, in the afternoon and the small hours of dawn. It even changes in relation to its own configuration, since it is in no way homogeneous. Maps and Barcelonans are divided on whether the Ramblas is one or many; perhaps the best answer is that there are five individual components of this street, each different from the other, but the whole is greater than the sum of its parts.

The Ramblas is the thoroughfare of Barcelona *par excellence*, the spinal cord either side of which lie the city's main attractions. What used to be a river bed is now a river of vital movement – of people: a torrent of humanity comprising bankers, beggars, artists, intellectuals, workmen, vagabonds, clergy, tourists, anarchists and aristocrats. It is a concert of many languages blending with the noise of the traffic, the sounds of the birds and the scent of the flowers from the stalls, whatever the season. But it doesn't do to travel its length at too fast a pace; that way these 5,000 ft (1,500 metres) of tarmac become just a blur of colour.

The world on stage: The main promenade is a unique world of art and fantasy, tradition and deception, luxury and misery. It constitutes a free show for both onlookers and performers, and may even cause you to ask yourself which you are, spectator or spectacle. Rubbing elbows with musicians, mimics, artists, fakirs and faith-healers are men and women who read Tarot cards, fortune tellers and gypsies who will read your palm, a living statue, a man hitting ping-pong balls with a hammer, a trumpet player, a violinist. All along the promenade, musicians from many nations perform a whole variety of music, from the Andean flute to modern jazz. And sometimes a couple of women will offer a free striptease show to passers-by.

Despite its dual personality – gay, flower-bedecked in the morning, sombre, disorderly but undeniably picturesque at night – the Ramblas continues to be the page upon which the throbbing history of this city is written. This is where rumours are generated, protests are raised and popular demonstrations take to the streets before marching to one of the squares.

This is the city's prime observation point, an immense gallery where every aspect of life is exhibited; to the extent where the city, in unconscious homage to the Ramblas, has invented two words: *Ramblejar*, a verb which means to walk down the Ramblas, and *ramblista*, an

Preceding pages: fiesta crowds on the Ramblas. Right, the Canaletas Fountain.

adjective which describes a person addicted to the act of the verb.

It is along this street that major football victories (which are like national battles to the Catalans) have been celebrated and where opera lovers have thrilled to the voices of Caruso, Pavarotti and Caballé. It is here that the best restaurants purchase their supplies, in the Boqueria market, and where the citizens of Barcelona enjoy one last refreshing drink after a long and heavy night of clubbing.

River to road: Originally, the Ramblas was the river bed (the Latin name *arenno* was replaced by the Arab word *ramla*) that marked the exterior limits of the city fortified by King Jaume I. But when the city expanded during the 15th century, the Ramblas became part of the inner city.

In due course a number of religious houses were built throughout the surrounding areas and the river bed came to be known as the "Convent Thoroughfare". It was not until the beginning of the 18th century that the Ramblas was to become a more clearly defined street, after permission was granted to build on the ancient walls in the Boqueria area. In 1775 a section of the city walls was torn down and a central walkway built, lined with poplar trees and higher than the roadway that ran along either side.

Within the small and densely populated area of the ancient fortified city, the Ramblas was the only street of any significance, and it became the city's focal point. Renovations were constantly under way during the 19th century, and the street settled down to become more exclusive and aristocratic; this change of status was aided by the disappearance of some of the surrounding buildings and convents, creating space for new plazas and mansions.

The Ramblas assumed its present shape between 1849 and 1856 when all the remaining fortifications were torn down. The first plane trees, brought from Devesa in Girona, were planted in 1851 and the street became "the fash-

Discussing the latest Barça match.

ionable promenade route, where the cream of Barcelona parades on foot, by carriage or on horseback," according to the 19th-century journalist Gaziel.

From the top: The course of this unique promenade (which runs from the Plaça de Catalunya to the Columbus Monument by the harbour) begins from the **Font de Canaletas**, one of the symbols of Barcelona. The uppermost section of the Ramblas is actually called the Rambla de Canaletas after the 19th-century cast-iron fountain on the right-hand side of the first pedestrian stretch. Here tramps wash themselves in the morning and executives drink in the evening; the flowing water is purported to have the power to convert all who drink there into true Barcelonans. To "drink the water of Canaletas" is synonymous with baptism for the true citizens of Barcelona.

For years the Fountain of Canaletas has been the favourite meeting place of casual visitors. In 1781, the "foremost and most distinguished" citizens of Bar-

Spectators or spectacle?

celona gathered here (according to the chronicles of the time) in such numbers that rented chairs were placed on either side of the promenade – a practice which continues today. Thirty pesetas will procure a chair for the whole day and a bootblack will never be far away. Over the weekends, football generally takes precedence in conversations here.

This stretch of the Ramblas is like the hallway to the city's great salon. Solitary people gather around the fountain or at the entrance to the metro, clearly waiting the arrival of a partner who never seems to materialise. Up above the shop fronts are numerous small and not so small hotels.

Hidden just down Carrer Tallers is the **Boadas Cocktail Bar**, the oldest in the city, and well known among the locals. Here, under the eagle eye of the first owner's portrait, or of his daughter who still runs the bar with some style, one can ask for the cocktail of the day.

At the junction with the Carrer Bonsuccés is the long-standing pharmacy of

Dr Masó i Arumí, complete with ceramic pill-boxes and of notable modernist decorative elements. If you walk past it some distance down the narrow Carrer and along Elisabets, you will reach Barcelona's latest arts extravaganza, MACBA (Contemporary Art Museum) and the **Centre de Cultura Contemporània** in the elegantly converted Edifici Pati de les Dones.

The MACBA, designed by Richard Meier and Partners, has similarities to Paris's Pompidou Centre, and its forecourt is a popular, multi-ethnic playground. This new powerhouse of contemporary art has been built on the grounds of the former Casa de Caritat, or poor house, and makes a startling contrast to its immediate surroundings. Its permanent collection includes Catalan, Spanish and international contemporary art and there are also visiting shows here.

Returning to the Ramblas between Carrers Bonsuccés and Tallers is Carrer Sitges, a narrow street of young bars, music shops and value for money restaurants. Opposite Bonsuccés are the diverging streets Carrer Santa Anna and Carrer Canuda, the former a good pedestrian shopping street. Just down here through a half-hidden doorway to the left, is the **Monestir de Santa Anna**, an oasis of peace amid the roaring traffic. The Romanesque church and Gothic cloister are marvellous examples of the architecture of their time.

Returning to the Carrer de Canuda, at number 6, is the **Ateneu Barcelonès**, a traditional cultural enclave with walk-in exhibitions located in a building that dates back to 1796. Of the original structure, only the stairway to the inner courtyard, the romantic rear garden and the paintings on the ground-floor ceilings remain. Notice the polished knockers on the main doors as you leave.

Bird life: Back on the Ramblas, this is a good moment to buy a foreign newspaper in one of the numerous kiosks. The colourful equivalent of the flower stalls a little further down, the stands **Stall on the Rambla de les Flors.**

here boast a particularly lurid display of pornography that proclaims post-Franco liberalism – no matter that you never see anyone actually buying any of the stuff. Beyond begins the Rambla dels Estudis, also called Rambla dels Ocells ("of the birds"). The name is due as much to the vast number of sparrows that nest in the trees as to the number of bird vendors. The name Rambla dels Estudis derives from the 16th century, when the Estudi General, or University, was located here. In 1714, as a result of the Catalan defeat at the hands of Castilian troops, the university was transferred to the township of Cervera in the province of Lléida. The building ceased to exist in 1843.

Here, on the right-hand side, in the 18th century, was the Jesuit Col.legi de Nobles de Cordelles, the convent of the same order and the church. Today, part of the plot is occupied by the Reial Acadèmia de Ciències i Arts and the **Teatre Poliorama**, with a ticket office looking like a massive ornamental wardrobe. On the exterior is the clock which

has been the official timekeeper of the city since 1891.

The **Viena Café**, elegant and often with a pianist upstairs, is worth a stop. Here, on the corner with Pintor Fortuny, is the new **Meridien Hotel**, where rock stars stay.

Of all the vast conglomeration of the former university, only the **Church of Betlem** (beyond the Filipino tobacco company) remains, a long and rather depressing bulk. The baroque facade on the Carrer del Carme was built in 1690 but the main structure was not completed until 1729. On the exterior wall, the dressed stone that decorates the facade and the main front are both well preserved.

Once it has passed the Ermita, the Rambla (here called Sant Josep) opens up again. On the left is the **Palau Moja**. This important neo-classical, 18th-century building is actually rather disappointing from the outside, although it houses a collection of beautiful murals by Francesc Pla. One, *El Vigatà*, in the

Below, bookstall postcards. Right, the Boqueria market.

GRAN TEATRE DEL LICEU

The origins of Barcelona's Gran Teatre del Liceu, the city's famous opera house, are curious. The Philanthropist Manuel Gibert i Sans, a national militia commander, started the "Liceo Dramático de Aficionados" with the idea of organising soirées to raise funds for his battalion. The theatre company was housed for a while in the former convent of Montsió, where the first opera staged was Bellini's *Norma,* on 3 February 1838.

In 1842, looking for a bigger venue, they bought the land of the former convent of the Trinitarios on the Ramblas. Around this time the militia was dissolved and the company became a wholly artistic and social foundation. Gibert recruited the aristocrat Joaquim de Gispert i Anglí and the banker Manuel Girona i Agrafel, a principal representative of the new industrialist upper class, as backers for his project for the creation of the Gran Teatre del Liceu.

Construction began in 1844 under the supervision of architect Miquel Garriga i Roca. This enormous project was second only to that of the Scala of Milan, with space for 4,000 spectators. The French designer Viguié added an eclectic facade. The theatre boxes were sold for 15,000 pesetas each, in perpetuity, to the grand families who collaborated in the venture.

The Liceu was inaugurated in 1847, but a fire partially destroyed the theatre and it was refitted in 1862. The architect, Josep Oriol i Mestres, followed the style of Viguié and the interior decoration was carried out by a number of respected painters, led by Josep Mirabent i Gatel.

In the same year the Círculo del Liceu was started. This club that functioned as a meeting place for the city's power brokers is described by the American social historian Gary Wray McDonogh in his book *The Good Families of Barcelona*: "The club was isolated [from the Liceu] as a prerogative of the upper class... The boxes, an extension of the family dwelling, were the dominion of the women where they held their meetings and socialising. El Círculo itself, on the other hand, was converted into an extension of the men's offices. Both were central parts of the Liceu as an institution."

Every type of performance, from musical galas, operas and ballets to rowdy carnival dances, were held in the theatre, attended by all classes of society, carefully segregated in their respective areas.

Throughout the theatre's history some of the world's greatest musicians and artists have performed here, including Stravinsky, Falla, Caruso, Domingo, Callas, Kraus, Pavarotti and Catalonia's own Albéniz, Casalls, Caballé, Aragall and Josep Carreras, who made his debut here.

But the sight of fur-coated Catalan bourgeoisie heading cautiously down the Ramblas to the Liceu was interrupted on 31 January 1994, by a dramatic fire which once again gutted the interior. After the initial shock, emotional reactions and only a small amount of questioning about the fire's origins, the authorities came together in a show of solidarity to announce that the opera house would be rebuilt. Earlier controversial plans for major expansion, involving the expropriation of private buildings, never really got further than the drawing board.

Architect Ignasi de Solà Morales, has modernised the acoustics, lighting and stage, and doubled the theatre's overall size to 350,000 sq. ft (32,000 sq. metres), while keeping to the original style of decoration. The plan for the future is to reopen the Liceu with two concurrent operas in spring 1999. ∎

Alfredo Kraus in the Liceu dressing room

main salon, was painted in 1790. Today, the palace (much diminished) has been converted into offices of the Department of Culture of the Generalitat (the Catalan government), with exhibitions (main entrance in the Carrer de Portaferrisa at the side). Its Ramblas frontage is occupied by an official bookshop with every volume on Catalan culture imaginable.

Opposite the Palau's entrance is the **Font de Portaferrisa**, one of the most ancient fountains of Barcelona, although its present location dates from only 1861. Earlier (from 1605) it was situated in the Carrer del Carme, at the site upon which the Church of Betlem was built. In 1951 an impressive mural of Valencian tiles, representing the Ramblas of the 18th century, was added. The legend on the mural describes the origin of the name, which means "iron gate".

Carrer Portaferrisa itself leads into a world of commerce and numerous fashion shops. Some metres in, on the right, is the picturesque and narrow **Carrer de Petritxol**, which dates from the 15th century but its ambience – despite its 17th and 18th-century buildings – is 19th-century. The street is lined with sumptuous small boutiques, with tile-pictures on the walls celebrating local events ("Montserrat Caballé lived here"). Shops include **Beardsley**, an emporium of anything imaginative, and the **Casa Parés**, Spain's oldest art gallery (1840) from where Ramon Casas and Santiago Rusiñol spearheaded the revival in Catalan painting. From the turn of the century it became a tradition here to drop by after mass, admire the art and sample a hot chocolate in one of the street's so-called *granjes* (tea and chocolate rooms).

Textile house: Back to the Ramblas, detour down the Carrer del Carme for the **El Indio** textiles shop (at number 24), founded in 1870, and little changed since. Its present aspect, with interesting carvings on the wooden facade and windows, is the result of renovations carried out in 1922. Inside there are long

Street dancer in the Plaça del Pi.

wooden trestle tables for proper display of the cloth, and wooden chairs for stout ladies to rest their legs.

At this point back on the Rambla de Sant Josep (better known as the Rambla de les Flors, or "of the flowers"), the air smells sweet. During the 19th century this was the only place where flowers were sold and each vendor had his favourite clientele. Artist Ramon Casas picked out one of the flower-sellers to be his model, and later his wife.

To the right is the **Palau de la Virreina**, a magnificent 18th-century rococo building set back from the road for greater effect. In 1771 Manuel Amat, Viceroy of Peru, sent a detailed plan from Lima for the construction of the house that he planned to build in the Ramblas. The final building was not completed until 1778 and the Viceroy died only a few years after taking up residence. It was his young widow who was left to enjoy the palace, which became known as the palace of the "Virreina" or vicereine. Today it is an excellent exhibition venue, the official information centre for all cultural events in Barcelona, and a booking office. To one side is an ancient music store.

Fresh food emporium: Next door rises one of the most representative and best loved symbols of Barcelona, the **Mercat de la Boqueria**. Neither the market of Santa Caterina, inaugurated in 1842 as Catalonia's first covered market, nor any of the other 40 markets in Barcelona today has achieved the popularity of the "Boqueria", which was opened on 19 March 1836.

The market occupies a square surrounded by smooth Ionic columns that support the front terraces. The roofing, designed by Miquel de Bergue, was not in place until 1914; the whole structure stands on part of what used to be the convent of the Carmelites Descalças de Sant Josep.

Within, all the produce is presented in a careful and orderly fashion (if it smells, it'll be at the back with the fish). The multi-coloured central avenue (a bit

Left, Santa Maria church in Plaça del Pi. **Below**, road to the Palau Güell.

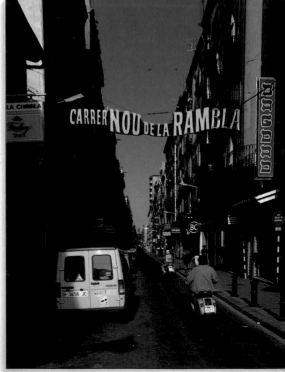

more expensive) is a particularly arresting sight, as much suited to an art critic as to a shopper. In season, look out for whole stalls selling truffles and different sorts of mushrooms.

Opposite the market is an unexpectedly modern building (uninspiring at street level) rather grandly titled the **Palau Nou de la Rambla**. The complex is supposedly completely automated, and includes "robot parking" on nine levels under the ground.

Executioner's spot: Beyond the market the Rambla enters the **Pla de la Boqueria** (marked only by a widening of the Rambla). This was the site of executions in the 14th century, when it was paved with flagstones. The name dates from the previous century when tables selling fresh meat, *mesas de bocatería,* were erected here ("boc" was the Catalan for goat's meat). In the 15th century the tables of gamblers and cardsharps replaced the meat stalls.

Today the flagstones have been replaced by a Joan Miró pavement created in the 1970s. The gallows, symbol of death, have been replaced by a neoclassical fountain, the symbol of life. At one corner is the **Casa Bruno Quadras**, built by Josep Vilaseca in 1891, in neo-Egyptian style. The decoration, complete with fans and a great Chinese dragon, demonstrates the oriental influence felt by the modernists.

The Carrer de Boqueria, which leads off the Rambla to the left, passes to the harbour side (dive up the tiny Carrer Alsina) of three hidden gems: the **Plaçeta del Pi**, the **Plaça de Sant Josep Oriol** and the **Plaça del Pi**. The last of these comes complete with a Gothic church of Santa Maria (14th and 15th centuries), displaying one of the greatest rose windows in Europe (stand in the square and look up after dark). There are a number of antique shops in the area and during the weekend craft and artistic fairs are held throughout this rosary of small squares, which make up Barcelona's Montmartre.

Theatreland: Beyond the Miró paving,

Caricaturist on the Ramblas.

the Ramblas changes character again, giving way to the bar terraces, hotels and restaurants of the Rambla dels Caputxins. This particular stretch is most enjoyable at night and is best witnessed from one of the terraces or from inside the **Café de la Opera**, one of the few remaining old-fashioned cafés in Barcelona.

Height of *bel canto*: The Rambla dels Caputxins (so-called because, until 1775, the left side was the site of the Capuchin Convent and its adjacent vegetable garden) is known also as Rambla del Mig or the Rambla del Centre. It did not acquire its present aspect until the mid-19th century, when it was the first of the component parts of the Ramblas to become a promenade. This section is dominated by the **Gran Teatre del Liceu** (1861) cathedral of the *bel canto* in Spain, and launch-pad for names such as Carreras and Caballé. Unfortunately much of the interior was destroyed by fire in 1994, and needed to be almost entirely rebuilt (*see page 118*).

On the left side of the Ramblas here starts the Carrer de Ferràn, pedestrianised, which leads to the Plaça Sant Jaume at the heart of the Gothic Quarter.

The **Hotel Oriente**, on the same side as the Liceu a little further down , preserves the structures of the Col.legi de Sant Bonaventura, founded by Franciscan monks in 1652. The convent and cloister, built between 1652 and 1670, are there in their entirety. The cloister is now the hotel ballroom, surrounded by the monks' gallery. A wall plaque reminds readers that this was the first public place in Barcelona to use gas lighting.

Down the Carrer Nou de la Rambla on the right, numbers 3–5 are occupied by the **Palau Güell**, a notable residence built by Antoni Gaudí between 1885 and 1889. With this structure, which looks like a giant organ, the architect embarked on a period of fertile creativity. Here Gothic inspiration alternates with elements of Arabic influence; the palau could be the set of a horror film.

The Plaça Reial.

The layout of the building is structured around an enormous salon, from which emerges a conical roof which is covered in bits of tiling and presides over an unusual landscape of capriciously placed battlements, balustrades and chimneys of differing shapes.

Popular square: Back on the other side of the Ramblas, the diminutive Carrer Colom leads past bootblacks' stalls to one of the liveliest parts of the city, the **Plaça Reial**, an eddy at the side of the Ramblas in which representatives of all types of ramblers, from the richest to the poorest, come to rest for a while.

Inspired by the French urban designs of the Napoleonic period, it is the only one of the many squares planned in Barcelona during the past century that was built entirely according to its original plan. Francesc Daniel Molina built an architectural grouping of uniform, arcaded buildings on the plot of land where the Capuchin Convent of Barcelona once stood.

This square contains terrace bars, res-taurants, jazz and flamenco clubs and discos, so it buzzes day and night. Stamp and coin collectors gather every Sunday around the Fuente de las Tres Gracias and the two *fanals* (street lamps) designed by Antoni Gaudí. During the rest of the week the square is a meeting point for the most diverse cross-section of people, and has a permanent police presence to discourage the seedier elements, who have traditionally adopted the square. The Plaça was the focus of some attention during the relatively successful pre-Olympic cleanup. Despite the police presence it has maintained its atmosphere of suppressed excitement.

At number 8, is the **Museu Pedagogic de Ciències**, with its exhibition of strange desiccated animals. At number 18, between Pasatges Colom and Bacardí, are two popular music bars, **Jamboree** and **Tarantos**, good for live music. Check out the **Herbolari Ferran** in the Passatge de Bacardí, for its array of spices in small wooden drawers. On the corner where the Pasatge rejoins the

Cosmopolitan bedmates.

Ramblas is the Arpi photographic shop, the best in Barcelona.

Tacky territory: Beyond the Carrer de Colom the Ramblas opens up again into the **Pla del Teatre** or **de les Comedies**, the second of the Ramblas' open areas. Here, during the 16th century, the city's first theatre was built. The present **Teatre Principal** has replaced the old wooden theatre building, which was for many years the only stage in Barcelona. Unfortunately, even the new structure has been seriously disfigured by various forms of mutilation and vulgar decorations. A 2,000-seater, it was built on the site of the historical "Corral de les Comédies", an early popular theatre, but it never appealed to the bourgeoisie.

On the other side of the promenade is a monument to Frederic Soler "Pitarra", founder of the modern Catalan theatre. Some of the few prostitutes that remain in this area choose the small square that surrounds the monument to offer their charms – almost as an epilogue of what once was, and a prologue of what still is

throughout the adjoining streets that make up the *barri* **Xinès** (still better known as the *barrio* Chino). It has been much cleaned up but there are still ladies of the night here, together with the neon signs of sex establishments. This is the beginning of the Rambla de Santa Mònica, the last stretch of the Ramblas before it reaches the sea.

This is a strange area, populated by fortune tellers, fakirs and gypsies. It is also the meeting place of artists, portrait painters and artisans, with a craft market during the weekend. Along these few metres the threads of past history and future events intertwine. This is where, in 1895, films were first shown publicly in Spain by the Lumière brothers. Here, too, stands the **Centre d'Art Santa Mònica**. And, opposite, there is the **Palau March** (1780), today the Generalitat's Department of Culture.

Along this same pavement, beyond the Passatge de la Banca, is the **Wax Museum**, popular with children on a rainy day. This is also the place to start a horse-and-carriage tour of the city.

The last building on the left side of the Ramblas (now occupied by the armed forces) has a curious history. In 1778 the foundry of the Royal Artillery, as well as its workshop, were transferred to this building, popularly known as El Refino. The foundry was one of the most renowned cannon factories of its time. From 1844 until 1920 it was occupied by the offices of the Banco de Barcelona (the first private Spanish bank) and, since the Spanish Civil War (1936–39), it has been converted into the offices of the military governor.

Beyond stands the **Columbus Monument**, with an internal lift and a great view of the city (10am – 2.30pm, 3.30 – 6.30pm, except Mondays). Cross the busy traffic here and you will reach the **Rambla del Mar**, a floating extension of the Ramblas that connects with the Moll d'Espanya, the Maremagnum leisure and commercial centre, and the newly redeveloped waterfront, of which Barcelona is now justifiably proud.

Left, Superman at the Wax Museum. **Right,** the Columbus Monument at the foot of the Ramblas.

THE GOTHIC QUARTER

The oldest part of the city of Barcelona is built around Taber Hill, a misnomer for that which is little more than a mound in an otherwise flat city. On the mound, the *barri* **Gòtic** (Gothic Quarter) is surrounded by the remains of Roman walls, within which very little has changed for centuries. The quarter, with narrow, tortuous streets of ancient stone, is an island within the metropolis.

Around the walls: From the newly-paved **Plaça Nova**, in front of the Bishop's Portal and Cathedral, wander briefly around the remaining Roman walls. Built out of massive stone blocks 12 ft (3.5 metres) thick and 30 ft (9 metres) high and punctuated with defence towers, they circle the quarter for more than a mile.

In the plaça itself the walls open to reveal the cathedral square, full of photographers trying to get to grips with the heavily ornate facade of the cathedral, which never seems to get much sun, and then curves along the Carrer de la Tapineria (*tapins* were a style of medieval footwear) to the **Plaça de Ramon Berenguer El Gran**. The equestrian statue of Berenguer, an 11th-century noble instrumental in the creation of the Catalan national identity, is the work of Josep Llimona.

The wall that fronts this square is the best preserved and restored of the Gothic Quarter. This section has nine towers, three of which were joined together during the 13th century to build the Royal Palace Chapel (the Capella de Santa Àgata). One of the towers was extended to house the chapel's belfry.

Beyond the Plaça de l'Angel, the street continues in the direction of Plaça d'Emili Vilanova to a point at which another stretch of Roman wall with seven towers still stands. All the structures built on Roman foundations date to the 12th century or later, when the city's limits were extended, allowing the original fortifications to be used as intermediary walls. Back at the plaça, opposite the Picasso doodles on the Architectural College, stand the cylindrical towers of the **Portal del Bisbe**, or Bishop's Gate, named in the Middle Ages because of its proximity to the Bishop's Palace. These constitute the northern entrance to the ancient Roman city. (The opposite axis of the city was Decumanus, located more or less where the Carrer de Ferran is today.) The towers were modified during the 12th century and windows were introduced two centuries later.

Inside the *barri*: If you enter the Gothic Quarter from the Plaça Nova, up the sloping Carrer del Bisbe Irurita, you are instantly among important historical landmarks. At number 5 (on the right) stands the **Palau del Bisbe** (Bishop's Palace). The entrance door opens on to a 12th-century courtyard, the only remaining evidence for the original palace after centuries of modifications. The frescoes on the facade (facing the Carrer Montjuïc del Bisbe) date from the 8th

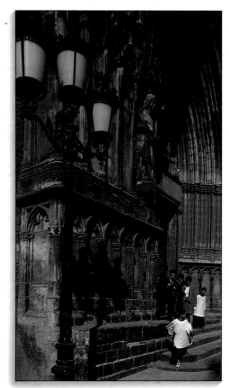

century, while the triple recess windows and large *flamígero* window in the courtyard are from the 14th century.

Opposite the palace the Carrer de Santa Llúcia leads towards the cathedral. On the corner is a chapel dedicated to Santa Llúcia, the patron saint of the blind and, curiously, of seamstresses. The chapel, built in 1268, is a fine example of Romanesque architecture with images of the Annunciation and the Visitation decorating the facade capitals. The holy water font inside the chapel is from the 14th century. A rear doorway leads into the cathedral cloister.

Opposite the chapel, on the other corner, is the **Casa de l'Ardiaca** (archdeacon's residence), presently the **Municipal History Institute**; it contains a valuable collection of historical chronicles and documents. The building as it stands today was reconstructed in the 15th century on 300-year-old foundations. A Gothic fountain is the centrepiece of the miniature oasis of the inner courtyard; the windows are Gothic

flamígero although the sculptures have overtones of the Italian Renaissance.

The dean's house, which forms part of the archdeaconery, was first modified at the beginning of the 15th century, but continued to undergo successive modifications as the cathedral esplanade was extended.

Magnetic point: The construction of the **Cathedral** itself began in 1298 under the patronage of Jaume II. The main area consists of three naves and an apse with ambulatory beneath an octagonal dome. Two 14th and 15th-century towers rise at each end of the transept. Beneath the main altar is the crypt of Santa Eulàlia and of particular note are the dome's multicoloured keystones. Some say that this is one of Catalonia's three "magnetic" points. The tomb of Santa Eulàlia, behind the altar, is an important work of art, executed in alabaster by a disciple of Giovanni Pisano (14th century) during the same period as the episcopal cathedral. The most outstanding of the aisle chapels behind

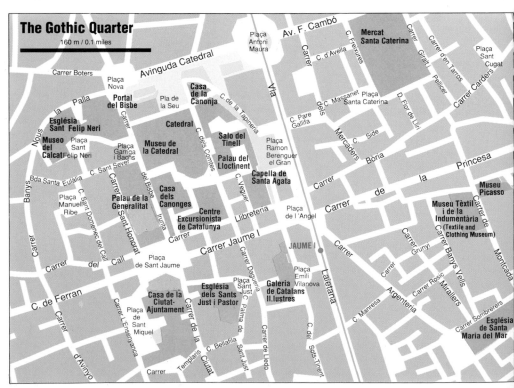

The Gothic Quarter
160 m / 0.1 miles

the altar is that of the Transfiguration, designed by Bernat Martorell. Considered as a masterpiece by art critics, the chapel is dedicated to Sant Salvador and was built in 1447.

The high-backed choir pews are by Pere Sanglada (1399), and the lower-backed benches were carved by Maciá Bonafé towards the end of the same century. The retrochoir was built at the beginning of the 16th century by the artist Bartolomé Ordoñez. The Capella del Santo Cristo de Lepanto (chapel of Christ Lepanto) contains the crucifix borne in the Christian flagship against the Ottomans in the battle of Lepanto. It was built in 1405 and 1454 and is considered to be the finest example of Gothic art in the cathedral.

The cathedral facade was finally finished during the 19th century by architects Mestres and Fontseré, modelled on a drawing by Mestre Carlí (15th century). The oldest part is that of the Porta de Sant Ivo (St Ives' Door) where some of the Romanesque windows and archways can still be seen. Although most of the cathedral's more antique furnishings are now housed in the city museum, there is a small collection in the Sala Capitular (Chapter House). A small pavilion beside the Porta de la Pietat still shelters a 15th-century terracotta statue of St George by Antoni Claperós, and the door that leads to the western end of the transept is made from the marble taken from the earlier Romanesque cathedral.

A few steps above the Plaça Nova the small cathedral square, known as **Cristo Rei** or **Pla de la Seu**, was, until 1421, an open space, part of the plot of land on which the deacon's house had been built, along with those of other canons, and part of the Roman wall.

On the far side is a singularly beautiful building, the 15th-century **Casa de la Canonja** (House of the Canonery). The oldest part is that which joins the corner of the Baixada de la Canonja (Canonery Hill). Later, in 1546, the building was extended and the wing that

overlooks the cathedral square was built, becoming the headquarters of the Pia Almoina, a charitable organisation created at the beginning of the century and charged with the feeding of a hundred poor people daily. The Museu Diocesà is housed here.

Down the road: Back past the bishop's palace and on to the Carrer del Bisbe Irurita once again, the street opens into the diminutive Plaça Bachs (which commemorates those who died in battle during the Napoleonic wars). On one side is the Santa Eulàlia Portal which leads into the **cathedral cloister,** a quiet, atmospheric place where pickpockets prowl. The sound of running water from the fountains can be drowned by the honking of the geese which live in the cloister. Four splendid galleries with pointed archways surround a romantic garden of elegant palms, medlars and highly perfumed magnolia trees, all enclosed by the 15th-century wrought-iron railings which surround the garden.

On the other side of Plaça Bachs, the Carrer Montjuïc del Bisbe leads off to the **Plaça de Sant Felip Neri**, a charming square further enhanced if, by chance, a wandering musician happens to have made his way here for the day. Excellent concerts are held in the church of the same name, either in one of the aisles or in the adjoining convent, both of which were built towards the end of the 18th century. These concerts are advertised in local entertainment guides and are worth watching out for.

On its way to the Plaça de Sant Jaume, the Carrer del Bisbe passes under a neo-Gothic bridge. This joins the **Palau de la Generalitat** (not open to the public) with the canons' residence, now used as the offices of the president of Catalonia. The Gothic doorway to the Generalitat, with its impressive St George medallion (wrought by Pere Johan), is the work of Marc Safont (1418) and opens first on to a typical Catalan-Gothic courtyard, complete with a loggia of pointed archways supported by slender columns of great beauty and supreme elegance. The

Gothic Quarter shopping.

Generalitat's **Capella de Sant Jordi** is also the work of Safont and is a magnificent example of Catalan *flamígero*.

Inside, there is a small 15th-century statue of the saint. The chapel was enlarged in 1620 and an interesting architectural feature is the dome with its hanging capitals.

The second courtyard, called **Los Naranjos**, is the work of Pau Mateu (16th century) and was completed by Tomàs Barsa. The original floors were of blue and white tiling but these were later substituted by marble from Carrara; the belfry is the work of Pere Ferrer (1568) and the bells toll a unique sequence of ancient melodies which imparts a singular and very special atmosphere throughout the surrounding district. The **Gold Salon** has magnificent examples of *artesanía*, delicate workmanship.

Through a Renaissance doorway is the **Saló de Sant Jordi**, designed by Pere Blai; it is a room of classical simplicity. The main, Italianate facade of the Generalitat, overlooking the Plaça de Sant Jaume, was begun towards the end of the 16th century and is of Italian style. The marble balcony is of a later date (1860) and includes a niche containing an equestrian statue of Sant Jordi (St George) by Aleu.

Civic heart: The area that today forms the **Plaça de Sant Jaume** was inaugurated in 1823, at the same time as the streets Carrer de Ferran and Jaume I. The square, with its restored **Casa de la Ciutat** (town hall) on the seaward side, is considered to be the civic heart of the city, not only because it is the scene of political meetings and has witnessed great historical events, but because the Barcelonans gather here to hold public and political demonstrations.

This is where President Tarradellas was given a clamorous reception when he returned from exile to attend the birth of the new democracy. Here the *castellers* or human towers are constructed and carnival "bigheads" (literally – heads made from papier-mâché) are greeted with great excitement during

Below, *casteller* in the Plaça de Sant Jaume. **Right,** in the archdeacon's courtyard.

THE JEWISH CITY

Throughout Catalonia the Jewish quarters of towns and cities are known as *call*, from the Hebrew *qahqal* which means "meeting". The most important *call* was in Barcelona. Situated west of the Roman metropolis on Mons Taber (now the Gothic Quarter), it reached the peak of its importance during the Middle Ages and had a remarkable cultural reputation. Many famous philosophers, writers, astronomers and intellectuals lived here between the 9th and 12th centuries. Among them were poet Ben Ruben Izahac, astronomer Abraham Xija, philosophers Abraham Ben Samuel Hasdai, Rabi Salomon Arisba and Bonet Abraham Margarit and the Biblical scholar Joseph Ben Caspí.

For centuries the only university institution in Catalonia was the "Universidad Judía" or "Escuela Mayor". This thriving community also had a talent for finance and monarchs were known to apply for loans. Their knowledge was so advanced that they were made ambassadors at court. But their display of wealth and their superior lifestyle created great jealousy.

The fortunes of the Jews began a slow decline in 1243 when Jaume I ordered not only the separation of the Jewish quarters from the rest of the city but that the Jews should wear long hooded capes with distinguishing red or yellow circles. From then on small fights began to break out, and became worse when the Castilians spread a rumour that the Jews were responsible for bringing the Black Death to Spain. Full-scale rioting erupted in several cities in 1391, provoked mainly by a group from Seville who encouraged the population to storm houses in the Jewish quarter and murder their occupants.

These riots began in Valencia on 9 July 1391 and spread to Mallorca, Barcelona, Girona, Lléida and Perpignan. But those in Barcelona were by far the most violent; the *qahqal* was virtually destroyed and about 1,000 Jews died. The survivors were forced either to convert to Christianity or flee, despite the efforts of the national guard who defended the lives and properties of the persecuted as best they could.

Joan I eventually ordered the arrest and execution of 15 Castilians responsible for the uprising; however, the monarch's good intentions could not prevent the fact that the *call* was never rebuilt. By 1395 the flow of anti-semitism had reached such proportions that the synagogue on the street then called "Sanahuja" was converted into the church of the Trinity (today Església de Sant Jaume, in the Carrer de Ferran). In 1396, the principal synagogue was rented to a pottery maker.

The *call* finally disappeared in 1401 when the synagogues were abolished and the Jewish cemeteries were destroyed. It was not until 1931 that the first Spanish synagogue since 1492 was established, at the corner of Balmes and Provença streets. It was shut down at the beginning of the Civil War, and reopened 1948, in the Avinguda de Roma. It later moved to its present site, 24, Carrer d'Avenir.

Today the only noteworthy evidence of the prosperous era of Jewish dominance are certain stretches of streets in the Carrer de Banys Nous and in the Carrer del Call, the Jewish quarter's main street. To a lesser extent, Carrer de Sant Domènec del Call, once the Carrer de la Sinagoga Major, preserves some historic buildings.

The Carrer de Marlet, by the Arc de Sant Ramon, has the most tangible evidence of the Jewish city. Here, a memorial stone dating back to 1314 reads: "Holy foundation of Rabi Samuel Hassardi for whom life never ends. Year 62." ■ **The memorial stone in Carrer de Marlet.**

the city's major festival, Mercè (in the week of 24 September).

But perhaps the key confrontation across the square these days is the opposition of the two main buildings, the Casa de la Ciutat and the Generalitat, whose occupants often have different political views, and both of whom are at work in the city.

The oldest part of the Casa de la Ciutat is the **Saló de Cent**, created by Pere Llobet in 1373; its baroque style was introduced during the 17th century. It was partly destroyed in 1842 during the Carlist War but its appearance today is essentially similar to that of 1925. Another room, the **Saló de Festes**, or Saló de Cròniques, was designed and decorated by the 20th-century muralist Josep Maria Sert. His paintings tell the tale of the Catalan *corps d'élite's* heroic feats, based on the chronicles of Muntaner and Declós.

The building's Gothic facade (finished in 1402) on the Carrer de la Ciutat is by Arnau Bargés and Francesc Mar-

enya. The portal that we can see today is somewhat smaller than its original size as a result of 19th-century modifications; the door is crowned by the figure of an angel attributed to Jordi Johan and the richly fluted windows on the upper storey correspond to those of the Sala d'Eleccions.

Quiet corner: Down the Carrer de Hercules (opposite this side entrance of the Casa de la Ciutat) is the **Plaça de Sant Just**, once the site of the cemetery of the same name. The fountain is dated 1367 and is in the Gothic style, albeit with certain details of later neoclassical influence, such as the balustraded enclosure which surrounds the overhanging terrace.

At the top end of the square is the **Church of Sant Just and Sant Pastor**, an ancient royal chapel until the 15th century. The actual building, by Bernat Roca, was begun midway through the 4th century. According to legend, it is built on the site of Barcelona's first Christian temple. Pere Blay's belltower

Preparing for wedding photos in the *barri.*

was the last phase to be completed, in 1567. The interior has several interesting features: the polychrome reliefs of the vault's keystones and, close to the apse of the chapel dedicated to Sant Fèlix, the altarpiece and holy water fonts which are Byzantine.

The **Carrer de Lledó** leads past a number of 14th and 16th-century merchants' houses, not in particularly good repair. At number 4 is the Palau de Filliver, while the inner courtyards at numbers 3 and 5 are beautiful examples of the architecture of 400 or 500 years ago. Next door, at number 7, is a building dating to the 15th century. At number 11, there is another of later date (18th century).

At the end of the Carrer del Bisbe Cassador is Barcelona's most important medieval palace – that of the Comtessa de Palamós, headquarters of the **Acadèmia de las Bones Lletres & Galeria de Catalans Illustres** (Academy of Literature and Illustrious Catalans), with a fine gallery of portrait paintings.

Facing once again towards the Plaça Nova, the Carrer de Dagueria, Carrer Llibreteria and Carrer Veguer lead to the **Museu d'Història de la Ciutat** (Museum of the City's History), located in what was once the house of Clariana-Padellás, built in the 17th century for a family of rich traders and only moved to this site in the 1930s. The museum is worth visiting for its architecture and to view the **Plaça del Rei** from its terrace, and in its basement are excavations of the Roman streets that stretch beneath the square.

This medieval square, living testimony to the nobility of the ancient city of Barcelona, was a cattle fodder market for three centuries. It was here that all the flour brought into the city in payment of taxes was collected. Little seems to have changed since then.

Royal Palace: At one end of the Plaça del Rei is the **Palau Real Major** with vast vaulted ceilings, 13th-century triple-recess windows and 14th-century rose windows. The silhouette of the

Left, Palau del Lloctinent and Rei Martí tower. **Below**, shop dummy.

136

box-shaped Renaissance tower of Rei Martí is an outstanding feature of the palace. Built like a dovecote, it has fine views down over the royal complex. The main room of the palace, the great **Saló del Tinell**, whose construction began with Pedro "El Cerimoniós" in 1359, was later converted to a baroque church, only to recover its original appearance after restoration works were carried out during and after the Spanish Civil War. During the 15th century this was where the Inquisition held court. Legend has it that the walls of the tribunal cannot bear a lie to be told and that, when this occurred, the ceiling stones would move, to the further terror of the unfortunate victims. These days it functions as an exhibition area.

On the north side of the Plaça del Rei is the **Palatine Chapel**, that of Santa Àgata, which apparently houses the stone on which the saint's breasts were mutilated. Construction began at the beginning of the 14th century and in its interior can be found the *Condestable*

altarpiece by Jaume Huguet. The centre depicts the Adoration of the Three Kings and, above, the Crucifixion. On both sides are scenes from the lives of Christ and the Virgin Mary.

Opposite the chapel is one of the sides of the **Palau del Lloctinent**. When the kingdoms of Catalonia and Aragón were joined with that of Castile, Carlos V created the office of Deputy (*Lloctinent*) for the court's representative, and this palace, the official residence, was built in 1549 by Antoni Carbonell. The facade is Catalan-Gothic; however, the inner courtyard is one of the few extant examples of Renaissance architecture left in the city. Today the palace is the headquarters of the **Arxiu de la Corona d'Aragó** (Archive of the Kingdom of Aragón).

The Baixada de Santa Clara leads up behind the cathedral's transept. To the left, down the Carrer de Paradís, is the **Centre d'Excursionistes de Catalunya** (a sort of Outward Bound headquarters) whose interior houses some of the Ro-

Religious icons a speciality.

man columns that belonged to the 1st/ 2nd-century Temple of Augustus.

The **Casas dels Canonges** (canons' houses) stand opposite the cathedral. This is where the canons were transferred when they abandoned the life of the cloister, hence the name. Once a typical 14th-century Catalan-Gothic building, the block was somewhat unorthodoxically restored in 1929. The house on the corner of the Carrer de Bisbe displays a series of serigraphs (silk-screen prints) carried out at the beginning of this century. Opposite, the **Porta de la Pietat** leads into the cathedral cloister.

During the Christmas period (8–24 December), the Fira de Santa Llúcia (Festival of Santa Lucia) is held in the area surrounding the cathedral. The narrow streets and alleyways are filled with crowds of festively dressed citizens and small handicraft gift stalls.

Museum district: A second itinerary leads through the Santa Maria district, starting at the Plaça de l'Angel and following Carrer de Princesa up to **Carrer de Montcada** (quiet on Mondays, when the museums are closed).

This latter street, named after the fallen during the conquest of Mallorca, was the city's most elegant district between the 12th and the 18th centuries. The street linked the waterfront with the commercial areas, such as that of Bòria whose enormous maritime and commercial industry reached its zenith between the 13th and 16th centuries, coinciding with the growth of Mediterranean trade. In 1947 the entire area was declared a national artistic monument and, in 1957, the town hall of Barcelona began to restore the most notable palaces, converting them into museums. These days the street has become a focal point for art galleries.

At number 12 Carrer de Montcada is the **Palau de los Marqueses de LIió** whose inner courtyard is the best preserved section of the original 14th-century building. The doors and windows of the palace are from the Renaissance **Gardening in the city.**

138

period and a result of the renovations carried out during the 16th century. The **Textile and Clothing Museum** is housed in the noble building, along with its own attractive café and shop.

The **Picasso Museum**, which no visitor should miss, is located in the 15th-century **Palau Berenguer d'Aguilar**. An outstanding feature is the courtyard which has a surrounding first-floor gallery with pointed archways resting on slender columns. In one of the rooms a huge 13th-century mural depicting scenes from the conquest of Mallorca was discovered and is now in the Museu Nacional d'Art de Catalunya. The adjoining Palau Castellet also forms part of the Picasso museum.

At number 25 on the same street is the 16th-century **Casa Cervelló-Giudice** whose facade is among the least decayed and where genuine Gothic elements blend with an essentially Renaissance ambience. The inner courtyard has suffered several drastic changes but still preserves a large *flamígero* Gothic window. The house belonged to the Cervelló family, aristocratic Catalans, and was later sold to the Giudices, a family of Italian merchants from Génova. The family aroused the anger of the local populace who burnt it down. Today it is the Barcelona branch of the **Maeght Gallery** which organises key exhibitions at regular intervals.

The **Palau Dalmases**, at number 20, was completely renovated during the 17th century with only a few features surviving from the original 15th-century building. The magnificent courtyard stairway is unanimously considered to be a baroque masterpiece. In the 18th century it housed the "Acadèmia dels Desconfiats" (the name of a group founded to defend the Catalan culture) and later it became the Acadèmia de las Bones Lletres; today it is the premises of the gallery "Omnium Cultural".

Among all this exhausting art are several venues for rest and refreshment. All of the museums have good cafés. Experts recommend that visitors sample

Street festival.

an aperitif in a local tavern: sherry, *cava* or cider, icy cold and accompanied by anchovies.

Carrer de Montcada leads eventually into the **Born**, the site of fairs, tournaments and jousts from the 13th to the 17th centuries. Here, too, were held the glass and tin fairs, and some of the surrounding shops continue to specialise in these articles.

At the far end of the Passeig del Born is the **Mercat del Born**, a massive building that looks like a cross between a railway station and a conservatory, built by Fontseré and Mestres between 1873 and 1876 and a fine example of wrought-iron architecture. The latest plan for its future is to be a library.

A Gothic Gem: The transept entrance of the **Church of Santa Maria del Mar** closes off the other end of the Born. It may not look much from the outside – grass grows on the frontage, and you'd have to be a pigeon to get a good view of the whole – but Santa Maria del Mar is probably one of Barcelona's most beau-

tiful Gothic churches; some call it the Riverside Cathedral. It was built between 1329 and 1384, a comparatively short time for churches of that size and that era, and a contributory factor to its great purity of style.

All the local corporations collaborated in the building of the church, and it became a symbol of the economic and political power of Catalonia in this period. The interior – best viewed from the main portal in the Plaça Santa Maria, which has glass doors expressly for that purpose – is built in what is known as a "salon" design. Three extraordinarily lofty and almost identical naves give it a feeling of great spaciousness and airiness. The octagonal columns are absolutely without ornamentation and are separated from each other by a distance of 43 ft (13 metres) – a distance no other medieval structure was able to achieve.

The church's magnificent glass windows allow the sunlight to filter through and bathe the interior in a captivating light. The central rose window is a product of the 15th century, as is the sculpture of the *Virgin and Child* on a pedestal near a side door. The church also houses some extremely valuable treasures such as a 16th-century silver cross, an equally old washbasin and an 18th-century jewelled chalice.

The facade (never mind the grass growing out from between the stones) exhibits all the characteristics of the Catalan-Gothic style: "prevalence of horizontal lines; flat terraced roofing; wide open spaces; strong buttresses and octagonal towers ending in terraces," which is how Cirici defines the style of the Gothic period in one of the best books on Barcelona.

Try to co-ordinate your visit to Santa Maria del Mar with one of the many events held in the church, particularly a concert. If you do, the performance will remain with you for a long time both for the quality of the music itself and for the manner in which the haunting notes seem to belong to another age – perhaps to the *barri* Gòtic itself.

Left, Montcada gallery. Right, Santa Maria del Mar, the Riverside Cathedral.

MONTJUÏC

"Before I came to Barcelona, I didn't know what a sporting city was."
– Baron de Coubertin, 1926

Montjuïc was once known as the "Exposition Mountain", referring to the Universal Exposition of 1929; in the early 1990s it became the "Olympic Mountain", hosting the 1992 Olympic Games which transformed its attractions and infrastructure.

From the first attempted urbanisation in 1890, Montjuïc has been used for a variety of purposes, ranging from a stone quarry to the orchard of Sant Bertran, from a military installation to a recreational park, with 540 acres (218 hectares) of landscaped gardens.

All this has happened on the flanks of a rocky hill just 570 ft (173 metres) high that rises from the estuaries of the Rivers Llobregat and Besós which was once the site of a primitive pre-Roman settlement and was later known as Mons Jovis (Mount Jupiter).

The beauty of this mountain was discovered by the Romanticists towards the end of the 18th century and in 1908 the town hall bought the Laribal Garden with its 9th-century Arab pavilion. But the real transformation of Montjuïc began with the celebration of the Universal Exposition of 1929, and was completed with the 1992 Olympics.

For 1929, the sides of the mountain were landscaped in accordance with a plan drawn up by the Frenchmen Forestier and Nicolau Maria Rubió i Tudurí. Fifteen palaces were built (most of them still standing as museums and part of the exhibition centre), together with national and commercial pavilions, a stadium, a swimming pool, the Spanish Village, ornamental fountains, the Greek Theatre, several towers and the access avenue.

The Exposition itself, opened by King Alfonso XIII, was a political *tour de force* of the Primo de Rivera dictatorship and was built around the themes of industry, art and sport. Its legacy, the **Fira de Barcelona**, is a complex with some 2 million sq ft (180,000 sq metres) of exhibition space and approaching 2 million visitors a year.

Front door: The first impressions of Montjuïc belong to 1929; on the crown of the hill are the jewels of 1992. The hill's main entrance – its most imposing aspect – is from the **Plaça d'Espanya**, by the architect Ramon Reventós. The central fountain of the plaça is the work of Josep Jujol, a disciple of Gaudí, and represents Spain's main rivers with marble and bronze sculptures by Miquel Blay. Reventós's square and rather modern-looking towers at the beginning of the Avinguda de la Reina Maria Cristina are of Venetian inspiration. Up the Avinguda there are impressive views of the fountains and the flights of steps up to the Palau Nacional.

Another unmistakable feature of the surroundings is the **Las Arenas** bull

ring, designed by August Font. It has a diameter of 170 ft (52 metres) and a capacity for 15,000 spectators, and when it opened on 29 June 1900 it put on a bullfight featuring the unusual number of eight bulls. These days, however, no bulls pass through its doors, Catalans not being great bullfight fans. The ring now hosts visiting circus troupes and open-air concerts.

Another singular building in the same area (on Carrer de Llansa, 2–12) is the **Pabellón** dog track which dates to the early 1950s.

From the twin Venetian towers the Avinguda de la Reina Maria Cristina passes between exhibition halls from the 1929 Exposition, up to the **Plaça del Univers**, an ideal place from which to see the magnificent **Fuente Mágica** or Magic Fountain, a spectacular interplay of moving water, coloured lights and music with a repertoire of 50 pieces which comes to life on Saturday and Sunday evenings from 9 to 11pm. Carlos Buigas engineered this work of art and he was also responsible for the lighting along the Avinguda, where glass lamps also constantly change colour during the show.

To the right of the Magic Fountain is an authentic architectural jewel: the **Mies Van Der Rohe Pavilion**, named after its German architect and built originally for the 1929 Exposition. It is a spare, plain, and surprisingly haunting building. Peter Berhens, the architect's professor, wrote: "This building will one day be remembered as the most beautiful of those built throughout the 20th century".

Nevertheless, there were those who couldn't comprehend this beauty, and it was dismantled. In 1985 it was rebuilt in its original location, and it doesn't seem dated, even now.

Unreal village: Behind the pavilion the road winds up the side of the hill to a convincing pastiche: one suddenly finds oneself confronted by a rampart and a doorway, through which lies the **Poble Espanyol** (Spanish Village). After pass-

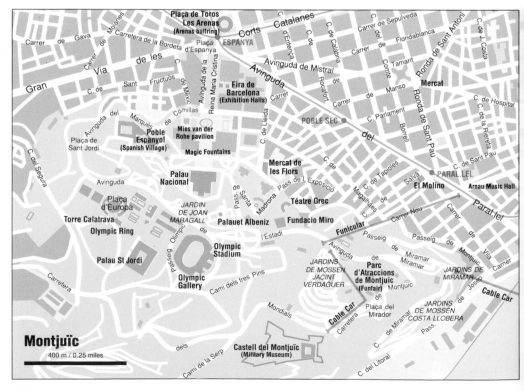

ing through a reproduction of the San Vicente de Avila Portal (imaginatively converted into a bar/nightclub with one of the strangest interiors of any in Barcelona, designed by Javier Mariscal) you find a group of buildings representing various styles of architecture from all over Spain; an explanatory plan is provided with your entrance ticket. This village was created, again for the Universal Exposition of 1929, as a stimulating architectural exercise, albeit only a temporary one. But the architects Miquel Utrillo, Xavier Nogués and Ramon Reventós did such a convincing job that the village escaped the bulldozer and has become one of the city's important recreational centres.

The concept of the village (which has a distinctly commercial bias) is the preservation of architectural styles, the development of handicrafts and the promotion of cultural events, with emphasis on regional gastronomy.

The gastronomic section is built around 14 restaurants (three of which include a cabaret), a cafeteria and six bars, supplemented by four night clubs and four music bars. There are also areas dedicated to museums and other cultural themes such as the **Museum of Popular Arts and Industries** in which, each weekend, a show is presented based on the traditions and lifestyle of Catalonia. The central square is a venue for artistic and musical events.

Crowning the hill: Returning to the main staircase, access to the **Palau Nacional**, a neoclassical building topped by a central dome, is by twin flights of steps, from the top of which there is a magnificent view of Barcelona. Escalators were installed to supplement the steps in 1992.

The palau, designed by the architects Enric Catà, Pere Cendoya and Pere Domènech, was conceived as a synthesis of different Spanish architectural styles; it works from a distance, but somehow loses its appeal close up.

Since 1934 this massive building has housed the **Museu Nacional d'Art de Catalunya** (**MNAC**), the most impor-

The Palau Nacional and Magic Fountain.

tant Romanesque art collection in the world. It includes murals peeled off the walls of tiny churches in the Pyrenees in the province of Lléida and brought down by donkey. There is also a good Gothic collection. The interior, originally re-modelled by Gae Aulenti, is still being renovated to house other collections, including the Museu d'Art Modern.

On the Carrer de Lléida side of the palace is a municipal theatre and con-cert venue known for its contemporary focus, the **Mercat de las Flors**. A short distance away is the **Greek Theatre** which was also built for the 1929 Expo-sition. Inspired by a model of Epidaurus, the theatre's backdrop is a solid wall of rock which was part of an old aban-doned quarry. During the Grec summer festival it is an important venue.

The Olympic Ring: Up behind the Palau Nacional the city turns its back on cul-ture and opens its arms to sport in a big way: here begin the installations of the 1992 Olympic Games, signposted the **Anella Olímpica** (Olympic Ring). There are eight Olympic-standard sports cen-tres and three tracks in the area, but if you stick to the road you will see only a fraction of what was created: fortunately there is access to the central square via a walkway on the inland (downhill) side of the main stadium.

The **Olympic Stadium** (usually open to visitors, with a coffee bar and souve-nir stall) was actually built for the 1929 Universal Exposition, designed by Pere Domenech i Roura, it fell into disrepair after hosting the Mediterranean Games in 1955. Extensive works for the 1992 Olympics involved lowering the arena by 36 feet (11 metres) in order to create extra seating for 70,000 spectators. Most of the track events and the opening and closing ceremony were held here, and an **Olympic Gallery** is maintained to house archives, including film footage, at the back of the far end of the stadium.

Below and west of the stadium stret-ches the immense **Olympic Terrace**, lined with pillars, and with a view of distant Barcelona as its backdrop. In the

Left and below, giants and spectators in a fiesta in the Poble Espanyol.

middle of the main terrace is a lawn with an artificial stream flowing through it; to the left side a small forest of identical sculptures.

The terrace drops down to a second level in the middle distance, and then to a third – the **Plaça d'Europa** – which is a circular colonnaded area built on top of a massive water tank containing 60,000 cubic metres of drinking water for the city. The whole has the atmosphere of a re-created Roman forum.

On each side of the terrace are key installations: to the left is the **Palau d'Esports Sant Jordi**, to the right the **Bernardo Picornell Olympic Pools**, and in the far distance the INEFC **Universitat de l'Esport**. All this is as planned, but there is one highly-visible landmark in the whole which caused great controversy at the time, not least with the architects who created the whole Olympic ring: the great white **Torre de Calatrava** communications tower (616 ft/188 metres), which looks like a great white thread being pulled through the great white eye of a great white needle.

Olympic architects Frederic Correa, Alfons Mila, Joan Margarit and Carles Buxade hated the tower project, and rallied dozens of intellectuals to their cause. Nevertheless the Telefonica tower went ahead, and the result is quite stunning, though it must be said it does rather contradict – even upstage – the cool space of the terracing.

Other than the stadium itself, the installation most in the public eye is the Palau d'Esports Sant Jordi, designed by the Japanese architect Isozaki. The roof – 525 ft (160 metres) long and 360 ft (110 metres) wide – was built on the ground in situ, covered in grey ceramic tiles, then raised in the air agonisingly slowly by hydraulic pistons. It took 10 days to reach its final height of 148 ft (45 metres). The result is an indoor stadium that can seat 15,000, without a pillar in sight. Since the Olympics the palau has proved very popular for concerts, exhibitions and sporting events.

Once it has passed the main stadium,

The Olympic Stadium.

the road starts to dip downwards. Up to the right is the **Parc del Migdia**, which extends to the top of the hill and includes the Botanical Gardens, with some 7,000 species. On the left, the peaceful and elegant gardens of **Joan Maragall** surround the **Palacete Albéniz**. This *palauete* or "little palace" is now the official residence of visiting dignitaries to Barcelona. It was built as a Royal Pavilion for the 1929 Exposition and during the years of self-government in Catalonia – from 1931 until the end of the Civil War – it was used as a music museum.

Next on the roadside are the Jardins de Laribal, breezy and shady and with a fine view of the city. Beyond, the white **Miró Foundation**, a cool, smart building in the heat of the day, holds a wealth of that artist's work as well as being an important study centre for modern art in general. The white block pavilion, which was designed by Josep Lluis Sert, a friend of Miró, and finished in 1974, seems rather understated after the im-mensity of the Olympic intallations, but it is deceptively large. It has a pleasant café with a terrace and an imaginative short menu. Below it is a sculpture garden (separate entrance, free).

Transport choice: The next corner offers a choice of routes: *up* to the castle, over the funfair using the cable car, or *down* to city-level in the funicular.

Upward travellers who resist the attractions of the fair reach **Montjuïc Castle**, built in the 17th century during the battle between Catalonia and Spain's Felipe IV, known as the "War of the Harvesters". At the beginning of the 18th century Bourbon troops ransacked the castle; it was rebuilt between 1751 and 1779. The new fortress was in the form of a starred pentagon, with enormous moats, bastions and buttresses. Today the castle is a military museum, and keen climbers spend their weekends abseiling down its walls.

Downward travellers who opt for the **funicular** are using yet another (refurbished) product of the 1929 exhibition.

Still shaking on the Paral.lel.

The rail descends a distance of 2,500 ft (760 metres) and disembarks at the **Avinguda Paral.lel**.

This is Barcelona's can-can district, under the shadow of three enormous 235-ft (72-metre) chimneys. The three are the remains of the "Grupo Mata", an electricity-producing plant dating from the turn of the century. As part of the urban development scheme, a "designer park" was created here, named after those towering landmarks, **Parc de les Xemeneies.**

Strange name: The Avinguda Paral.lel was originally the Calle Marqués del Duero, in honour of the man himself. Then, in 1794, a Frenchman, Pierre François André Méchain, discovered that the avenue's pathway coincided exactly with the navigational parallel 44°44'N. In honour of this discovery a local cook (influenced no doubt by her astronomer husband) opened a tavern which she called "El Paralelo". The popularity of the place did the rest.

The Paral.lel has been called the "El Pigalle" of Barcelona. This is the quarter of Barcelona that lived between innocence and sin. However, the closure of **El Molino** in 1998, after various reprieves, could be a symbol of change. This historic music hall was a Barcelona tradition, and anyone who hadn't stepped inside the smoky, alcohol and fume-laden premises – where silence is a forbidden commodity – could not say they truly knew Barcelona. Younger audiences are attracted to the plethora of music bars, jazz venues and discotheques in and around the city, and here the cinemas and many of the theatres have disappeared. The **Arnau** hosts variety shows and light comedies and the Apolo is known as a dance club. However, the **Baghdad**, which offers some of the hardest porn shows to be seen in Europe, is still open, and nearer the Ramblas in Carrer Lancaster is the unrivalled **Bodega Bohemia**. A famous Barcelona haunt, where old music hall stars present their old repertoires. Glimpse the former glory of the Paral.lel.

Barcelona's bit of Paris.

THE WATERFRONT AND CIUTADELLA

The rediscovery of Barcelona's waterfront began in the late 1980s, prompted by the 1992 Olympics. The development is perhaps the most radical transformation of any city in Europe and represents an investment of some 400 billion pesetas (£2 billion). For years city planners have been reproached for having turned their backs to the sea. Until recently the port areas had been progressively abandoned in preference for the foothills of what is today the smart residential district of Pedralbes.

But now several miles of beaches have been renovated and provided with first-rate facilities. Along the coast Nova Icària, the site of the Olympic Village, is a whole new city district, the work of intelligent architectural design with an eye for future as well as present needs. The old city wharves, once hidden under tumbledown sheds, have emerged, blinking, into the sun. Barceloneta is transformed, and there is more to come on the harbour quays. Barcelonans can now promenade the length of their seafront with pride; not so long ago this was an unpleasant and hazardous journey.

Starting point: Any waterside strolling begins beneath the feet of the rather over-enthusiastic monument to the adventurer and discoverer Christopher Columbus, here pointing in the wrong direction for the sake of simplicity (lifts to the top every day except Monday).

To the right are the sheds of the **Drassanes**. Although the buildings do not look exceptional from the outside, this is the world's greatest extant medieval shipyard. The enormous sheds were begun in 1378, but the extensions were not completed until the 18th century. Even for the more modern additions, the original design and lay-out of the construction was adhered to – simply because it was considered impossible to improve upon. The shield above the doorway on the facade is a fine example of Gothic sculpture. To the right of the entrance are three 17th-century halls used for displays and exhibitions. To the left are the eight huge sheds, covered by a continuous peaked roof, which gives them an elongated appearance.

The magnificent interior area is such that it allowed the simultaneous construction of 30 galleons. Today it is the location of the **Maritime Museum**, recently remodelled to include an exciting interactive display "La Gran Aventura del Mar", which charts Catalonia's seafaring history, and includes the reproduction of Juan of Austria's flag-ship, which led the Christian fleet to a decisive victory over the Ottomans at Lepanto in 1571.

Fragments of the medieval wall can be seen opposite the main entrance. Extensions carried out during the 16th century include the Sea Tower and the Tower of Sta Madrona.

Between the Drassanes and the sea is the **Duana Nova** (new customs house), which was built between the years of

1895 and 1902 from a project drawn up by Enric Sagnier and Pere García. Crowned by a massive winged sphinx and various other mythical flying beasts (Barcelona's port buildings seem to specialise in fine roof-top silhouettes), the Duana Nova is designed in the form of the letter "H", the most practical design for processing cargoes.

To the left of the Columbus Monument is the **Junta d'Obres del Port** (Port Authority Building), designed by the engineer Julio Valdés and built in 1907. Its original use was as the reception for passengers arriving in the city from the sea. The interior is in a variegated, eclectic style, rather ornamental for its now mundane function.

Ferry passengers are still in the vicinity, however, notably at the **Portal del Pau**, a set of steps (once a wooden footbridge) which is the starting point for golondrina ("swallow") boat tours of the harbour. Between it and the Junta building is an extension which allows the Ramblas to walk on water, the **Rambla del Mar**. This moveable walkway links with the Moll d'Espanya.

To the right, the **Moll Barcelona** still retains the terminal where the ferries to the Balearics berth. The jetty also has the Torre Jaume I link for the cross-harbour cable car, which has the most stupendous views of the city from the top. Right at the end of the moll, however, is another ambitious and unmissable project: a huge commercial block called the World Trade Center.

Modern mole: This is just part of Barcelona's recent harbour improvements. Stretching north from the Moll Barcelona is the **Moll de la Fusta**, a new promenade on the site of the old wooden cargo sheds, studded with palms and bar-restaurants – including the Mariscal-designed **Gambrinus** where the speciality is obvious from the massive plastic lobster on the roof. The Moll de la Fusta project was designed by the architect Manuel de Solà-Morales i Rubio, who made laudable efforts to minimise the noise of an increasingly traffic-satu-

Café on the Moll de la Fusta.

rated highway (the Passeig de Colom) with surrounding recreational zones.

On the city side of the passeig is the 17th-century convent of La Mercè which has been used since 1846 as the **Capitania General** (army headquarters). The facade built by Adolf Floresa on the occasion of the Universal Exposition of 1929 and the restored cloister columns and the facings of blue Valencian tiles within the convent are an architectural delight. Ask before taking pictures, however, as the military is liable to confiscate cameras.

The Moll de la Fusta turns the corner of the harbour, passing the base of the Moll d'Espanya, and a departure point for smaller – and cheaper – harbour tour boats. On the corner just inland stands the unmissable sculpture *El Cap de Barcelona* by Roy Lichtenstein, created for the Olympics, and with obvious reference to both Miró and Gaudí.

The **Moll d'Espanya** sticks out into the port here, with a walkway that sweeps up to a small viewpoint, and then down

into a new development: the **Maremagnum** centre contains 100 shops, a multi-screen cinema, restaurants and bars. Also on the Moll is the Imax (semicircular screen) cinema and the **aquarium**, the largest in Europe. Not long ago this was all disused warehouses. Old-timer tenants of the wharf are the Reial Club Nautic and the Reial Club Maritim, two of the city's most elite sports clubs.

A detour inland: Although the new promenade – and the traffic arrangements – tend to restrict visitors to the harbourside at this point, there are several key buildings to the left, inland. On the corner of Via Laietana is the headquarters of the **Correus** (Post Office), a rather pompous and grand building completed in 1927. The architects charged with the design of the building, Josep Goday and Jaume Torres, were obliged to bow to the wishes of the General Post Office Ministry who required "suitable" offices, hence its somewhat monumental appearance. The enormous vestibule

Refreshment, señor?

COLUMBUS ON THE QUAY

Once, passengers arriving in the port of Barcelona disembarked across a wooden footbridge at the Portal de la Pau – near the start of the new wooden walkway of the Rambla del Mar – and through an open doorway that led on to the Ramblas. Today only travellers who have booked a passage aboard the *golondrinas* (sightseeing boats) arrive by sea in this way. Tradition has it that the name *golondrinas* was given to these vessels because, like the swallows they are named after, they always returned to port after each passage.

When the traveller boards any of these boats, he or she is embarking on an adventure at a speed of four knots for a two-hour voyage to the Olympic port or a more traditional 30-minute round trip through the litter of ships, yachts and fishing boats that crowd the port, to the end of the breakwater. The journey starts and ends under the eye of someone whose adventure involved going much further: Christopher Columbus.

The monument to the tireless explorer at the foot of the Ramblas was built to celebrate the Universal Exposition of 1888, nearly 400 years after the actual discoveries it celebrates. Columbus himself, the Italian-born navigator for whom Spain was his adopted homeland and sponsor, arrived in the port of Barcelona from the newly discovered Indies in April 1493 with his wife, three sons (Diego, Cristóbal and Fernando) and a small escort including seven Indians, the survivors of the many who had embarked from the island Columbus christened "Española" (Cuba).

The 233-ton monument, designed by Gaietà Buïgas, celebrates that first voyage. It is divided into three parts. The first part is a circular podium reached by four stairways and supporting eight wrought-iron heraldic lions, cast by Josep Carcassó. The eight bronze bas-reliefs on the pedestal illustrate the feats of Columbus. The second part is the column's base in the form of an eight-sided polygon, four sides of which act as a counterbalance, each displaying four stone sculptures representing the kingdoms of Catalonia, Aragón, Castilla (Castile) and León.

Backing the four sides are four more sculptured groups depicting the Montserrat missionary monk, Fra Bernat Boil, representing civilisation; Captain Pere Margarit, symbol of Spanish might in America; Jaime Ferrer de Blanes, a famous astronomer representing the link between the sciences and the discovery; and Luis de Santángel, who financed Columbus's fleet. On the side walls are eight medallions, each carrying the likenesses of other personalities connected with the voyage.

The third part is the column itself, Corinthian in style and reaching 170 ft (51 metres). In the lower part is a bronze sculpture of a caravel, two griffins and four winged figures representing Fame.

On the top of the column Europe, Asia, Africa and America are represented. Finally, on a prince's crown and a semicircle that evokes the globe's newest discovery, stands Rafael Atché's bronze statue of Columbus, 25 ft (7.6 metres) high.

The interior of the iron column has a lift to a viewing platform dominating the port and city of Barcelona, open to the public for a small entrance fee from 10am until 7pm (not Mondays). The view gives a good impression of the new seafront developments. The visit can be combined with a tour of the nearby Maritime Museum, or to the Maremagnum complex in the middle of the harbour, or a walk along the waterfront to the Olympic Village. ∎

Columbus points out to sea.

was decorated by the prestigious *noucentistes* (from the 1900s) artists Canyellas, Obiols, Galí and Labarta.

Money market: On the other side of the Via Laietana, behind the monument to Antonio Lopez, rises the **Llotja** (exchange market), a rather subdued building which used to house the stock exchange and is also the headquarters of the Acadèmia de Belles Arts, where Picasso and Miró were pupils. The entrance is in the Carrer de Consolat de Mar. Within the Llotja, the Saló de Contració is the work of Pere Arberí and was built between 1380 and 1392. Four hundred years later a series of extensions and modifications were carried out and the courtyard and vast hall have both been preserved in excellent condition. A remarkable feature (go up the stairway) is the timber roofing which rests on archways and not on columns, as would be usual at this period. The enormous 14th-century salon has been the scene of masquerade balls.

The Llotja's main facade (not used as an entrance) overlooks the **Pla del Palau** (Palace Square) where, as the name indicates, a royal palace once stood. Although now rather isolated, during the 18th and 19th centuries the square became the city's political centre – previously, as now, this honour was held by the Plaça de Sant Jaume. The reason behind the change was the loss of Catalan power, as represented by the Generalitat (which occupies Sant Jaume), under the dominant viceroy.

Opposite the Llotja, on the other side of the Passeig d'Isabel II, is a neoclassic arcade known as the **Porxos d'en Xifré**, built by the "Indiano" (a name given to anyone who left Spain to make their fortune in the Americas) Josep Xifré, between 1836 and 1840. The main facade, which appears as one whole block, is actually divided into three sections: a ground floor composed of shop premises and three lofty storeys of living accommodation.

The archways and the pilasters are adorned with terracotta medallions by

Sailors onshore.

Damià Campeny depicting commercial and industrial events. Also there is a series of busts of personalities connected with the conquest of America such as Juan Sebastián Elcano, Cortés, Ercilla, Colón, Magellan and Pizarro.

One of these apartments was the first home of the Picasso family in 1895 when they arrived in Barcelona from Málaga. The artist, then 13 years old, was enrolled in the Belles Arts de la Llotja school, where his father was a professor. Five years later the local *Vanguardia* newspaper was to write: "almost a child, Picasso has organised an exhibition [in the Quatre Gats café]".

On the ground floors of both this building and its neighbour, a unique, densely populated area of port bazaars has developed, with a strong oriental atmosphere. Traditionally, the goods sold – mainly watches and clocks, electrical goods and naval artefacts – are cheaper than in other parts of the city.

Great eating place: The arcade is also the site of one of Barcelona's most his-toric and exclusive restaurants, the **Set Portes,** first established in 1838 by Josep Cuyás. According to the journalist Josep Carandell, who wrote the history of the restaurant, the name Set Portes (Seven Doors) comes from the original owner's desire to suggest the Masonic Doors of Knowledge. Other design elements have masonic echoes: the iron columns, the tiled floor resembling a chess board, and the branches of the acacia tree which are painted on the blue tiles of the walls.

It is also true that the cafés surrounding the Pla de Palau were popular meeting places of the Barcelona Freemasons and that Cuyás owned two more establishments in the area: the Café Aurora and the Café Constitució, both names with Masonic connotations.

Set Portes was the very first bar to have an outdoor terrace set with tables and chairs and was among the city's leading café-theatres. Now it offers elegant, old-fashioned dining, but at a fair old price.

Opposite the restaurant on the other **Tour boat.**

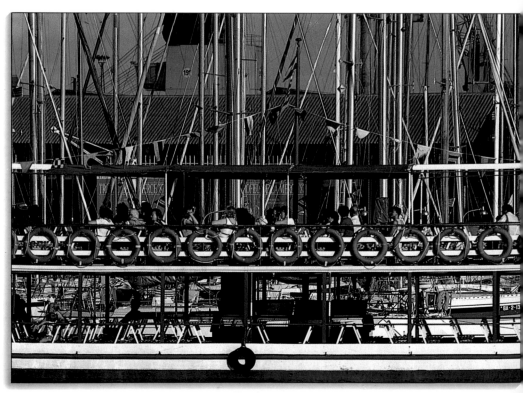

side of the square is the **Civil Governor's Palace**, the original "Antiga Duana" designed by Count de Roncali, who personally directed the construction works between 1790 and 1792, replacing the first "Antiga Duana" which was destroyed by fire in 1772. Count de Roncali's desire to pretend to a greater nobility than was actually the case has made it rather over-blown.

On the port side of the square, where the historic Portal del Mar crossed the Roman walls, is the **Escola Nàutica** (Naval Academy), which once faced the palace that gave its name to the Pla de Palau. Since 1714 this has been the official residence of the Chief of Naval Operations, and it was also a court house until the fire of 1875.

Today the **Font del Geni Català** (literally the fountain of the Catalan genius), built in 1855, is isolated by traffic in the middle of the square. The fountain is in memory of the Marquis de Campo Sagrado and commemorates the installation of the first fresh-water conduits to the city. The "Geni Català" is in the form of a winged figure, symbolising Catalonia, with four mouths allegorising the Rivers Llobregat, Ter, Ebre and Segura which, in turn, correspond to the four provinces of Catalonia represented by statues at each corner.

Meanwhile, back on the mole: Once it has passed the *El Cap de Barcelona*, the jolly sculpture by Roy Lichtenstein and the Moll d'Espanya, the promenade sweeps on round to the **Moll Diposit** and the marina, Port Vell, which hosts some of the most exclusive motor yachts in the Mediterranean. In 1992 the former warehouse complex, the Magatzem General de Comerç (1878) by Elias Rogent, was eye-catchingly transformed into the **Palau de Mar** by architect Ebertrard Zeidler. Its upstairs floors house the **Museu d'Història de Catalunya**.

There are a couple of government offices in the back of the building, but the key attraction here are the restaurants that line the front. Sunday lunch in

Waterfront restaurant.

the Palau de Mar has become an institution for those who can afford it. The view is of the harbour – and many a local yachtsman takes advantage of his in-town mooring for an on-board barbecue on a Sunday – and is an excellent place to watch the flow of people enjoying the promenade.

Skating – roller-blading – is the hip way of getting about the Moll Diposit and the broad **Moll Barceloneta** beyond. There are even a couple of specially created skaters' courses. The Moll Barceloneta, now the favourite place of lovers and Sunday newspaper readers, was once covered in crumbling *tinglados* (sheds), and the decision to knock them down for the new-look Barcelona of the 1990s was greeted with cries of outrage. The loudest cries were over the fate of a shanty-town of popular beachside seafood restaurant shacks or *chiringuitos* on the other side of Barceloneta, swept away to make space for the continuing promenade.

In truth, there is no shortage of seafood restaurants in the vicinity, and no doubt the proprietors were offered generous resettlement terms elsewhere, but the *chiringuitos* had a cheerful, tacky atmosphere of their own and added real colour. Meanwhile the seafood restaurants on the Passeig Joan de Borbó – the main road which runs out along the port side of Barceloneta – still continue to attract good business, and are happy to have been given their own view of the harbour. To make a choice, follow the crowds and your nose, and don't expect to eat particularly cheaply.

Downtown Barceloneta: The rigidity of the street plan gives a clue to the origin of what is misleadingly called the fishermen's quarter. Barceloneta was born of a political, military decision. It was to this area that the inhabitants of La Ribera were relocated when their homes were demolished to give way to the building of a fortress after the siege and conquest of Barcelona by Felipe V.

The military engineer/architect Juan Martín Cermeño was the author of the project; his plans were based on the construction of 15 short, identical, streets giving rise to a series of narrow, rectangular blocks all facing in the same direction (towards Ciutadella), facilitating easy military control. During the second half of the 19th century the lack of living accommodation in the city and pressure from the local proprietors resulted in the buildings being raised to three storeys.

The first inhabitants of Barceloneta were therefore refugees under careful military control, but from this inauspicious beginning, the suburb has gradually emerged as one of the most appealing areas of the city.

The road that heads off from the other side of the roundabout leads to the **Moll de Pescadors** – the "fishermen's wharf" with the distinctive clock tower or Torre del Rellotge, which started life as a lighthouse. Close by is the Market Exchange (first opened in 1924) where auctions are held twice a day on weekdays: one at six o'clock in the morning

Promenade to the Olympic Village.

to auction the blue fish caught during the previous night, and the other at five o'clock in the afternoon selling the same day's trawler catches.

Beyond the roundabout the Passeig Joan de Borbó passes the **Torre de Sant Sebastià** whose 257-ft (78-metre) height marks the end, or the beginning, of the cable car's route which completes its 3,876-ft (1,292-metre) journey at Miramar, on Montjuïc. The "Aeri del Port" as the cable car is known, is the result of an idea conceived in 1926 by Carles Buigas. It began operating four years later. The 390-ft (119-metre) Torre de Jaume I, on the Moll Barcelona beyond the ferry port, is a popular halfway stopover. If you have the time and the head for heights for this trip, you will be rewarded spectacular aerial views over the city and the port.

Brave new world: If you are now on the seaward side of Barceloneta and have resisted the restaurants so far, then continue to do so for a little longer. A mile or so along the promenade at the back of

the beaches (including Barcelona's own Muscle Beach) which were specially created for the Olympics – Barcelona now claims 3 miles or 5km of downtown beaches – stands the **Olympic Village**, unmissable by virtue of its two skyscrapers and the golden fish sculpture (*Pez y Esfera* by Frank Gehry) rippling in the sun. All that you see before you was created on the pretext of the Olympic Games, and it is quite an achievement. Meanwhile, on your left before reaching the village, note the modernist **Watertower** (1905) by Jose Domènech Estapá, virtually the only original industrial building left standing in this area.

The Olympic Village was built on land formerly occupied by ramshackle warehouses and tumbledown factories, according to a master plan developed by architects Mackay, Martorell, Bohigas and Puigdomènech. In order to assimilate the village into the city, the major railway lines into Estació de França, the international train terminus, had to be

The beach beyond Barceloneta.

buried below ground. The village itself cost three times the money spent on the installations on Montjuïc: here are two of the highest towers in Spain: one the chic Chicago-designed Arts Barcelona Hotel, intended for the Olympics but opening two years too late, the other the Mapfre tower of largely offices.

The 140,000 sq ft (13,000 sq metres) of commercial and recreational space includes some of the most exclusive shopping in Barcelona, and the immediate vicinity of the Olympic Port alone (300 moorings) has more than a dozen restaurants and seven bars, and people head here every night of the week.

Twenty-eight different architects went on the rampage in the Olympic Village: the 200 new buildings cover 183 acres (74 hectares), and are in 200 different designs. Many appartments have been slow to sell since the Games, although the Olympic Village and Port are undeniably popular with locals, who flock here at weekends.

Also here is the Centre Metereològic,

a strangely shaped tower designed by Alvaro Silva for the study of weather.

The Olympic Village now shares its metro station with the zoo side of the **Parc de la Ciutadella**. The name (citadel) has its origins in the use to which Felipe V put this land when, after the fall of Barcelona in 1714 following the siege by Franco-Spanish troops, he ordered a fortress to be built capable of housing 8,000 soldiers, thus ensuring control of the city. To achieve this it was necessary to demolish most of the district of Ribera; 40 streets and 1,262 buildings disappeared completely.

Exhibition park: In 1869 General Prim ceded the land to the city for conversion into a public park; the town hall issued a public tender for the landscaping and construction of the gardens which went to Josep Fonseré, whose plan was approved in 1873.

The project also included model arcade buildings which were to surround the park; however, it was not until 1888, the year of the Universal Exposition,

Montaner's Castle (Zoological Museum) in Ciutadella Park.

that the park began to be a reality, emerging in a shape later to be damaged by bombing in the Civil War.

Of the original idea, only the Governor's Palace, the chapel and the arsenal (today the site of the Catalonian Parliament, inaugurated in 1932) remain. When Francisco Franco became dictator of Spain in 1939 the Parliament House was once more relegated to its original function of military barracks and the Salón de Sesions (which had, even earlier, been the throne room of a royal palace), became a warehouse. In 1945 the building was converted once again, this time becoming the **Museum of Modern Art**.

The French landscape architect, J.C.N. Forestier, created the oval plaza (Plaça d'Armes) facing the main facade, of which the great beauty of the "El Desconsol" statue – the work of Josep Llimona – is an important feature as it emerges from the central pond. The plaça is well stocked with benches and chatting Catalan old-timers.

Other elements of note in the park are the rather overwhelmingly grotesque modernist cascade in the far corner and the artificial lake, both designed by Josep Fonseré. In fact both the cascade and the lake were intended to camouflage a huge water deposit; in the central section of the waterfall, which can be reached by two flanking, symmetrical stairways, a statue of Venus predominates, sculpted by Venanci Vallmitjana; he was assisted in his labours by a young student of architecture working with Fonseré: Antoni Gaudí.

There are further important architectural buildings, such as the very noticeable pseudo-castle **Castell dels Tres Dragons** (Castle of the Three Dragons), built by Lluís Domènech i Montaner as a café-restaurant for the 1888 Exposition; however, the works were not finished in time and the café never opened. Today it is the **Zoological Museum** but it was one of the first modernist projects and home for years to the architect. Close by is the **Hivernacle**, designed by

Snowflake poses prettily.

Josep Amargós, and recently restored to house a café and summer evening concerts. Next to it is the **Umbracle**, a wood-and-brick structure designed by Josep Fonseré.

Bohemian quarter: The Passeig Picasso separates the Ciutadella Park from the old quarter of Ribera, and features the **Porxos d'en Fonseré**, the arcade that was designed by Fonseré as part of the park environs; Antoni Tàpies's statue *Homenatge a Picasso*, a bizarre and not particularly attractive work on the *paseo*, is worth a moment's contemplation, if just to conclude that it looks rather like a shower cubicle. Old gents gather here to play *petanca* (a game normally associated with France).

The **Ribera** district, behind the massive Mercat del Born, which was opened as Barcelona's central market place in 1876 (now destined to become a library), has enjoyed a renewed lease of life thanks to the proliferation of bars, restaurants, night clubs and art galleries. With its narrow streets and histori-cal features, it is an appealing district for slow meandering. It is, according to designers Juli Capella and Quim Riera, "the ugliest and the most beautiful place in Barcelona". This is one of the city's oldest suburbs, and has appealed to artists such as Gargallo, Nonell and Picasso, all of whom, successively, set up their studios on the top floor of Carrer de Comerç number 28. This was Picasso's last studio in Barcelona.

On the port side of Ribera the Avinguda del Marquès de L'Argentera was once the "Jardí del General" (General's Garden), created in 1815 only to be demolished again in 1877. In 1848, Spain's first railway line was inaugurated here with a route that ran from Barcelona to Mataró.

The railway station was little more than a shack, close to the modern-day **Estació de França** (half-way down the avenue) which at the time of its opening, in September 1929, was the largest station in Europe. Closed for years while the tracks were buried underground for the Olympic Village, today its pristine, airy interior of polished marble and sweeping ironwork echoes to classical music, and is almost unsullied by passengers – even though it is Barcelona's key station for long-distance and international trains.

From under the shadow of the nearby church of **Santa Maria del Mar** (one of the finest interiors in Catalonia), narrow streets lead back to the Carrer Consolat de Mar. This atmospheric street has existed since the 14th century, and its name alludes to the book, also titled *Consolat de Mar*, the first-ever treatise on maritime law. Two special features of the street are the groups of arches, the **Voltes dels Encants** and the **Voltes dels Pintors**, now rickety constructions which existed even before the port itself was built. Despite the fact that the buildings appear to be from the 18th century, it is probable that the prismatic stone columns of the Voltes dels Pintors date back to the 1400s, making them the oldest part of the waterfront.

Left, nightspot on the quay. **Right,** cable-car tower on the ferry terminal.

THE EIXAMPLE, MODERNIST QUARTER

Virtually every city can be identified by one monument. In Paris it is the Eiffel Tower, in New York the Statue of Liberty; Rome wouldn't be the same without the Coliseum, nor London without Big Ben.

Barcelona's most identifiable monument has to be Antoni Gaudí's modernist skyscraper, the Sagrada Família, the city's as yet unfinished cathedral. But all around the Sagrada is another important distinctive entity which, although it is less showy, is at least as important to the city as Gaudí's creation. This entity is the grid-like expansion outside the old walled city which is known as the **Eixample**, loved and hated by locals and visitors alike, and on rather too large a scale to be easily walkable.

At the end of the 19th century, while the rest of Spain was fighting against a growing decadence, Barcelona's flourishing industrial middle class aspired to create a new city. They wanted to break out of the medieval walls, so they created the Eixample. Within its confines they sponsored the creation of some of the most ludicrous and imaginative buildings in the world – examples of modernist architecture that today symbolise the city.

Expansion areas: The original design of the Eixample was the work of a liberal-minded civil engineer, Ildefons Cerdà i Sunyer. The actual work began in 1859 when a Royal Decree finally gave the green light. The Eixample (Catalan for "expansion") was to cover the areas between the old city centre and the equally historic municipalities of Sants, Sarrià, Sant Gervasi de Cassoles and Gracia.

The plan's principal characteristic, and one which broke completely with the tradition of urban planning in Spain, was its absolute adherence to geometric forms. The concept was of a grid of streets running parallel to the seafront, crossed perpendicularly by others running southeast to northwest, rather in the style of an American city.

The concept has not been well received. Carles Soldevila writes in *Barcelona*: "We are not going to try and hide the fact that we Barcelonans tend to speak very badly of our Eixample. We deride it (above all) as being monotonous. The rigorous parallel streets, the unvarying width of 20 metres, the inexorably perpendicular crossroads, the total absence of squares and gardens, the impossibility of separating an outstanding building and providing it with four facades…"

Cerdà is not responsible for this state of affairs. He planned a garden city in which only two of the four sides of each block would be built on. The other sides, together with the central open space, were to have been attractive, shady squares and the *chaflanes* (angled street corners) were meant to be open spaces, not packed with double-parked vehicles as they are today. Cerdà's plan was not

Preceding pages: office buildings on the Diagonal. **Left**, the roof of Gaudí's La Pedrera. **Right**, arresting shop display.

adopted in its entirety for a number of different reasons. He came from a liberal background, and was at the time strongly influenced by the prevailing doctrines of so-called "Utopian socialism" – which did not appeal to the more conservative elements in the city. His original concept for the devolopment caused immediate controversy.

The Eixample is broken down principally into two halves, La Dreta (right) de L'Eixample and L'Esquerra (left) de L'Eixample, which are defined as the areas on both sides of **Carrer de Balmes** as one looks inland towards Tibidabo. Within the two halves are well-defined neighbourhoods such as those of the Sagrada Família and Fort Pius (on the right) and Sant Antoni and a *barri* near the old municipal slaughterhouse called L'Escorxador (on the left).

The right side: Most of Barcelona's greatest landmarks can be found in the right-hand sector, the Dreta, while the Esquerra tends to be more modern and residential. Since the 1960s La Dreta

has undergone a profound transformation. With the earlier inhabitants moving to other districts such as Bonanova, Pedralbes and the upper reaches of Carrer de Balmes and Carrer de Muntaner, the larger houses have been converted into offices and multi-family dwellings.

To start with some points of historical and architectural interest: at the junction where the Carrer d'Ali Bei leaves the Ronda de Sant Pere is a monument to **Rafael de Casanova**, a politician who was injured in this place on 11 September 1714, during the siege in which the city was sacked and its special privileges abolished by Felipe V. The defeat is remembered every year in the Diada de Catalunya – the Catalan national day. The statue and monument are by Rossend Nobas and Josep Llimona respectively.

Directly opposite – and a taste of what is to come – is a modernist building by Telm Fernández i Janot, with another in the same style on the corner of Carrer de Girona, the work of the architect Enric

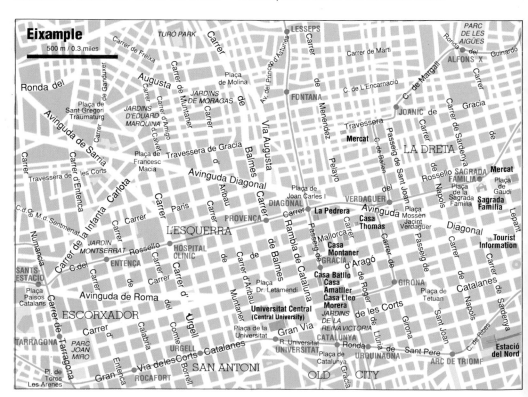

Sagnier. A group of pre-modernist "eclectic" buildings is further up the street. Also close by, at Carrer d'Ausias Marc, 42–46 bis, is still another block in the modernist style, this one noted for its asymmetric tribunals (enclosed balconies or window boxes) and iron railings.

In front are two examples of Sagnier's mix of the eclectic and medieval in houses built for Tomàs Roger and Antoni Ricard. Toward the Plaça Urquinaona is the **Farmàcia Izard**, which dates to 1903, and **Casa Puget**, with exceptional wrought-iron balconies.

Stiff-neck streets: Admirers of modernism will also get a stiff neck from walking up Carrer de Casp. The eclectic facade of number 46 – **Casa Salvado** – shows the clear influence of the Renaissance on architect Juli Batllevell i Arus. Next door, at number 48, is the first of the works by Antoni Gaudí encountered in the Eixample. **Casa Calvet** was built at the beginning of the 20th century and clearly reflects the fashion for borrowing from other periods of architecture.

Scurrying around these streets are journalists from the nearby radio stations of Cadena SER, Radio Nacional and Radio Miramar, all within a few hundred feet of each other.

One block up is the Gran Via de les Corts Catalanes, a major transport artery though pedestrian-friendly since its recent repaving. Along it to the north is the **Plaça Tetuán**, with another monument by Josep Llimona, dedicated to Doctor Robert, who was both a politician and a doctor of medicine. The bronze represents the *pàtria* with a great Catalan flag, and the monument's base has so much in common with La Pedrera (one of Gaudí's best-known works) that experts speculate that the master must have had a hand in its design.

Further north on the Gran Via is Barcelona's second *plaça de braus* (bullring), the **Monumental**, at the intersection of the Gran Via and the Passeig de Carles I. It was built just after Les Arenas, the ring in Plaça d'Espanya, and the two show considerable similarities –

The Rambla de Catalunya.

although this one has more strongly Islamic influences in its architecture.

From the Plaça de Tetuán, the Passeig de Sant Joan leads back down to the Arc del Triomf, a rather overlooked imitation of the arch of the same name in Paris. To the northeast is the **Estació del Nord**, now a bus station. Originally built in 1861 for the Lléida railway line, the neoclassical facade of this depot is actually its side. It was enlarged in 1910 with the addition of an enormous iron roof and a principal entrance, by Demetri Ribes. The building gives character to a neighbourhood situated between the old train tracks and the Gran Via, once the site of the old Roman thoroughfare out of the city.

Return to the Passeig de Gràcia, where the city block bordered by the streets Consell de Cent, Pau Clarís, Diputació and Roger de Llùria was built in 1866 with a small walking street in the middle. The architecture along this **Passatge de Permanyer**, which was built towards the end of the 19th century, has echoes of a British inner-city mews and is a worthwhile detour.

At 299 Carrer d'Aragó is the *claustre* (cloister) and the **Church of the Conception**, one of the very few really old buildings in the Eixample, dating back to the 14th and 15th centuries. Nearby (at number 317) is a **market** of the same name, with a fine array of fresh produce and groceries. Towards the Passeig de Gràcia is a once traditional restaurant, the **Madrid-Barcelona**, unfortunately refurbished recently, perhaps to keep up with the imposing and modern **Fashion Café** opposite.

Elegant avenue: The monotonous uniformity of the Eixample has always been a sore point among the Barcelonans. Yet they complain, maybe with tongue in cheek, that even this very dullness is inconsistent, broken by the beauty, diversity and enchantment of the **Passeig de Gràcia**.

This wide, tree-lined avenue was designed to link the old city and the outlying neighbourhood of Gràcia even be-

The Mansana de la Discòrdia with buildings by Cadafalch (**left**) and Gaudí (**right**).

fore the ancient walls of the city were torn down. The broad promenade is still in a state of excellent preservation due to the prosperity of the period in which it was built, which ensured the use of prime quality materials only in its construction. In his plan Cerdà increased its width to 180 ft (60 metres), which gives it more exclusivity among the uniform streets of the rest of the Eixample. The eye-catching iron street lamps were designed by Pere Falqués.

Where Passeig de Gràcia intersects with Carrer Consell de Cent is the location for the key art galleries in the city (on Consell de Cent – although the Carrer de Montcada area is challenging that title). Here also is **El Golfiño,** a pleasant bar with a selection of excellent *tapas*, or an equally excellent although expensive restaurant, the **Orotava**, which specialises in seasonal game.

The most famous block on the Passeig de Gràcia, between the streets Consell de Cent and d'Aragó, is popularly called the **Mansana de la Discòrdia** (the Block of Discord). The name stems from the close juxtaposition of four buildings, each of which is in a conflicting style, although they are all categorised as modernist. **Casa Lleó Morera,** by Lluís Domènech i Montaner and decorated with the sculptures of Eusebi Arnau, is the first. Next to it is the less spectacular **Casa Mulleras,** by Sagnier; slightly further along stands the outstanding **Casa Amatller** by Josep Puig i Cadafalch, next door to which is Gaudí's **Casa Batlló,** remodelled in 1906. With the Ruta del Modernisme, ticket entry to those and other buildings is possible (*see page 78*).

In the same block, but around the corner on Carrer d'Aragó, sits yet another building by Domènech i Montaner, **Casa Montaner i Simón**. Originally built for the editorial house of Montaner i Simón, it has become, in its new designation as the **Fundació Tàpies**, a much discussed structure due to the "sculpture" called *Núvol I Cadira* (cloud and chair) which Tàpies designed for the roof. Observers' opinions vary from "Genius!" to "If I had done that, they would have put me in jail".

This architectural richness continues on Passeig de Gràcia at number 74 with **Casa Coma,** another modernist building by Enric Sagnier, while at the next corner is **Casa Enric Batlló**, displaying pre-modernist Gothic elements by Josep Vilaseca. Close by, on Carrer de Mallorca (253–257), is the **Casa Angel Batlló**, built in the same prolific years (1893–96) by the same architect.

World favourite: Perhaps the best-known building on the Passeig de Gràcia is Antoni Gaudí's **Casa Milà,** more popularly known as **La Pedrera** (the quarry), at number 92 on the corner of Carrer de Provença. At the time of its construction in 1910 it was the subject of passionate debate between enthusiasts and denigrators. For many years it was left to fall apart, but UNESCO recently declared it a monument of world interest and it is now cared for by a Catalan bank. Inside is an exhibition space and

Passeig de Gràcia street lamps.

guided tours include the spectacular roof where the chimneys are so weird they have been dubbed the "witch scarers".

The best area for refreshment after visiting the Pedrera is the nearby Rambla de Catalunya, a quieter extension of the more famous Ramblas. Here the pedestrian area is lined with *granjes, xocolateries* and ice-cream shops, such as the **Jijonenca**, **El Turia** and maybe the city's best venue for breakfasts and sandwiches, the **Confiteria Mauri** (on the corner with Carrer Provença).

Back on the other side of Passeig de Gràcia is the **Palau Montaner**, built in 1893 at the corner of Carrer Roger de Llúria and Carrer de Mallorca. Decorated with multi-coloured ceramic murals and a bas-relief facade, it was the work of one of the principal architects of the time, Domènech i Montaner.

The palace, owned by the Marquis de Júlia, was one of the great buildings of the new architectural style. The same architect then built **Casa Tomàs**, also on Carrer de Mallorca (number 293).

Not far away, Josep Puig i Cadafalch's **Casa Quadras** was unveiled in 1897 on the Avinguda Diagonal (number 373). The house, erected for the Barón de Quadras, has since been converted into the Music Museum, which is due to be relocated in the new Auditorium. The following year, Puig completed the **Casa de les Punxes**, a little further up the road.

Both of these, together with the **Casa Serra** on the last block of the Rambla de Catalunya, show definite influences of Nordic neo-Gothic. But, while Casa de les Punxes has been declared of world interest by UNESCO, Casa Serra, which was originally a monastery, needed a massive campaign in the press and among local residents and architects in order to save it from being torn down.

The **Diagonal** (so called because it runs, perversely, across the rigid grid of the Eixample) is the city's main business thoroughfare, lined with buildings in the latest architectural style and shops and office blocks for much of its length. To embark on the Diagonal, you really

In the neighbourhood of the Sagrada Família.

need to know where you plan to end up.

Turning right down the Diagonal, the Carrer de Mallorca leads off into the heart of the *barri* of the **Sagrada Família**, the neighbourhood at the northern extreme of the Eixample. The area has Gaudí's staggering temple – still only 40 percent finished – at its centre (*see page 83*). Work is currently in progress on the nave, and plans are being studied for a massive central tower to soar above it all. Models of the finished work are in the small museum in the crypt.

The Sagrada is not the only monument of interest around here. At the end of the Avinguda de Gaudí is the **Hospital de Sant Pau**. The complex, made up of over 20 buildings, is another of the many buildings designed by Lluís Domènech i Montaner between 1902 and 1912. If you can spend half an hour walking through the public areas of the hospital, you are in for a treat which serves as a reminder that, although Gaudí is the best known of the modernists,

there were others just as creative.

The left side: Although the Dreta (right side) of the Eixample attracts most of the visitor's attention, the **L'Esquerra** (the left side) is not unimportant.

In the two neighbourhoods of L'Escorxador and Sant Antoni, the dominant architectural structures were built by *mestros d'obres* (master builders). For example, there is a modernist building by Jeroni Granell at number 260, Carrer de Corsega, although it is not considered one of his best works. Nearby, at number 271, is another house with its vestibule decorated in the modernist style. The building on the corner with Carrer d'Enric Granados is the work of Ruíz i Casamitjana, with outstanding railings on the balconies.

The Carrer d'Aribau is known for several restaurants. At the corner where Aribau and Carrer d'Aragó meet, the **Gargantua I Pantagruel** offers the best in cooking in the style of the province of Lléida. Not far away, at number 73, the **Chicoa** serves one of the best cod dishes

Not all eyes are on the architecture.

in the city as well as *calçots* (roasted spring onions) when they are in season.

In the **Sant Antoni** region, delineated by the Gran Via de les Corts Catalanes, the Avinguda del Paral.lel, the Ronda de Sant Pau and the Ronda de Sant Antoni, the Avinguda de Mistral makes interesting walking. It leads to the **Mercat de Sant Antoni**, a bigger and more diverse market than its more famous colleague on the Ramblas. Within its eye-catching columns and beams, among other things, are inexpensive clothes, paintings, comics, pirated computer programs and, on Sundays, a market for collectors of old books. On the northwest corner of the market is a bar which specialises in *tapas* of mussels, crayfish and clams.

Situated at the southwest corner of the Eixample is the neighbourhood which takes its name from the ancient slaughterhouse which once stood here, the **Escorxador**. This region, bordered by Hostafrancs to the south, is a relatively recent development. Its landmark

in the neighbourhood is that of the **Parc de L'Escorxador** itself. The park (sometimes known as the **Parc de Joan Miró**, because of the artist's sculpture) is on the site of the municipal slaughterhouse, and was built 100 years after the Plan Cerdà which had provided for it.

Further out: Recent years have seen the development of a smart residential area away from the centre. This focuses around the Diagonal particularly at **Plaça Francesc Macià** and **Plaça Reina Maria Cristina**, where the shopping is select. Up the hill above the Diagonal live the smart people, with their nannies and extensive families. **Pedralbes** is exclusive. Down by the Diagonal the university gives the area a misleadingly rebellious flavour. The **Palau Reial de Pedralbes**, tucked away behind its lovely park, filled with students revising or making love with equal intensity, is a handsome building which dates from 1929. It was designed by Eusebi Bona i Puig to be a residence for the royal family, but today it serves as the home for the **Ceramic Museum**.

Up the hill behind the palace is one of the finest examples of Catalan church architecture and one of the most peaceful corners of the city: the **Monestir de Pedralbes**. The monastery was founded in 1326 by Queen Elisenda de Montcada, fourth wife of King Jaume II. One of its chapels is covered with typical Catalan paintings by Ferrer Bassa, but otherwise the monastery's simplicity adds to its quiet power, and its cloisters are now an unusual museum of monastic life.

Part of the complex also houses some 72 canvasses and eight sculptures from the **Thyssen-Bornemisza Collection**, of which the bulk is now housed in Madrid. That's not to denigrate the Pedralbes selection, however, which includes work by Canaletto, Velazquez and Tintoretto. Even if you don't get in to see the collection, it is worth coming out to Pedralbes to enjoy the atmosphere of this small cobbled world, tucked away up the hill out of the hubbub of the city. Here you can hear the birds sing.

Left, modern imitates modernism. **Right,** Eixample shopping.

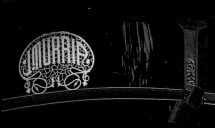

VICENTE BOSCH
BADALONA

OUE

CHARTREUSE

TAR

CITY PARKS AND URBAN SPACES

The avant-garde thinking which recently transformed Barcelona's architecture and design also permeated what the town planners call the *espais urbans* (urban spaces), both green and concrete. Architects were commissioned to create new spaces and upgrade existing ones, though "traditional" parks have been left essentially untouched.

Barcelona's public parks date from as far back as 1869 (Parc de la Ciutadella) up to the most recent transformations of city centre plazas and demolished buildings created in the late 1980s and 90s. Some are little more than a rearrangement of the benches and flower-pots at the convergence of two or three streets and consequently of far more benefit to the locals than to visitors. Others, such as the Parc del Clot, which today occupies the ruins of a Renfe (Spain's national railway) shunting shed and roundhouse,

Preceding pages: in the Maragall Gardens. **Left,** the Parc de l'Espanya Industrial.

are large, complex and interesting for everyone.

The **Parc del Clot** (Metro line I to Clot station) is an excellent example of the latest thinking in urban planning by the architects Dani Freixes and Vicenç Miranda. The word *clot* means "hole" in Catalan, and, like the modern urban parks, this one was partially created within a large depression in the ground. In this case, the basin is a natural amphitheatre housing a sizeable playing field which even on the gloomiest winter day sees its fair share of children playing football. A long bridged walkway passing overhead links the sunken portion of the park with a grass park of equal size sporting a long geometric pergola, trellises and sculptures by Bryant Hunt.

But the one element which makes this park worth a visit is the remains of the old train roundhouse; its walls and arched windows enclose and criss-cross the site, creating an area where people can walk or play among the remnants of the not-too-distant past.

Slaughter quarter: The **Parc de Joan Miró** is on the site of a slaughterhouse and consequently it is sometimes nicknamed the Parc de l'Escorxador (Slaughterhouse Park). The cement square, which covers an entire city block, has undeservedly become something of a mecca for tourists because of the enormous phallic sculpture called *Dona i Ocell* (woman and bird) by the genial Catalan artist Joan Miró, which towers 70 ft (22 metres) above the concrete.

But, apart from the sculpture and its surrounding pool, the park shows none of the imagination which has pushed Barcelona into the forefront of Europe's urban renewal schemes and the visitor is better off buying a postcard and skipping the trip. If you insist, Metro line III, station Tarragona, or line I, station Plaça d'Espanya, or a variety of bus routes will get you there.

Other spaces catalogued as parks, such as La Plaça de la Palmera, El Parc de la Crueta del Coll, El Fossar de la Pedrera, Moll de la Fusta and the Jardins d'Emili

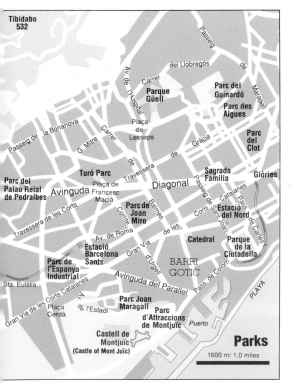

Vendrell, are a notable combination of the natural and the man-made.

A good example of this innovation is the park of the **Estació Nord** (Metro line I, Arc de Triomf station). The park was built around the abandoned train station, now a major bus terminal. In keeping with the policy of preserving existing structures, the station's covered platform area has been converted into a multi-sports centre and the abandoned shunting yards have become the site of an auditorium and a national theatre. It is visually enlivened by Beverly Pepper's enormous multi-toned blue-and-white ceramic sculpture (a wave or a hill, according to your point of view) and an avenue-wide path.

Meeting point: At the junction created by the convergence of three of the city's principal arteries, Gran Via de les Cortes Catalanes, the Meridiana and the Diagonal, a single pole tower spoked with suspension cables supports a series of elevated curving ramps which unite three sections of the small but interesting park

called the **Glòries** (Metro line I to the station of the same name). From various vantage points on the overhead walkways view alternating areas of grass, flower beds, a man-made river and a children's playground. The park is also an indication of where Barcelona, and perhaps Europe, is heading in terms of urban leisure spaces. This area at Glòries has been developed as a commercial centre with an arts complex comprising the **National Theatre of Catalonia**, styled like a great Greek Temple, by Ricardo Bofill, and a music auditorium.

The most remarkable modern urban space has to be the **Parc de l'Espanya Industrial**, situated on the west side of the Sants railway station. It can be reached on Metro line 5 or 3, Sants-Estació, or by bus. The park, built between 1982 and 1985 by architects Luis Peña Ganchegui and Francesc Rius i Camps on a parcel of land which once supported a textile factory, has both a romantic and an industrial face. The lower and more romantic part comprises

Beverly Pepper's sculpture in the Estació Nord.

a large lake, usually complete with teenagers splashing one another from rented rowing boats, and an expansive lawn area with paths, willow trees and sculptures by such notable Catalan artists as Fuxa, Casanovas, Alsina, Anthony Caro and Palazuelo.

The upper esplanade is the industrial area and by far the most controversial section. It is dominated by 10 towers, each with megaphone-shaped spot-lights and lookout platforms which would not be even slightly out of place in a German Stalag of World War II. Happily, Andrés Nagel's immense play-sculpture, *Drac de Sant Jordi* and a series of water spouts and cascades help to contradict the concentration camp atmosphere of the upper levels. It is a park that few love at first sight, but it has a habit of growing on people.

Green zones: The concrete parks aside, a second group of *espais urbans*, including Parc Pegàs, Turó Parc, Aigües, Parc de Cervantes-Roserar and Guinardó, demonstrates the broad spectrum of styles and ideas which make up the green zones of the city.

An interesting walk for adults and an adventure for children is **Parc Pegàs**, which can be reached on Metro line I, station Fabra i Puig. The park is principally made up of a long serpentine lagoon with rowing boats for rent. A path snakes along the edge of the waterway, crossing it from time to time on a variety of bridges, climbing uphill to lookout areas and descending again to the water level. Stands of heavy tree growth and flower gardens enclose the entire area and turn it into a labyrinth.

Turó Parc, which is also known as Parc del Poeta Eduard Marquina, is a short walk from Plaça de Francesc Macià, and any of the buses which run westward along the Diagonal stop at the roundabout. The park, a project of Rubió i Tudurí, has two distinct areas. One is made up of lawn, hedges and flower beds laid out in a classic geometric pattern. The other contains children's playgrounds, a small lake with lilies and

The Parc del Clot, brightening up a large depression.

an open-air theatre with the polyglot title Teatret del Turó Parc.

The entrance to the park is divided by a monument dedicated to Catalan cellist Pau (Pablo) Casals. The sculpture, by Valls, is aptly composed of a host of angels playing trumpets and violins and a poem by Catalan poet Salvador Espriu. Other sculptures by Clarà, Villadomat, Eloïsa Cerdan and Borrell i Nicolau dot the interior of the park.

The **Parc de les Aigües** or water park is named after the massive reservoir upon which it sits. On top of the underground cistern, part of Barcelona's water distribution system, is a small, well-trimmed classical garden. Because it is owned by the city water company, it is closed to the public, though parts may be glimpsed through the fence. The surrounding public park, whose entrance lies close to the Alfons X station on Metro line IV, is an ideal place for a picnic or just to watch the local *petanca* (boules) matches.

The **Parc de Cervantes-Roserar** is, as its name suggests, a rose garden. Located near the Zona Universitaria station (on Metro line III), the 20-acre (8-hectare) park is a little boring for those who have no particular penchant for roses. But, with 11,000 bushes comprising 245 different varieties, the park is an essential visit for devotees of the plant.

One of the last of the Barcelona parks which refuses to fall easily into any category is **Guinardó** (Metro line IV to Guinardó). Although the greatest part of this park is hill-side forest, the most southerly tip holds the most interest. This is a *torrent ajardinat*, or "cultivated water course". In Guinardó, a section of a shallow gorge has been made into a garden by the French gardener with the appropriate name, Jean Forestier. The water, when there is any, spills from a small reservoir and passes through a series of tiny dykes and canals between trimmed shrubs and over a series of terraces and flower beds.

Fort park: The great-grandfather of all green spaces is **El Parc de la Ciutadella**

Shady walk in the Parc Pedralbes.

186

(citadel). Ciutadella is today the site of Barcelona's zoo, various museums and the Catalan parliament, and has a well-documented history dating back more than 250 years. At one time a fortress stood on this site. In order to accommodate it a whole neighbourhood was razed to the ground and the evicted population moved to the newly created Barceloneta district by the port.

Beginning in 1869, a Catalan botanist and gardener named Oliva was put in charge of the project to transform the whole area into a park, but it wasn't ready until the opening of the 1888 Universal Exposition. The remains of its pre-park military past are still present in the names of its buildings, such as the **Arsenal de la Ciutadella** and the ancient **Plaça de les Armes** which is now the central ornamental garden.

Besides the Arsenal, which houses both the **Museu d'Art Modern** (MNAC *see page 195*) and the Catalan **Parliament**, landmarks are the **Museu de Zoologia** in the pseudo-castle former café-restaurant of modernist architect Lluís Domènech i Montaner, the **Museu de Geologia,** the **Hivernacle**, a tropical greenhouse, and another structure for heat-loving plants called the **Umbracle**. Paths zig-zag through the park, around the boating lake and the cascade and among orange groves and palms where parrots, escaped from the Ramblas, squawk. Beside them are statues of Catalan writers, artists and politicians.

The park is permanently changing as the neighbouring zoo bites into it in an attempt to simulate the natural habitats of the species it houses; some observers believe that the zoo is disfiguring the park, but it is a popular disfigurement – particularly its superstar "Snowflake" (*Copo de Nieve),* an albino gorilla. Zoo and park are reached by Metro line I, station Arc de Triomf, or line IV Ciutadella station or bus.

Forgotten classics: At the city's opposite extreme, along the Diagonal, is one of the few parks which has been passed over by the avant-garde regime in the

present-day Town Hall. Next to the Palau station on Metro line III is the **Parc del Palau Reial de Pedralbes**, the result of a 1919 conversion of the antique Can Feliu into a residence for the Spanish Royal family.

Today the elegant palace hosts a large classical garden built to a "geometric decorative outline". It was designed and built in the 1920s by landscape architect Nicolau Maria Rubió i Tuduri and integrated the existing palace garden with land ceded by the Count Güell. After various uses by kings and heads of state, the garden and the palace were opened to the public in 1960. Today the palace is home to the Ceramic Museum, and the park around it is the haunt of lovers of classical gardens.

As "traditional" as the Parc Pedralbes may be, it is almost modern when compared to the **Parc del Laberint**. The garden dates back to the 18th century and is the work of Joan A. Desvalls – the Marques of Alfarràs – and Domenic Bagutti. Entered through the grounds of the Velòdrom in the Barri Verge del Cami, the garden is Barcelona's best example of Romantic-neoclassicism, with strong Italian influence.

As well as a labyrinth of trimmed hedges, Laberint is composed of a system of visual axes, reservoirs, bowers, niches, temples, water channels and a series of icons depicting love in various aspects. The nucleus of the estate was a medieval tower around which the Marques built his fortress-like house in the eclectic style of the 19th century, with more than a touch of Arabic fantasy.

Twin pleasure peaks: Playgrounds always have a section for children, and Barcelona is no exception. But as well as the "in park" play areas the city boasts two outstanding parks of year-round attraction: Montjuïc and Tibidabo.

Montjuïc hill, the site of the 1992 Olympics and Barcelona's best-known natural landmark, is a mecca for Sunday hikers, playing children and courting couples. As well as its parks, its Olympic installations, its museums, its ferris

wheels and its roller-coaster rides, it has two outstanding gardens. The largest, **Mossen Costa i Llobera**, specialises in exotic tropical plants and cacti. **Joan Maragall**, the garden of the king's residence in Barcelona, the *palauete* (small palace) of Albéniz, is in classical style with illuminated fountains and a large area for concerts and theatre.

This is the most inviting garden in the city, unfortunately open to the public only on Sunday and holidays (10am– 2pm), due to its official role as a venue for diplomatic meetings and conferences. Montjuïc's immense size is best managed with the help of bus number 101 (from Plaça d'Espanya) or number 13 (from El Polvori), or by the funicular from Metro Paral.lel or a series of escalators from Plaça d'Espanya.

For an adult, getting to **Tibidabo Park** is almost more fun than being there. First, take the FGC train from Plaça Catalunya to Av. del Tibidabo station, then the semi-open tram to the end of its line. From there the funicular climbs the

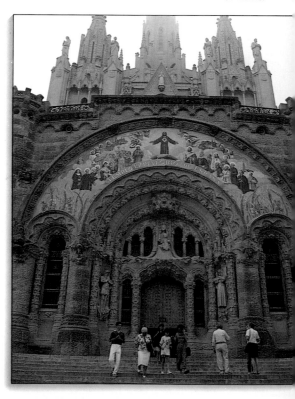

Sacre Cor church, on Tibidabo's summit.

steep hill to the park. Two interesting sidelights are the climb to the top of the church steeple for the highest look-out you're going to get without an aeroplane (ride the latter in the fairground below), and the **Museu d'Autòmats**, inside the amusements area. If the view from Tibidabo is not good enough, then try the nearby **Torre de Collserola**, the communications tower by Norman Foster for the 1992 Olympics.

Modernism rampant: Without a doubt Barcelona's best-known park is **Park Güell**, designed by Antoni Gaudí i Cornet. The present-day park was originally planned to be a garden city (English-style, hence the spelling of "park") encompassing 60 building plots on the estate of Eusebi Güell. Happily, the development was a flop. The only buildings which were completed were two pavilions flanking the entrance and two houses inside the park, one of which is today the **Casa-Museu Gaudí**, where Gaudí himself lived from 1906 to 1926.

In creating Güell, Gaudí used shapes which harmonised with the landscape. Always aware of the struggle between man and nature, he built a complex garden of staircases, zoomorphic sculptures, sinuous ramps and viaducts. The most important single element of the park is a two-tiered plaza 280 by 130 ft (86 by 40 metres). The lower part, made up of a series of columns in the form of a *sala hipóstila*, was designed to be the development's market-place. The upper portion is an open area with grand views over the city, surrounded by an undulating bench of mosaics, whose detailing is largely the work of Josep Jujol. The park, built between 1900 and 1914, has been declared a monument of world interest by UNESCO.

Park Güell has become one of the symbols of the city, along with the monument to Columbus and the Sagrada Família. But that isn't to say that there aren't *espais urbans* of equal interest within the capital. Barcelona has a spectrum of parks broad enough to satisfy every green or urban taste.

The "airport" in Tibidabo's amusement park.

MUSEUMS

The cultural activity in Barcelona is intense: in an average year there are more than 1,000 art exhibitions city-wide – many of them within the city's 65 museums. The recommendations that follow are very much a selection, therefore, and have been grouped by area. The Palau Virreina, on the Ramblas, has details of cultural events. Remember that most collections remain closed to the public on Mondays.

Montjuïc's collections: One of the most attractive places in Barcelona is the hill of Montjuïc (Metro lines I and III to Plaça d'Espanya). The **Museu Arqueològic** (Archaeological Museum) is on Passeig de Santa Madrona. It has recently been rearranged and in a new part of the building a section has been dedicated to the *Mundo Ibérico* (the Iberian world). These rooms contain important discoveries from Catalonia, the Balearic Islands, the rest of the Iberian peninsula and parts of Europe. The museum has collected evidence of the different phases of man's evolution from the Palaeolithic to the Visigothic ages.

Next door is the **Museu Etnològic** (Ethnological Museum). This is a modern structure (built in 1973) and is one of only three buildings in the city (the others are the Joan Miró Foundation and the new Museu d'Art Contemporani) constructed specifically for the purpose. All the others, former palaces and historic buildings, have been converted into museums by private foundations.

The Ethnological Museum houses a collection of more than 25,000 pieces, which can be visited by specialists with prior authorisation. Open to the public are exhibitions on two floors. Every exhibit is clearly marked with texts in both Catalan and Castilian.

On the Mirador de Palau, the imposing Palau Nacional houses the **Museu Nacional d'Art de Catalunya** (MNAC), recently remodelled by the Italian Gae

Aulenti, who also created the Musée d'Orsay in Paris. The museum has the most extensive and valuable collection of Catalonian Romanesque art in the world, including ancient church frescoes brought down from the Pyrenees by donkey. There is also a display of Gothic art and a somewhat fragmented collection of 16th and 17th-century art including works by Tintoretto, El Greco and Zurbarán. Building works continue to eventually house the Museu d'Art Modern and other smaller collections under the same roof.

New on Montjuïc is the **Olympic Gallery**, located in the back end of the Olympic stadium, where reference material and archive film for the 1992 Games are kept.

The **Fundació Joan Miró**, founded by the artist himself in 1971, is between the stadium and the Montjuïc Funicular Railway in a striking, luminous building designed by his friend and leading Catalan architect Josep Lluís Sert. The foundation exhibits a large selection of

Miró's art and is also dedicated to the promotion of contemporary art in general. Every year it organises the "Premi Internacional de dibuix Joan Miró" (International Joan Miró Drawing Prize) and a constant round of conferences and debates on cultural and artistic subjects. Contemporary music concerts are held here as well as a programme of children's theatre.

The museum's library of contemporary art is extensive. A highlight is the *Mercury Fountain* by Alexander Calder, now back in operation after years of disuse due to a lack of enough mercury.

On top of the hill is the **Museu Militar** (Military Museum), in Montjuïc Castle (bus number 11 from the Plaça d'Espanya; the *teleferique* will take you to the castle gates). The museum houses collections of military artefacts and arms, models of the castles of Catalonia and an excellent library of the history of light and heavy armaments.There are great views to the south beyond the commercial port.

The Montjuïc venues are completed by those in the Poble Espanyol (a mock Spanish village built for the 1929 Exposition). Here is the **Museu d'Arts, Indústrias i Tradicions Populars** (Museum of Art, Industry and Popular Traditions) only open by prior arrangement (tel: 93 423 6954) and the **Museu de les Arts Gràfiques** (Museum of Graphic Arts) also visits by appointment (tel: 93 426 1999).

On the Ramblas: In the Ramblas itself is the **Palau Virreina**, an 18th-century palace which is the city's cultural information centre, and a vital stop to update on cultural activities and purchase tickets. It also holds exhibitions and is the temporary home to the **Gabinet Numismàtic** (Coin Collection) before it is moved to the MNAC on Montjuïc.

Down the Carrer Bonsuccés from the Ramblas is the **Museu d'Art Contemporani**, a huge, pure white modern building by the American architect Richard Meier beside the CCCB (Contemporary Culture Centre of Barcelona).

This is a wonderfully spacious gallery for large sculptures and installation art.

At the bottom of the Ramblas is the **Museu Marítim** (Maritime Museum) in Drassanes Reials, the medieval covered shipyard. Thanks to recent intensive restoration, the museum is in impeccable condition and now incorporates *La Gran Aventura del Mar*, a very effective interactive installation on seafaring through the ages. There are also extensive documentary and photographic libraries, a reference section and a workshop specialising in the preservation and restoration of models.

Also at the end of the Ramblas, in the Passatge de la Banca, is the **Museu de Cera** (Wax Museum), with 300 waxworks enhanced by sound effects. And a short walk along the Moll de la Fusta leads to the **Museu d' Història de Catalunya** in the impressively converted Palau de Mar. An interactive tour through the history of Catalonia, it works well as a more universal history museum. Entertaining for the whole family.

The Miró Foundation.

194

Cathedral quarter: There are four museums close to the cathedral: the Museu d'Història de la Ciutat (Museum of the History of the City), the Museu Frederic Marés, the Museu Diocesà and the Museu de la Catedral (Museum of the Cathedral).

The **Museu d'Història de la Ciutat** in Pl. de Veguer is interesting because it conserves archaeological finds from the first Roman city, the Iulia Augusta Paterna Barcino colony. Excavations carried out in the subsoil beneath the building can be visited under the Plaça del Rei, Tinell, Plaça Sant Iu, Carrer Comtes de Barcelona and the cathedral.

The impressive **Museu Frederic Marés** in the Plaça Sant Iu was created by sculptor Frederic Marés and donated to the city in 1946. It has 48 galleries covering both mainstream and folk art. The sculpture section exhibits pieces from the classical period to the present day. The folk art area has magnificent collections of unusual objects, including fans, dolls, bicycles and toys.

The **Museu Diocesà** is in the Pia Almoina building just in front of the cathedral, Pla de la Seu. It has a collection of religious art and interesting temporary exhibitions. Worth visiting for the beautiful building.

The **Museu de la Catedral** is located in the Sala Capitular, and is largely dedicated to Catalan Gothic paintings and sculptures from the 16th, 17th and 18th centuries.

Paintings and jeans: Not far from the cathedral, on the other side of the Via Laietana, are the Museu Picasso and the Museu Tèxtil i d'Indumentària, both on the Carrer de Montcada.

The **Museu Picasso** is spread through the Gothic palaces of Berenguer, Aguilar, Baro de Castellet and Palau Meca. An entire day can easily be spent in this well-designed museum, which presents the artistic evolution of the artist from his earliest works, and also has a pleasant café/restaurant. The quality of the lighting reveals the magnificence of *Las Meninas* (a series of 58 works on a theme of Velázquez) as well as the mastery of his graphic art, bullfighting themes, etchings and lithographs. The museum, which possesses its own teaching facility, also contains a comprehensive library.

Just opposite is the **Museu Tèxtil i d'Indumentària** (Textile and Clothing Museum). The exhibits follow a strict chronological order from the 14th century right up to the blue-jeans era, even though explanations of the beautiful displays are scant. Worthy of mention is a hand-operated silk weaving machine from València. An attractive café and shop are located in the patio of this medieval palace.

Park places: The third corner of Barcelona with various museums is the Parc de la Ciutadella (Metro line IV, Barceloneta station). At one end of the park is the **Museu d'Art Modern**, soon to be relocated to the MNAC in the Palau Nacional on Montjuïc.

The collection includes paintings, sculpture, drawings, engravings and

The Textile and Clothing Museum.

decorative arts from the 19th and 20th centuries, but particularly from the second half of the 19th century and first quarter of the 20th. These are the works of Catalan artists from the neoclassical period up to the present time, including names such as Casas, Mir, Nonell and Rusiñol. In order to follow a logical and chronological sequence, the visitor should start at the left of the entrance. All explanatory notes are, as usual, in Catalan.

At the opposite end of the Park, in the Passeig dels Tillers, are the museums of geology and zoology, both in striking modernist buildings built for the 1929 Exposition. The **Museu de Geologia** is actually the oldest museum in Barcelona, founded in 1878. The **Museu de Zoologia**, housed in the extravagant modernist castle built by Domènech i Montaner which was originally used as a café/restaurant in the Exposition, has two halls: the ground floor is used for temporary exhibitions relating to fauna and biology, including a section dedicated to zoological taxonomy, and the upper floor is entirely given over to exhibits of stuffed animals, birds and reptiles.

One of the most important functions of this museum is education. Staff attempt to bring an awareness of environmental problems to the whole of society, not just to visitors. The administration has organised mobile exhibitions and short lectures for schools on such topics as recycling.

The museum also has an active research function whose work is reflected in its two publications, *Miscel.lània Zoològica* (a multi-author periodical) and the monograph series *Treballs del Museu de Zoologia*, which are exchanged with publications of a similar nature from other countries.

Citywide exhibits: Numerous other museums are dispersed far and wide. The eye-opening **Museu de la Ciència** (Science Museum), well-funded by the La Caixa bank, is at 55 Carrer de Teodor Roviralta (accessible by bus numbers

Roman Casas and Pere Romeu on a Tandem, by Casas, in the Museu d'Art Modern.

17, 22, 58 or 73, or train to Av. Tibidabo station). Its prime objective is education: through a series of interactive displays and well-researched temporary exhibitions it makes science fun and palatable for all ages.

The **Museu Clará** at 27–29 Carrer de Calatrava (FGC line, Tres Torres station) houses the work of the great sculptor Clará along with personal memorabilia and the works of several friends. It is a pity that such a beautiful museum should be so poorly cared for.

Beyond the Tres Torres station the same line continues to Reina Elisenda; get off here for the **Museu-Monestir de Pedralbes**, Carrer de Baixador del Monestir, 9. Built in the 14th century, the church consists of only one nave and the Gothic cloister is built on three floors. This peaceful spot is a haven and gives visitors a fascinating glimpse of monastic life. Its own art collection is interesting (notably the 14th century paintings of Catalan Ferrer Bassa) and it now houses part of the **Thyssen-Bornemisza**

collection, of which the bulk is in Madrid. Paintings by the Old Masters Canaletto, Velázquez and Tintoretto, in a superb setting.

Down the hill from the monastery on the Diagonal is the Palau Reial de Pedralbes, now home to the impressive **Ceramics Museum** and the Postal Collection (the latter by appointment only). The ceramic collection includes pieces of historical interest as well as contemporary ceramics from such hands as Picasso and Miró. The palace has a lovely formal garden.

The **Museu de la Música** is in the beautiful modernist Casa Quadras restored by Puig i Cadafalch at no. 373 Diagonal (Metro lines III or V, Diagonal station) though soon to be relocated to the Auditorium. The exhibits are grouped together into families of musical instruments. On the mezzanine floor are the keyboard instruments, the second floor houses percussion, and the string section is on the third floor. The building alone is worth the visit.

On the road from Vallvidrera to Tibidabo, on Tibidabo itself, is the **Gabinet de Física Experimental Mentora Alsina** (the Mentora Alsina Experimental Physics Collection), reached by the funicular railway which stops very near to the museum.

Here are all kinds of apparatus and instruments related to classical physics (optics, electricity and magnetism). Entry is free and the museum is open every morning from Monday to Saturday, but visitors must call beforehand (tel: 2475734).

The association "Amics de Gaudí" founded the small **Casa-Museu Gaudí** in Gaudí's former residence inside the Güell Park. And another admiration society founded **Museu de Jacint Verdaguer** (open mornings only) in Villa Joana in a beautiful setting in the Collserola woods, (FGC train to Baixador de Vallvidrera), where the great writer and poet, who played a key role in preserving the Catalan language, spent his last years.

Gallery on the Carrer de Montcada.

SHOPS AND SHOPPING STREETS

Barcelona is a commercial city and a correspondingly excellent shopping centre. Not without reason, the Catalans are popularly known as a "nation of shopkeepers". Here, emporia from the last century coexist with avant-garde shops of the latest design. Most shops are open from 9.30am to 2pm and from 5pm to 8pm on weekdays and Saturday mornings, and department stores dispense with the midday break. However, thanks to the Catalan instinct for commerce, many shops stay open late and on Saturday afternoons.

From its vantage point as Barcelona's centre, a large part of the city's commerce gravitates around the Plaça de Catalunya, on one side of which is **El Corte Inglés**, whose name – the English Cut – derives from a small Madrid tailor's shop. It is Barcelona's largest department store, where everything imaginable can be acquired including baked beans in the well-stocked supermarket. Shopping here can be quite a scrum, though its air-conditioning is an attraction during the hot summer months. Not the place to seek the famed Barcelona style.

On the other side is a new commercial centre El Triangle and on the sea side is Spain's largest Marks & Spencer (due to open in 1999) confirming Plaça Catalunya's new role as a shopping centre. Adjoining El Triangle is the Carrer Pelai, good for moderately-priced fashion and shoes.

Leading towards the Gothic Quarter from El Corte Inglés is the Avinguda del Portal de l'Angel, which has a personality all of its own: classic fashion shops rub shoulders with modern boutiques specialising in younger fashions. A refurbished majestic building houses a new branch of El Corte Inglés. Fashion stores include **Podium**, **Zara**, **Cortefiel** and excellent children's wear in **Kiddy's Class**. There are numerous shoe shops and leather goods stores as well as the old-style haberdashery **Santa Anna** which has a beautiful selection of embroidered and lace articles. On the pedestrianised side streets of Carrer Comtal, Carrer de Santa Anna or Carrer de la Canuda are many bookshops, ceramic and art shops as well as a few antique dealers.

From the Plaça de Catalunya you can opt for the elegant and expensive in the Eixample by going up Passeig de Gràcia or Rambla de Catalunya which runs parallel to it; or you can head down the Ramblas in the direction of the port.

The Ramblas: Barcelona's main promenade starts at the Plaça de Catalunya and ends almost at the sea's edge. The shops on the Ramblas, apart from a few exceptions, are mainly dedicated to the sale of cheap souvenirs and leather goods. Far more colourful are the stalls on the Ramblas promenade itself, which sell flowers, birds, animals and books and magazines of all descriptions. At weekends the lower part of the Ramblas

becomes a hive of activity with an arts and crafts market selling anything from clothes and ceramics to costume jewellery and silver.

Opposite the La Boqueria market (open for fresh foods until 8pm), **Carrer de la Boqueria** is lined with long-established family businesses offering gloves, fans, hats and Spanish shawls, together with numerous costume jewellery shops aimed particularly at tourists. In the side streets and nearer Plaça de Sant Jaume (where the Town Hall and Generalitat are situated), are several ceramic and toy shops and others selling typical artisan stoneware.

The old quarter: The main shopping area in the old city is bordered by the Plaça de Catalunya, the Ramblas, Carrer de Ferran and the cathedral, with two of the most bustling streets being the the narrow Carrer Santa Anna and Carrer Portaferrissa.

The pleasure of shopping down the narrow streets of Barcelona's *barri* Gòtic is heightened by the street shows which spontaneously appear throughout the intimate little squares. One of the most popular is the **Plaça del Pi**, which can be reached from the Ramblas down the Carrer Cardenal Casañas. The surrounding buildings and church create an atmosphere not unlike Paris's Montmartre. On the square itself is an old knife and scissors shop as well as another tiny business dedicated to the sale of antique engravings and postcards.

Off the corner of the square behind the knife shop is the narrow **Carrer Petritxol**, typical of this quarter with its overhanging balconies adorned with ferns and cascading hanging plants catching what little sunshine they can. Wall tiles depict various scenes from the history of the tiny street. Up here, the **Sala Parés** gallery (founded in 1840) is well worth a visit; each work of art is accompanied by a guarantee of authenticity. Perhaps you are looking for a wastepaper basket? There is a grand selection in the eclectic **Beardsley**, opposite. Another feature is the number of shops

Servicio Estación, an eclectic hardware store.

202

with home-made chocolate and pastries.

The Plaça del Pi joins with the charming **Plaça Sant Josep Oriol** where, every weekend, an art fair is held. Artists fill the square with their easels – but they don't start early in the morning. Surrounding the square is a number of small shops selling products typical of the region, particularly terracota and glazed ceramics and papier-mâché dolls. At one corner is **Cosas de Casa**, a long-established shop that sells everything for the home and whose multi-coloured display windows add a bright note to the little square, as does the display in the **comic shop**. Just off the square is Carrer del Pi that has attractive fashion and gift shops and a charming grocery shop **La Pineda**, where a glass of wine can strengthen weary shoppers.

Antiques tradition: A tiny street, Carrer Ave Maria, leads from the Plaça Sant Josep Oriol to the no less narrow **Carrer dels Banys Nous**, once the Jewish quarter, with antique shops at every step. Barcelona has a long tradition in the antique trade and this street is the tradition's most popular exponent. All purchases carry a guarantee of origin.

In the heart of the Gothic Quarter is the **Carrer del Bisbe Irurita**. An old candle shop, a stamp shop, one selling babies' clothes and another selling trendy odds and ends are the only commercial enterprises along this ancient street which leads to Barcelona's cathedral. However, there are many other narrow alleys leading from the Plaça Sant Jaume, whose shops offer a wide variety of ceramics, souvenirs and even recycled paper transformed into original and colourful articles.

The **Carrer de Ferran**, which leads back to the Ramblas from Plaça Sant Jaume, has recovered some of its former elegance recently and has crafts, souvenirs, leather shops and cafés.

Eixample shopping: Inland from the Plaça de Catalunya and up the **Rambla de Catalunya** there is a wealth of sophisticated stores specialising in furs – a traditional Barcelona trade, such as

the **Peletería Solsona** and **La Siberia**.

Among the haberdasheries, with their embroidered shirts and quality bed linen, are famous-name boutiques such as **Massimo Dutti** (on the corner of Carrer d'Aragó), **Zara** and **Japan**, as well as several good shoe shops, including **Vogue** and **Tascòn**.

On the way up are entrances to the exclusive shopping malls **Bulevard Rosa** and **Catalunya Center**. Don't be misled by the low-key entrances: the former in particular opens up into a warren of boutiques and restaurants.

The traditional centre for art galleries in the city has always been Carrer de Consell de Cent, near its crossing with the Rambla de Catalunya. At number 333 is the **Galeria Salvador Riera**, and just down the road, another well-known venue, **Sala Gaspar**. On the Carrer de Mallorca at number 291 is the **Barcelona Edicions de Diseny** which displays a wide range of furniture based upon designs by Gaudí, Thonet and Le Corbusier, among others.

For gastronomy, the **Colmado Quilez** on the Rambla and Carrer d'Aragó offers a wide selection of Spanish and international food products. A little further on, at the corner with Carrer de Provenca, is the sweet and cake shop **Mauri**, one of the most famous in Barcelona with an irresistible variety of chocolates and pastries. No less well stocked a window, although of a totally different flavour, is that of **Servicio Estación** on Carrer d'Aragó, an irresistible mecca for those enthusiastic about do-it-yourself. Across the road is the new Fundació Tàpies topped by the controversial "cloud and chair" sculpture by the artist himself.

On the avenue: The broad avenue of the **Passeig de Gràcia** was chosen by the Catalan bourgeoisie in the late 19th and early 20th century as the most select residential area in the city. The avenue continues to preserve its original elegance, particularly in the tasteful shops lining either side of the promenade — mainly art galleries, jewellers, lingerie

Weird welcome to a designer mall.

204

shops and hand-tooled shoe and leather shops. New and sophisticated shopping malls in no way detract from the original charm of this street.

At the beginning of Passeig de Gràcia is **Gonzalo Comella**, housed in a magnificent towered building at the corner with Carrer de Casp, offering its own line of men's and women's clothing. A little further on, at number 12, is **Casa Furest**, reputed to be one of Barcelona's finest men's shops. **Loewe**, at number 35, is a traditional fashion and accessory shop, specialising in leather goods which, although of Spanish design, follow marked Italian, French or English style. It is on the ground floor of one of the best-known modernist buildings, Casa Lleó Morera, and rather disfigures the frontage. By contrast, at number 41, the **Bagués Joieria** derives some of its style from the Casa Ametller in which it is housed.

The **Roca** jewellery shop, founded in 1858, oozes elegance and distinction and occupies a place of honour at num-

ber 18; every article purchased here carries the company's own guarantee. Nearby is Adolfo Dominguez, which stocks Spanish designer wear for men and women.

From the junction of Carrer d'Aragó, the Passeig de Gràcia changes its commercial look – dominated by banks and airline offices – to one that combines typical family businesses and modern boutiques. A classic example of the former is **Santa Eulàlia**, at number 60, traditional outfitters to the female Catalan bourgeoisie and in marked contrast to newcomers Fashion Café, Replay and Zegna, Bulevard Rosa shopping mall is full of trendy fashion boutiques with Spanish and international labels.

Further towards the Diagonal, and next door to Gaudí's La Pedrera mansion, is **Vinçon**, at Passeig de Gràcia, number 96. This shop is regarded as the ultimate authority in design in a wide range of products, from tableware, bed linen and bathroom products to garden articles and many other unusual items.

Barcelona has a strong textile tradition.

Its window displays are always entertaining and the shop also has its own art gallery. Despite its elegant, up-market appearance, prices can be a pleasant surprise.

Designer Diagonal: The "designer" shops along the Avinguda Diagonal, in the direction of the Plaça de Francesc Macià, are in the most exclusive area of Barcelona and reflect local spending power. **Conti**, at number 512, is a good example, displaying Lanvin, Valentino and Ermenegildo Zegna fashions. Almost on the corner of Via Augusta, at number 462, is the **Cinc d'Oros**, a small, unassuming bookshop specialising in art. Just over the road is **Pilma**, a leading store in home design, now facing up to competition from the newcomer **Habitat** (on the corner of Carrer Tuset) with its graphically designed products in a magenta-coloured building that seems made for the company.

Along the length of the tree-lined Diagonal, an air of sumptuousness prevails above the noise of the traffic.

At number 469 is **Jean Pierre Bua** which has the best range of Spanish and international designer fashion for men and women. Nearing the Plaça Francesc Macià is a smaller El Corte Inglés store.

Beyond the plaça the Diagonal continues through a modern architectural landscape of office blocks. About halfway to the university is a small shopping oasis with another comprehensive **El Corte Inglés** and **Bulevard Rosa** shopping mall. Before, on the left, is **L'Illa**, including the smart hotel L'Illa Husa, a branch of **Marks & Spencer**, a hypermarket, FNAC (books and music), and numerous fashion shops. And if your desire for shopping still remains unfulfilled, then **Carrer Muntaner** north of the Diagonal is thick with both local shops and international designer boutiques.

Variety of markets: Barcelona has its own very special flea market, **Els Encants**, situated at the end of Carrer Dos de Maig and the Plaça de las Glòries (Metro line I from Plaça de Catalunya). This little market-place is redolent of a Moroccan *souq* and bartering is the order of the day. Everything imaginable is sold here. The market is open Monday, Wednesday, Friday and Saturday.

On the **Av. de la Catedral** (the Cathedral Square) an antiques market is held every Thursday. Also by the port, Moll de les Drassanes, another antiques market is open at weekends.

Yet another open-air market is that of **Sant Antoni**, at the junction of Carrer Comte d'Urgell and Carrer de Tamarit (near the permanent market of the same name). It is held on Sunday morning and offers book collectors an opportunity to browse among old books, magazines and back copies of newspapers.

Finally, there is also a **Philatelic and Numismatics** market, held on Sunday morning in the Plaça Reial (close to the Ramblas), which draws a considerable number of collectors and admirers. The charm of the square itself lends a special ambience to those who come here to buy, sell, swop or browse.

Left, Ramblas cake shop. Right, bargain hunting at a Christmas market.

Portbou

FRANCE

Estagel

Sournia

Millas

Perpignan

Madres ▲ 2471

Boule d'Amount

Thuir

Tute de l'Ours ▲ 2259 m

Pic de Montcalm ▲ 3141 m

Casamanya ▲ 2707 m

Font-Romeu

Mont Louis

Pic du Canigou ▲ 2785 m

Amélie-les-Bains

Argelès

Collioure

Port-Vendres

Banyuls

ANDORRA

Andorra la Vella

PYRENEES

La Jonquera

Portbou

Les Escaldes

Puigcerdà

Puigmal ▲ 2913 m

Camprodón

Castelló d'Empúries

Cap Creus

Figueres

Cadaqués

Roses

Segre

SERRA DEL CADI

Guardiola de Bergueda

Ripoll

Olot

Fluvià

l'Escala

Viladamat

Gallina Pellada ▲ 2307 m

Emb. d'Oliana

Berga

SPAIN

Ter

Banyoles

Ter

Torroella de Montgri

Solsona

Prats de Lluçanès

Emb. de Sau

St. Gregori

Girona

Cap de Begur

Anglès

Cassà de la Selva

Palafrugell

Navars

Vic

Palamós

Cardona

St. Hilari Sacalm

Llagostera

COSTA BRAVA

Torà de Riubregós

Súria

Moià

Sta. Coloma de Farners

St. Feliu de Guixols

Calaf

SRA. DE MONTSENY

Manresa

St. Feliu de Codines

St. Celoni

Tossa de Mar

Lloret de Mar

Blanes

Monasterio de Montserrat ■

Tarrasa

Granollers

Calella

Mataró

Igualada

Llobregat

Sabadell

Arenys de Mar

MERESME

Martorell

Badalona

Sant Sadurní d'Anoia

St. Feliu

Barcelona

La Llacuna

Vilafranca del Penedés

Hospitalet de Llobregat

Castelldefels

✈

El Prat de Llobregat (Airport)

El Vendrell

Sitges

Vilanova i la Geltrú

Tarragona

COSTA

DAURADA

Mediterranean

Sea

Around Barcelona

40 km / 25 miles

210

AROUND BARCELONA

Trips out of Barcelona by car or train are an important part of city life. Beaches, mountains, wine country, religious retreats and provincial cities are all within reach for day trips or overnight visits. Travelling to and from these places can be a nightmare, particularly on Sunday evenings, and visitors should try to avoid coinciding with the so-called "operation return".

Ten trips: Of excursions, two are to the south (Sitges and Tarragona), two to the west (Sant Sadurní and Montserrat) and the remaining six are northward: Montseny, Vic, Santa Cristina, Figueres and Girona, Núria and Puigcerdà. This last, which is in the Pyrenees on the border with France two-and-a-half hours away, is the only trip which may be too far for a one-day excursion.

Sitges and Santa Cristina have fine beaches; Montserrat and Montseny are natural and religious mountain-top retreats virtually overlooking Barcelona; Vic, Tarragona, Figueres and Girona are provincial towns; Sant Sadurní d'Anoia is wine country; Núria is a sanctuary high in the Pyrenees, and Puigcerdà is the central town of the Pyrenean Cerdanya valley.

Best beaches: Less than an hour south of Barcelona, the town of **Sitges** is the closest clean and uncrowded bit of the Mediterranean coast. While sand and sun can be enjoyed in Castelldefels, 20 minutes from Barcelona, or even on Barcelona's beaches around the Olympic Village, the gleaming, whitewashed houses and flower-festooned balconies of Sitges are well worth the extra time on the train.

On the other hand a tour through the vineyards and olive groves of the Penedès via the *Autovia* to Tarragona makes a good drive.

A day on the beach at this convenient watering spot, with a *paella* for lunch at one of the many places available on or very near the beach itself, is a good idea at any time of the year. All you need is good weather. If it's raining, change plans and stay in Barcelona. A train leaving at 9 or 9.30am allows plenty of time to get installed on the beach before 11 o'clock. Paella can probably be organised as late as 3.30 or 4pm or as early as 1.30 or 2pm, according to hunger and strategy.

Fringed by palms and populated by an intriguingly cosmopolitan range of bathers, the gently curving **Platja d'Or** (golden beach) runs from the rocky point, La Punta, at the northeast end of Sitges Bay; it starts from the simple white facade of the 17th-century Sant Bartomeu i Santa Tecla Church and extends 3 miles (5 km) south and west past the Hotel Terramar.

The **Cau Ferrat Museum**, **Maricel** and the **Museu Romàntic** are the prime points of interest in the town of Sitges, although the tiny streets and bite-sized houses are no less charming. Cau Ferrat, in a 16th-century house built over

the rocks next to the sea, has two El Greco paintings, several Picasso drawings, and a unique collection of Catalan wrought iron. The work inside and the waters of the Mediterranean close by outside are a powerful combination of art and nature.

Maricel (*mar i cel* means sea and sky in Catalan), two buildings connected by a small bridge over the street, is most notable for the mural paintings by Josep Maria Sert, while the Museu Romàntic at number 1, Sant Gaudenci, allows a fascinating insight into well-conserved 18th-century living conditions.

A cosmopolitan and international party in summer, Sitges is quieter from October to May except during *Carnaval* when it becomes wilder and stranger than Rio de Janeiro itself.

Roman remains: Ninety minutes from Barcelona by train or car, **Tarragona** still has the feel of a provincial capital of the Roman Empire. Captured by Rome in 218 BC and later the capital of the Spanish province of Tarraconensis un-der Augustus, the town was the major commercial centre on this part of the Mediterranean coast until Barcelona and Valencia overshadowed it after the Christian Reconquest of Spain in the early 12th century.

Rich in Roman ruins and stunningly beautiful ancient buildings, Tarragona may be approached from top to bottom, beginning within the walled upper part of the city surrounding the cathedral, continuing on for a tour of the wall itself, the **Passeig Arqueòlogic** or Archaeological Promenade. One can then descend to the next level of the city, featuring the Rambla and the **Balcó del Mediterrani**, and conclude with a stroll through the fishing port and lunch on the quay.

Tarragona's cathedral, the centrepiece of the top part of the city, has been described by Catalonia's own travel writer Josep Pla, who had something to say about every town, as "easily and serenely mighty, solid as granite, maternal – a cathedral redolent of Roman

On the beach at Sitges.

212

virtues projected on to carved stone – a lion in repose, drowsy, unabashedly powerful". The mass of the wall itself and the tiny perforations in and out of this ancient cloister are hauntingly archaic, as if leading to some secret older than time itself.

The Passeig Arqueologic offers views south over the city itself, west out to the mountains, north to the hills and trees surrounding the city, and finally east to the coastline and the sea.

Below the walls is the middle section of Tarragona, with the wide and stately Rambla ending in the Balcó del Mediterrani (Mediterranean Balcony) suspended over the ocean below. The city's luminosity at this point has been much commented on and is indeed remarkable: a crisp elegance and clean air shimmer over the golden sandstone of Roman structures which are more than 1,000 years old.

The **Serrallo** section of the port is the main attraction in the lower part of the city, the multi-coloured fishing fleet unloading the Mediterranean's varied marine life every afternoon, the fish auctioned off within minutes. A late lunch at a dockside restaurant – featuring Tarragona wines, fundamental to the Roman Empire, and seafood just out of the nets – makes a delicious ending.

Wine routes: Sparkling wine made in Catalonia is not champagne; it is *cava*. And don't confuse **Sant Sadurní d'Anoia** with Vilafranca del Penedès. Both towns are fundamental to the wine industry, but Sant Sadurní is closer to the production end of the process and is the true founder and home of *cava*.

A 45-minute train ride from Sants station in Barcelona will drop you in Sant Sadurní d'Anoia next to Freixenet, the world's leading producer of *cava* sparkling wine, with vineyards in California and operations in the People's Republic of China.

Freixenet is by no means the only sparkling wine producer in the Penedès, but it offers the most spectacular tour, including a screening of its famous se-

Tarragona's Roman remains.

ries of Christmas greetings featuring such stars as Liza Minelli, Gene Kelly, Raquel Welch, Plácido Domingo and Paul Newman.

Cava, produced in Sant Sadurní since 1872 by Jose Raventós, who carefully studied the wine-making techniques, the *méthode champenoise*, of Dom Perignon, is an important part of life in Catalonia: baptisms, weddings, even routine Sunday dinners are occasions for popping corks. On 20 November 1975, the day Franco died, *cava* was given away free in Barcelona.

In addition to tours of the Freixenet or Raventós Codorníu wine cellars, Sant Sadurní offers excellent gastronomical opportunities at local restaurants well-known for fine *cava* and seafood. Held between late January and mid-March, the *calçotada* is a traditional feast starring the long-stemmed white leeks, *calçots*, dipped in a kind of *romesco* sauce made of oil, peppers, garlic and groundnuts. *Cava*, of course, flows freely at these earthy banquets, accompanied by lamb or rabbit grilled, as are the *calçots*, over coals.

The Penedès region, one of the world's leading wine producers, is to landscape what Bach is to music: spare, pure, geometrically logical, moving. The Montserrat massif to the north rises above rows and rows of vines stretching down to the Mediterranean in the south, with moist sea breezes and 2,500 hours of sunshine a year. Around Sant Sadurní even children have opinions on *bruts*, *secs* and *brut natures*; in the Penedès, Bacchus reigns.

Mountain retreats: Catalonia's most important religious retreat is **Montserrat.** Here athletes pledge barefoot pilgrimages if prayers are answered and vital competitions won. Groups of young people from Barcelona and all over Catalonia make overnight hikes at least once in their lives to watch the sunrise from the heights of Montserrat. "La Moreneta" (the black virgin), Catalonia's favourite saint, resides in the famous sanctuary of the Mare de Deu de

The monastery at Montserrat.

Montserrat, next to the Benedictine monastery nestled among the towers and crags of the mountain.

Montserrat (*mont*, mountain; *serrat*, serrated), 30 miles (48 km) west of Barcelona, can be reached easily and spectacularly by train and funicular, starting from Sants station. The advantage of going by car, on the other hand, is the opportunity of seeing this landmark from different angles, especially from the northern or southern sides. In the words of the Catalan poet Maragall, from varying perspectives Montserrat can look like "a bluish cloud with fantastic carvings, a giant's castle with a hundred towers, thrown toward the sky, its needles veiled by the fog hanging among them like incense: Montserrat, above all an altar, a temple".

Looming nearly 4,000 ft (1,200 metres) over the valley floor, Montserrat, the highest point of the Catalan lowlands, stands central to the most populated part of Catalonia. Visible from Barcelona, Sabadell, Terrassa, Manresa,

elow, altar screen with a Moreneta. Right, wine making in the Penedès.

Igualada, and Vilafranca, the massive conglomerate stone monolith is ideally located to play an important role in the cultural and spiritual life of Catalonia. During the 40-year Franco regime, when the Catalan language was officially forbidden, baptisms and weddings in Catalan were still held at Montserrat.

The basilica itself is packed with works of art by a long list of prominent painters and sculptors, including works by El Greco in the sanctuary's museum. Catalan poets have dedicated some of their most inspired verse to Montserrat while maestros such as Nicolau and Millet have composed some of their finest pieces in honour of this mystical Catalonian retreat. Goethe is said to have dreamed of Montserrat and Parsifal sought the Holy Grail here in Wagner's musical drama. The monastery's famous choir sings twice a day.

Montserrat's highest point, **Sant Jeroni**, can be reached by funicular from the Romanesque monastery of Santa Cecilia. From Sant Jeroni almost all of

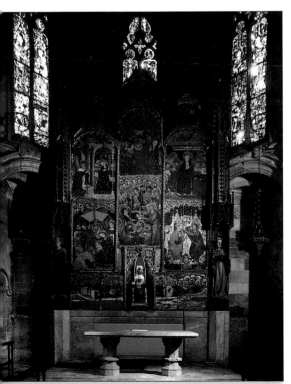

Catalonia can be seen; the Pyrenees, Mount Canigó in France and even, on a clear day, as far away as Mallorca in the Balearic Islands.

Rugged forest: The **Serra de Montseny** and Montserrat occupy, in some way, polar extremes in Catalonian spiritual life. Whereas Montserrat is dramatically vertical, acute and passionate, Montseny is smooth, horizontal, massive and placid. *Seny* in Catalan means sense, restraint, patience, serenity; and Montseny, well-named, seems to be a rich lode of this resource.

Best explored by car, this monumental mountain forest, considered one of Europe's most important sources of oxygen, is presided over by four peaks: Turó de l'Home, Agudes, Matagalls (all around 5,000 ft or 1,500 metres) and Calma i Puigdrau, a lower peak at 4,050 ft (1,215 metres). Lesser terrain features and water courses connect and define these four pieces of high ground, tracing out an autonomous geographical entity which always appears hulking and mist-shrouded on the horizon, often confused with cloud formations.

The village of **Montseny** itself, an irresistible nucleus of stone and vegetation attesting to sounder, saner times and places, can be reached via Palautordera and Sant Esteve de Palautordera. This road continues on to Brull, through the pass at Collformic and over to Tona, near Vic on route N 152, thus traversing the entire Montseny massif. The road up from Sant Celoni, just off the *autovia* towards France, via Campins and Fogars de Montclus, arrives at the **Santa Fe hermitage**, a vantage point which seems little more than a stone's throw from Montseny's highest points at Turó de l'Home and Les Agudes.

Santa Fe, surrounded by oaks and poplars, becomes bright with colour as the leaves turn in autumn, an unusual sight in Catalonia where forests and deciduous trees are uncommon. **Viladrau**, to the north, and **Riells** are two more delicious villages, spiritual redoubts for thought and solitude.

The port at Blanes.

Montseny, no more than 40 minutes from Barcelona, is a botanical anthology, including some of the southernmost fir trees in Europe, other specimens from all over the continent, and evergreen oak which is found as far south as Andalucía. This rich natural treasure, a symphony of greens, along with the sweep and force of the massif, make Montseny Barcelona's reservoir of thought and reflection, to be drawn upon in times of turmoil.

Country towns: An easy hour north by train or car, **Vic** is the meeting place of industry, commerce and agriculture, a mixture of rural and urban life with a strong ecclesiastical and cultural tradition. Especially known for its Romanesque bell tower, Josep Maria Sert's epic murals, and the wide, arcaded Plaça Major, Vic is an entity distinct from Barcelona. The Vic accent in Catalan is unmistakable and becomes, if anything, more acute in the Catalonian capital as natives of this small city emphasise their separate identity.

Rupit, a medieval town in the green and rocky Collsacabra region east of Vic, is a 40-minute drive from Vic for lunch. Built on a rock promontory over a stream, it is known for its unique *patata*, a baked potato stuffed with duck, beef, lamb and secret ingredients.

Vic's **cathedral**, a neoclassical structure completed in 1803, is known for its graceful 11th-century bell tower. But the real story of Vic cathedral is that of the Herculean labours of the painter Josep Marià Sert who decorated the walls with murals in 1930, and again, after fire destroyed them at the beginning of the Civil War in 1936, working until he died in 1945.

Sert, a powerful, vital artist, left his personal vision in these voluptuous, neo-baroque figures performing colossal deeds, muscles bulging, building, straining. His triptych on the back of the cathedral's western door depicts the injustices in the life of Christ and, by association, in the history of Catalonia. With the cathedral in ruins as his back-

Evening *passeig* on the Costa Brava.

ground, Jesus expels the moneylenders from the Temple and is, in turn, condemned to be crucified while Pilate washes his hands and Barabbas, the thief, is cheered by the crowd. Certain faces (Pilate, Barabbas) are said to be those of Franco's lieutenants, but El Generalísimo himself, during a visit to Sert's work while it was in progress, did not seem to see the resemblance.

Philosopher Jaime Balmes (1810–48), a native of Vic, is buried in the 14th-century cloister, as is Sert. The **Museu Episcopal** contains a series of altarpieces and sculpted figures collected from local chapels and churches. One of the best of these is *El Davallament de la Creu* (The Descent from the Cross), an especially fine 12th-century sculptural work in carved, polychrome wood.

The Plaça Major, or central square, surrounded by low arcades, is a metaphor for the sense and feel of this agro-industrial town. Open, unrelieved by the equestrian statue some critics feel it should have, the square stands on its own, as the city itself does, flat and firm on the plain, the Plana de Vic.

Costa Brava: An hour north of Barcelona, between Blanes and Lloret de Mar, **Santa Cristina** is one of the first *calas* or inlets of Catalonia's famous Costa Brava. Whether by train to Blanes and bus to Santa Cristina, or by car along the coast, Santa Cristina's proximity to Barcelona has made this sandy enclave popular with Barcelonans. Other visitors might do well to stay in town at the weekend and save this trip for the week.

With its twin beaches bordered and divided by rocky promontories, Santa Cristina's lovely **hermitage** stands at the top of the steep paths down to the water. The chapel and house were left to the town of Lloret de Mar by a wealthy 18th-century landowner who moved to Cuba. At that time the shorefront was worth nothing; the valuable property in those days was inland, where there were arable fields.

The Costa Brava, which officially begins at **Blanes**, is distinguished by its

Girona rises beside the River Onyar.

bold, rocky shoreline punctuated by small sandy inlets. There are beaches all the way northwards from Barcelona, but the clear, bright water and rocky coastline make the coast unique.

During the summer months, passenger boats work in and out of the *calas.* You can board a boat at Blanes for Santa Cristina or be dropped at some remote *cala* which may be at the bottom of a sheer cliff and inaccessible from land.

At Santa Cristina there are several simple restaurants on the beach where paella can be prepared anytime during the afternoon. These places are relaxed, outdoor spots where dining in bathing suits is normal, and they might not mind adding a few crabs or mussels to the *paella* if you find any among the rocks. They also serve excellent seafood *tapas* or small specialities of squid, sardines, wild mushrooms, shrimp or prawns.

Below, Girona Cathedral. Right, the Arab baths. A day at Santa Cristina, especially if you can manage a drive up the NII coast road in an open-top car, is a breather from a heavy diet of museums and Ro-

manesque art. The only architecture available is the Santa Cristina chapel, a five-minute visit; the landscapes are provided by the Costa Brava and the Mediterranean.

Northern culture: The cities of Figueres and Girona can be combined for a memorable excursion. **Figueres**, 90 minutes north on the *autovia*, is the major city of the **Alt Empordà** (Upper Ampurdan), a fresh, busy country town which, in many ways, could be on either side of the border with France.

Like many provincial cities in Spain, Figueres seems to have some time on its hands, certainly in comparison to Barcelona where time is, somewhat ironically, a thing of the past. The Figueres Rambla is the scene of the traditional *passeig*, the constitutional, the midday or evening stroll, which is a chance to run into one's friends, share an aperitif with an old chum you haven't seen for years, an encounter tailor-made for a 20-minute chat.

A visit to the spectacular **Salvador**

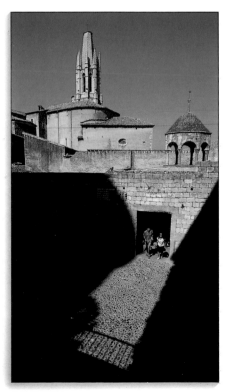

Dalí museum (closed on Mondays) and lunch in one of the excellent gourmet bistros scattered throughout the town would complete an excellent tour.

Girona, 30 minutes back towards Barcelona, is known for its *Ciutat Antiga* (Old Town) and especially for its 13th-century **Jewish quarter** which is considered, along with Toledo's, one of the two most important and best preserved in Spain. The Onyar river separates Girona's old section from the modern part of the city which lies west of the river. The footbridges over the Onyar provide some of Girona's most unforgettable views into the old city, including reflections of the buildings on the banks of the river as well as taller structures such as the Sant Feliu bell tower or the cathedral. The 12th-century **Sant Pere de Galligants** church is one of the city's oldest monuments, with a delightful Romanesque cloister built before 1154.

Girona's old city, built on a hill, is known for its lovely stairways, such as the baroque *escalinata* leading up to the cathedral or the stairs up to Sant Martí church. **Santa Maria Cathedral**, described by the ever-present Josep Pla as "literally sensational" in its force and magnitude, was built by architect Guillem Bofill who succeeded in covering the structure with Europe's largest Gothic vault.

The cathedral's **museum** is most notable for its *Tapis de la Creació*, a stunning 11th-century tapestry depicting God surrounded by all the flora and fauna, fish and fowl of Creation. Equally impressive is Beatus's *Llibre de l'Apocalipsi* (Book of the Apocalypse), dated 975. **Sant Feliu Church**, the **Arab baths** and the lofty plane trees of **Devesa Park** are other important landmarks of this ancient city of sunless alleys, graceful stairways, and the Onyar flowing through as imperceptibly as the millennium itself.

Into the Pyrenees: Riding the cogwheel train up to **Núria** is an adventure not soon forgotten. Connections up to Ripoll

Green folds of the high Pyrenees.

and Ribes de Fresser by train from Barcelona are simple enough. There are departures from Sants station (stopping at Plaça de Catalunya) every three hours or so. The morning train connects with the midday cogwheel. From Ribes, the cogwheel train, known as the *cremallera* or "zipper", clicks up, via Queralbs, to Núria, the first winter sports resort of the Catalan Pyrenees.

The shrine of La Mare de Deu de Núria (the Mother of God of Núria), La Verge de la Vall de Núria (The Virgin of the Valley of Núria), follows the Marian cult of Montserrat, the most important in Catalonia. Montserrat and Núria are Catalan women's names, perhaps the two most common. Núria, associated with the purity of the upper Pyrenees and all its natural connotations, has a spiritual image which is, if possible, even more pristine and unspoiled than the somewhat more suburban monastery of Montserrat.

Rolling out the barrels at Puigcerdà.

Until 1916 Núria was open only in summer. The construction of the *cre-mallera* railway in 1917 connected the town of Ribes with the sanctuary at Núria, and since that time the town has been accessible all year round.

According to legend, Sant Gil from Nîmes did penance in the valley of Núria during the 7th century, leaving behind his wooden image of the Virgin Mary, the bell he used to call the shepherds of the region to prayer, and his cooking pot. A Dalmatian pilgrim came to Núria several centuries later, around the year 1072, and discovered Sant Gil's cave with the wooden statue of Mary, the bell and the pot; these are still kept in the sanctuary.

The polychrome wood sculpture is a simple Romanesque carving which the poet Josep Maria de Sagarra described as "rigid and palpitating reality of wood and colour, dark rose of the Divine Shepherd". The bell and the pot came to have a special religious significance: the story is that, by placing their heads in the pot and pulling the bell cord, barren women desiring children would

have as many children as the number of times the bell pealed above them.

The **chapel of Sant Gil** lies at the foot of Puigmal, near the sanctuary. Next to the chapel is a spring, La Font de Sant Gil, famous for its freezing waters. The wooden image of Maria, La Verge de la Vall de Núria, sounds an essential chord in the Catalan spirit: remote, intimate, pristine, mysterious – a natural presence who, in the words of the poet Sagarra, "anoints in ecstasy the eyes of the sheep and the blue of the sky until the eagles tremble".

Last resort: Three hours away by train, two and a half by road, **Puigcerdà** has long been Barcelona's favourite mountain resort. Built on a small rise in the Cerdanya valley, *Puig* (hill) *Cerdà* (Cerdanya) the town is the county seat and key commercial centre of the Oriental Pyrenees.

The **Cerdanya Valley** stretches from Prades and Mont Louis in France all the way down to Martinet in the Catalonian province of Llèida, thus fragmenting this whole geographical entity into two countries subdivided by two provincial administrations and further complicated by the Spanish enclave at **Llivia**. The latter is a town surrounded by French territory yet remaining Spanish under the terms of a 17th-century treaty which declared all "villages" north of a certain point to be French. However Llivia, which was incorporated as a "town", remained part of Spain.

The Cerdanya, an east–west valley with an exceptional number of hours of sun each year, is rich pastureland bordered by two *cordilleras* of the Pyrenees, to the north and south. Primarily dedicated to the breeding of cattle and horses, the Cerdanya is also known for pears and pigs and, increasingly, for tourism since the construction of the Cadí tunnel provided four million Barcelona residents with a safe, quick way to reach Puigcerdà.

The valley floor is dotted with lovely Pyrennean villages and farmsteads lying behind huge gates. Some villages, such as Aja or Guils, are within walking distance of Puigcerdà. **La Tour de Carol**, an hour's walk north of the town in France, is a good hike via back roads, keeping the Carol stream on your left.

Llivia, 10 minutes away by car, has a lovely church, Europe's oldest pharmacy, and **Can Ventura**, a rustic village farmhouse which has been converted into a restaurant by the owners of the Hotel de Llivia, one of the finest in the Pyrenees. Surrounded by 15 ski resorts in France, Spain and Andorra, Puigcerdà has enough excursions and activities to last a lifetime: horseback outings, jeep safaris, trout fishing, cross-country skiing, wild mushroom hunting, or just sightseeing.

A night at the **Hotel Maria Cristina** in Puigcerdà should provide a spectacular evening and morning overlooking the Cerdanya, an opportunity to watch the sun drop off the far end of the valley at dusk and to catch its first rays hitting the top of the rock walls of the Serra del Cadí at dawn.

Left, the Spanish enclave at Llivia. **Right**, harvesting the hills. **Overleaf**, the Magic Fountain, Barcelona.

222

INSIGHT GUIDES
Travel Tips

Simply travelling safely

American Express Travellers Cheques

- are recognised as one of the safest and most convenient ways to protect your money when travelling abroad

- are more widely accepted than any other travellers cheque brand

- are available in eleven currencies

- are supported by a 24 hour worldwide refund service and

- a 24 hour Express Helpline service provides assistance and information when travelling abroad

- are accepted in millions of shops, hotels and restaurants throughout the world

Travellers Cheques

Getting Acquainted

Barcelona is the capital of the semi-autonomous region of Catalonia in northeast Spain.

Area: 99 sq km (38 sq miles)

Population: 1.6 million, 2.9 million in the greater metropolitan area. Forty percent of the population is from other parts of Spain.

Currency: Pesetas.

Electricity: 220 volts, two-pin plug.

Weights and measures: metric.

Language: Catalan and Spanish (Castilian).

Religion: Predominantly Roman Catholic, though there is a strong anti-clerical tradition.

Highest point: Mt Tibidabo, 516m (1,700 ft).

Time zone: One hour ahead of GMT in winter, two hours in summer. Six hours ahead of Eastern Seaboard Time.

International Dialling Code: 34 (Spain), 93 (Barcelona).

Climate

Average temperature: 54° F (10° C) in winter, 75° F (25° C) in summer.

December and January have the lowest temperatures, though the cold is often accompanied by bright sunshine.

Rains tend to be in November and February/March. Spring and autumn are pleasant with mild, sunny days. July and August are aggravated by humidity, Sunlight: 2,500 hours a year.

Government

Spain is a constitutional monarchy headed by King Juan Carlos I, who came to the throne in 1975. He appoints the prime minister from the party which has a majority in the Cortes (parliament). This has a Chamber of Deputies (Lower House) with 350 members elected by proportional representation every four years. The

14 Autonomous Regions (of which Barcelona is one) elect 49 members to the Senate (upper house). The Autonomous Region of Catalonia is governed by the Generalitat in Barcelona, opposite which is the Ajuntament (town hall) where the mayor and the city council preside. For more than two decades after free elections, the Generalitat has been governed by the conservative Convergencia i Unió under Jordi Pujol, and the town hall has been socialist, now under mayor Joan Clos. Municipal and Autonomous elections take place in 1999.

Economy

Catalonia, and in particular Barcelona, is of outstanding economic importance to the Spanish state. It has 25 percent of the nation's industry, and supplies nearly 20 percent of the Gross Domestic Product. In European terms, the economy of Catalonia has a greater turnover than Portugal or Ireland. Foreign investment has increased in recent years, a reflection of confidence in Catalonia as a progressive region. However, the Spanish economy took a downturn in 1992 and successive devaluations of the peseta have been to the visitor's advantage.

Planning The Trip

What to Bring

Catalan men and women dress elegantly, though men rarely wear ties In July and August; cotton and loose-fitting garments are necessary. Respect local traditions: bathing costumes and bikinis are strictly for the beach. Fashionable shorts are fine, especially for men, but avoid really short shorts. A light jacket is useful any time of the year. In winter, bring a warm jacket which can accommodate various layers especially in January and February, when the wind blows. Be sure to bring comfortable shoes – Barcelona is a very walkable city.

Entry Regulations

Passports are required for all nationalities entering Spain. Carry a photocopy for everyday use so that the original document can be left in a secure place (such as a hotel safe).

Visas are needed by non-EU nationals unless their country has a reciprocal arrangement with Spain.

If your passport is lost or stolen, report the fact immediately to the National Police.

Animal quarantine: There are no regulations in Spain but you will need health certificates before you bring your own animal into the country: the regulations vary according to country of origin; the airline with which you are travelling should be able to provide the information required.

Duty free: There is no limit now to what passengers from European Union countries can bring in to the country. For other countries the allowance is 2 cartons of cigarettes, 2 bottles of alcoholic beverage and 50 cigars.

Health

Drink: In most areas of Barcelona tap water can be drunk without fear, but it is often dosed with purifying salts which make the taste unpleasant. Mineral water is easily available and Vichy Catalan is soothing for queasy stomachs. Cheap wine can be rough, so take it easy.

Food: Catalan cooking is healthy and nutritious, but a change of diet can affect some digestive systems. Avoid bars and restaurants where oil is obviously used to excess.

Another danger area can be in *tapas* (snacks), which in the hot weather can be a source of infection. Most notorious is anything mayonnaise-based, such as *ensaladilla rusa*, a potential source of salmonella; in some parts of Spain home-made mayonnaise has been banned. With common sense it is easy to spot the "tired" *tapas* which should be avoided being well past their eat-by date.

Sun: don't overdo it, especially in July and August: break yourself in gently.

Insight Guides portray destinations in depth, providing the complete picture and the top photography

Insight Pocket Guides focus on the best choices for places to see and things to do and include large fold-out maps

Insight Compact Guides' portability makes them the perfect books to carry with you for on-the-spot reference

Three types of guide for all types of travel

INSIGHT GUIDES Different people need different kinds of information. Some want *background information* to help them prepare for the trip. Others seek *personal recommendations* from someone who knows the destination well. And others look for *compactly presented data* for on-the-spot reference. With three carefully designed series, Insight Guides offer readers the perfect choice. Insight Guides will turn your visit into an experience.

The world's largest collection of visual travel guides

Planespotting

Get a passport ✈ get some cheap tickets ✈ get a plane ✈ get some sun ✈ get a tan
get some friends ✈ get another plane ✈ get some laughs ✈ get some great photos
get another plane ✈ get some memories ✈ get some weird clothes ✈ get to the clubs
get another plane ✈ get some more sun ✈ get some strange food ✈ get another plane
get some adventure ✈ get some thrills ✈ get to the sea ✈ get another plane
get to the cities ✈ get to the action ✈ get away ✈ get Young Europe Special ✈ get a life!

Young Europe Special –

 tickets are sold in packages of four to ten.

See Europe from only £49 for the first flight coupon! This price *includes* UK airport departure tax but not any other security charges/airport taxes applicable to your selected European destinations.

Get a free info pack by:

Filling in the coupon below and sending it to us FREEPOST.

Calling us on **0800 214 493.**

Finding us on the Internet at:

http://www.lufthansa.co.uk

What are *YOU* doing this year?

Lufthansa ⊗   B**M** British Midland   SAS

Please send me my free YES info pack.   ⊗ Lufthansa   B**M** British Midland   ////**/SAS**

Title   Initials   Surname

Address

Postcode   Are you a full time student ? Yes ☐ No ☐   Date of birth

Please complete and return this coupon to: **YES**, FREEPOST LON 7242, LONDON EC1B 1PH.

INSIGHT

Money

Most banks have automatic tills or cashpoints, operating 24 hours a day, where money can be withdrawn by credit card and personal identification number.

Keep a record of the individual numbers of your travellers' cheques. If they are lost or stolen they can be quickly replaced if you have this information.

Be sure to always carry small change as notes larger than 2,000 pesetas are a cause of consternation though taxis are now obliged to change a 2,000 pta. note.

Banks

Bank opening hours vary, but as a general rule are Monday to Friday, 8.30–2pm, and on Saturday between 1 October and 31 May, 8.30–1pm. The Cajas or Caixes (savings banks) offer the same service, but are open on Thursday afternoons instead of Saturday mornings between 1 October and 31 May. They also have 24-hour cashpoints.

There are currency exchange offices in the centre, particularly the Ramblas and a good service in the Plaça Catalunya Information Centre.

Foreign banks in the city:

American Express has an office in Passeig de Gràcia, 101, offering the usual services to clients including poste restante, tel: 93 217 0070.

Lloyds Bank, Rambla de Catalunya, 123.

Banco Natwest March, Passeig de Gràcia, 8–10.

Bank of America, Bori Fontestá, 23.

Barclays Bank, Passeig de Gràcia, 45.

Credit Cards

Major international credit cards, Visa, Eurocard, MasterCard, Eurocheque, can be used. The larger hotels also exchange money, though usually at a less favourable rate.

American Express, tel: Madrid (91) 572 0303.

Diner's, tel: 302 1428/Madrid (91) 547 4000.

Eurocard, MasterCard, Master-charge, Servired and **Visa**, tel: (93) 315 2512; Madrid (91) 519 2100.

Visa International, tel: 900 974 445.

Public Holidays

Many bars, restaurants and museums close in the afternoons and evenings on public holidays and Sundays. If a holiday falls on a Tuesday or a Thursday it is common to take a *puente* (bridge) to link the interim day with the weekend. August is the annual holiday month and many businesses, including restaurants, close down for three or four weeks.

These are the public holidays:

1 January – New Year's Day
6 January – Reis Mags: Epiphany
Good Friday – variable
Easter Monday – variable
1 May – Festa del Treball: Labour Day
21 May – Whitsun
24 June – Sant Joan: Summer solstice
15 August – Assumpció: Assumption
11 September – Diada: Catalan national holiday
24 September – La Mercè: Barcelona's town fiesta
12 October – Hispanitat/Pilar: Spanish national day
1 November – Tots Sants: All Saints
6 December – Día de la Constitució: Constitution Day
8 December – Immaculada Concepció: Immaculate Conception
25-26 December – Christmas

Festivals

Apart from the main fiestas described here, every district (*barri*) of Barcelona has its own, known as the Festa Major, centred on its own patron saint. These usually last several days and have certain key ingredients:

Sardanas: the national dance of Catalonia, can also be seen every Sunday and holiday in Plaça Sant Jaume at 7pm (6.30pm in winter), and in the Plaça Catedral on Sundays at 12 noon.

Gegants and *Cap Grossos*: Giants and Big Heads. Giant figures and comic characters with large heads parade the streets and usually reunite in the evening at a Grand Ball in one of the public squares.

Castellers: human towers reaching nine-man storeys, capped with the youngest and smallest.

CALENDAR OF FESTIVALS

Christmas, during December the Santa Llùcia Fair is held in the streets around the Cathedral.

Sant Esteve, (St Stephen's) 26 December: families meet for an even larger meal than on the 25th.

Reis Mags, Epiphany, 6 January: children receive presents from the Three Wise Kings, though modern commerce now indulges them in presents at Christmas as well. In Barcelona the Kings arrive from the Orient by boat.

Carnival, Carnestoltes, pre-Lent: wild celebrations which close with the "Burial of the Sardine" on Ash Wednesday. The best celebrations are at Sitges, on the coast.

Sant Jordi, 23 April: A traditional Catalan festival now known as World Day of the Book, in which men give a rose to their lady, and receive a book in return.

Fira de Sant Ponç, 11 May: Aromatic and medicinal herbs, crystallised fruit and honey sold in Carrer Hospital.

Sant Joan, 24 June: celebration of the summer solstice on the eve, with fireworks, cava and "coca", a Catalan cake made with pine nuts and crystallised fruit.

Diada de Catalunya, 11 September: the Catalan National Holiday, consists of political demonstrations.

The Feast of La Mercè, Barcelona's patron saint, 24 September: the city's main fiesta, with a week of merriment, including fire-breathing dragons.

Getting There

By Air

Iberia is the national carrier and major airlines connect with most parts of the world, sometimes via Madrid. Various companies compete over cheap deals to Barcelona, especially off-season, and there are charter flights in summer: when booking try to get a contact number in Barcelona as information locally is not always easy to find.

The airport is 12 km (7 miles) south of the city. The distribution of airlines in the three terminals is to change, so confirm on arrival where to depart. Tel: (93) 298 3838.

Iberia head office:
Diputació, 258. Information and bookings: tel: 902 400 500.

Internal airlines:
Air Europa (Tel: 93 298 3328).
Aviaco (part of Iberia: Tel: 93 478 24 11, fax: 93 478 03 27)
Spanair (Tel: 902 131 415).

By Sea

There is a regular passenger and car service from Barcelona to Mallorca, Menorca and Ibiza with the Trasmediterránea company, based at the Estación Marítima, Moll de Barcelona. Tel: 902 454 645 for information, or through travel agents.

By Train

An international service, the Talgo, runs daily to Paris, Milan, Zurich and Geneva. It is a high-speed, comfortable train. All other international connections involve a change at the French border, in Port Bou on entering Spain and Cerbère when leaving. These have few facilities, so travel prepared if you cannot get on the Talgo.

The direct trains (Talgo) terminate in the Estació de França (Av. Marquès de l'Argentera, near Parc de la Ciutadella) and the rest go to Sants. For international train information and reservations, tel: (93) 490 1122.

National long-distance trains terminate in Estació de Sants, Barcelona's central station, Plaça Països Catalans and some in Estació de França. For national train information, tel: (93) 490 0202).

By Bus

The international bus companies Julià, Via (Eurolines) and Linebús run a regular service all over Europe, linking up with the national bus companies in each country. Julià has a daily bus to and from the main European cities. Buses arrive and depart either from Estació d'Autobusos Sants (tel: 93 490 4000), or Barcelona Nord (tel: 93 265 6508).

By Car

Barcelona is 149 km (92 miles) from La Jonquera on the French border and easily reached by the A7 motorway (autopista, toll payable) and then, nearer Barcelona, the A17. Be careful when you stop in service stations or lay-bys: professional gangs work this route, engaging travellers in conversation, or seeking help, while their companions skilfully rob them. If you stop for a drink or a meal try not to leave the car unattended.

The worst times to travel throughout the year, particularly June to September, are Friday night, Sunday evening, or the end of a bank holiday, when tailbacks of 16–19 km are common. Normal weekday rush hour is from 8–10.30am and from 7–9pm.

Practical Tips

Emergencies

Security and Crime

Take care as in any large city. Loosely swinging handbags and ostentatious cameras are easily snatched by the desperate. Don't tempt them. Do not be alarmed either: Barcelona is not a den of vice, and with due attention and common sense you can avoid dangerous situations.

The old town has a bad reputation so be aware when wandering through it or watching street artists. Wear your handbag across your chest, keep your camera hidden and do not flash your wallet around. Carry enough money for the day, leaving the rest in the safe deposit box of your hotel.

At airport, railway and bus stations, keep your luggage together and don't leave it unattended. Never leave anything valuable in a car, especially radios, even in a crowded street.

Don't get caught by a few small gangs who perpetrate various tricks to waylay you, like commenting on the dirt on your back and while "helping" you to remove it, slip the purse from your pocket. Another is a game known as trila, a variation of the three-card trick, played by crooks in the guise of innocent bystanders.

There are three kinds of policemen:
Policia Municipal: the City Police, known as Guardia Urbana, responsible for traffic, civilian care and security; recognisable by the blue-and-white checked band around their caps and on their vehicles. Tel: **092.**
Policia Nacional: the State Police, who wear navy-blue uniforms. They are responsible for law and order and civilian security. Tel: **091.**
Mossos d'Esquadra: the autonomous police of Catalonia, in Toni Miró-designed navy-blue and red. They are mostly responsible for the Generalitat buildings.

In the case of a theft, assault or loss, you should first contact the Policia Nacional to make a statement (denuncia). This is vital if you want to claim on an insurance or seek further help from the City Police or your consulate. The main police station is in Via Laietana, 49.

Tourist help: For further help, contact the City Police who have a special scheme for tourists at their headquarters (Ramblas, 43, tel: 93 301 9060, 7am–12pm, 7am–2am summer) offering legal advice, medical assistance, provision of temporary documents in the event of loss or robbery and an international telephone line for the speedy cancellation of credit cards etc. They can cope in French, English, German, Italian or Russian.
Police assistance for tourists: tel: 317 7020.
Police station with interpreter service available: Via Laietana, 49, tel: (93) 302 6325.

Loss of Belongings

There is a Lost Property Office in Carrer Ciutat, 9 just off Plaça Sant Jaume, 9.30am–1pm, tel: (93) 402 3161.

Medical Services

Residents of EU countries, Iceland, Finland, Sweden and Norway are entitled to receive state medical treatment in Spain if they present a form known as an "E111", which must be obtained in their own country. In the UK this can be done through the Post Office. For greater peace of mind, take out a private insurance which can be organised on arrival through any travel agency.

HOSPITALS

In an emergency go to "*Urgencias*" at any of the main hospitals:

Hospital Sant Pau, Carrer de Sant Antoni Maria Claret, 167, tel: (93) 291 9000.

Hospital Clínic, Carrer de Casanova, 143, tel: (93) 454 6000.

Hospital Cruz Roja, Carrer de Dos de Maig, 301, tel: (93) 433 1551.

Or visit an **Ambulatorio**, (clinic/medical centre) which can be found in every district. With private medical insurance (or a large wallet) the scope widens to include the many private doctors. Consulates can advise on those who speak your language.

DENTISTS

Dentists are not covered by any of the reciprocal agreements. The following clinics offer an emergency service:

Clínica Janos, Carrer de Muntaner 375, 6º 2ª, tel: (93) 200 2333. Open: 8am–1.30pm and 4–8.30pm daily (including Saturday).

Institut Dexeus, Passeig de Bonanova, 67, tel: (93) 417 9578. Famous for its gynaecological work and for producing the first test-tube baby in Spain, this clinic also provides a dental service daily from 9am–9pm, and on fiestas (etc.) and in August when many dentists are away on holiday.

Amesa, Gran Vía, 680, tel: (93) 302 6682. Open: 9am–9pm and 9am–3pm (Saturday).

EMERGENCY PHONE NUMBERS

Fire Brigade, tel: 080.
Ambulance services, tel: 061.
Road accidents, tel: (93) 352 6161.

Business Hours

Business hours vary according to the nature of the business, its location and the season: in general offices are open 9am–2pm and 4–8pm though some open earlier, close later and have shorter lunch breaks. Most official authorities are open 8am–3pm and close to the public in the afternoon. Companies in the outer industrial zones tend to close at 6pm. From mid-June to mid-September many businesses practise *horas intensivas*, from 8am–3pm in order to avoid the hottest part of the day and to get away early on a Friday.

Tipping

If you feel the need to tip, make it a token rather than an extravagant one. As a yardstick, in restaurants it should be around 5–10 percent and about the same in a taxi. In a bar or café 15–100 pesetas is enough depending on the size of the bill.

Religious Services

Mass is usually said between 7am and 2pm on Sunday and Feast days. Evening mass between 7pm and 9pm on Saturday, Sunday and Feast days.

Mass in English: Parroquia Maria Reina, Ctra. d'Esplugues, 103. Sundays 10am.

Anglican services: in English are held at Saint George's Church, Carrer Sant Joan de la Salle 41. Sunday 11am.

Judaism: The Synagogue, Carrer d'Avenir, 24, tel: (93) 200 6148.

Islam: Centro Islàmico, Av. Meridiana, 326, tel: (93) 351 4901.

Toarek Ben Ziad, Hospital, 91, tel: (93) 441 9149.

Media

Print

The main daily papers are:

El País: Based in Madrid but with a Barcelona edition, *El Pais* is probably the most respected Spanish paper internationally.

La Vanguardia: The traditional newspaper of Barcelona has good coverage of Barcelona news and activities. Conservative.

El Periodico: The more popular Barcelona newspaper, but limited on international news, published in Castilian and Catalan.

Avui: The original Catalan paper.

For sport enthusiasts there are two daily papers, *Sport* and *El Mundo Deportivo*.

International newspapers can be found on the newsstands on the Ramblas and Passeig de Gràcia, and in some international bookshops, like Libreria Francesa (Passeig de Gràcia, 91) or Collector (Carrer de Pau Claris, 168).

A wealth of magazines cover every interest and indulgence. The main fashion magazines, such as *Vogue*, *Marie Claire* and *Elle* publish a Span-

ish edition. Most notable of the national magazines are:

Cambio 16: A weekly news magazine, good on politics and controversial issues.

Hola: The most famous Spanish magazine, with fully illustrated scandal and gossip on the rich and royal.

On Barcelona:

Guia del Ocio: The best weekly listings magazine.

English language:

Metropolitan: Barcelona's first monthly magazine in English now becoming well established. Targeted at residents it nevertheless makes interesting reading and carries useful listings. Distributed free at key points in (and around e.g. Sitges) the city – bookshops, bars and cinemas. Check their web site before travelling: www.showcom/metropolitan.

Barcelona Business: suitably pink monthly newspaper with perspicacious comments on business affairs, unveiling some of the mysteries of local law and politics. Circulation growing fast, it is distributed free at over 100 points across the city.

Television

The principal channels are TVE1 and TVE2 (state-owned), TV3 and Canal 33, the autonomous Catalan channels. Private channels include Antena 3 (general programming), Tele 5 (directed towards housewives) and Canal Plus (mostly films, but for subscribers only). Satellite programmes are obtainable in many of the larger hotels.

News bulletins in various languages are on TVE and TV3 from July to September. Check the daily press.

Postal Services

Stamps for letters, post cards and small packets can be bought very conveniently in the many *estancos* to be found in every district. These are state-owned establishments licensed to sell stamps, cigarettes and tobacco, and easily recognisable by their orange and brown logo, Tabacs S.A. Opening hours are loosely 9am–1.30pm and 4.30–8pm. Post boxes are yellow. Express letters can be posted in special red boxes, marked *Urgente*, but it is easier to find the post office than one of these, and possibly more direct.

The main post office is at the bottom of Via Laietana near the port, in Plaça Antoni López. It has collections every hour and is open Monday to Friday 9am–9pm, Saturday 9am–1pm. Other post offices close at 2pm, apart from the one in Carrer d'Aragó, 282 (near Passeig de Gràcia) which is open until 7pm but with limited services. *Poste Restante* letters can be sent to the main post office addressed as follows:

Name
Lista de Correos
08000 Barcelona

Be sure to take personal identification with you when claiming letters.

Telephone & Fax

Telephone boxes and booths are well distributed throughout the city. They are easy to use and efficient, especially for international calls. Most bars have either a pay-phone or a metered telephone, but be tactful and at least have a coffee while you are there. Public telephones take all coins and some accept credit cards. The minimum charge for a local call is 20 pesetas. Telephone cards to the value of 1,000 and 2,000 pesetas are available in *estancos* and post offices. International reverse charge calls cannot be made from a box.

There are several central exchanges, where you talk first and pay after; they are convenient, but beware the bill that follows. Telephone rates are surprisingly high in Spain.

Principal walk-in exchanges are situated in Sants railway station (fax service), Barcelona Nord bus station and La Rambla, 88 (fax service).

Operator Services & Codes:
Directory enquiries: 1003.
International operator (Europe) 1008; (Rest of the World) 1005.
Information 1003; International information 025.
International direct dial: 07 (await signal) + country code + town code + number.

Country codes:
(These are written in phone boxes)
Australia: 61
Canada: 1
Eire: 353
United Kingdom: 44
United States: 1

Telegrams: can be sent from the main post office from 8am–10pm Monday to Saturday or from a small office in Ronda Universitat, 23, from 9am–7pm. Alternatively they can be sent by telephone, tel: (93) 322 2000.

Both telegram offices have a **telex** and **telefax service**, but will not receive a telefax unless the recipient is present. A more convenient and cheaper service is offered by **Prismafax** (Carrer Jaume I, 18, fax: (93) 310 5865) who will accept in-coming faxes.

Tourist Offices

Plaça de Catalunya, the main city tourist information centre (underneath the plaça). Well-equipped and helpful for hotel and theatre bookings, tel: (93) 304 3135. Bank, shop. Open: 9am–9pm.
El Prat Airport, tel: (93) 478 4704. Open: Monday to Saturday 9.30am–8.30pm, Sunday 9.30am–3pm.
Sants Station, open daily: 8am–8pm (summer). Rest of year: Monday to Friday 8am–8pm, weekends/holidays 8am–2pm.
City Hall, Plaça Sant Jaume. Open: Monday–Saturday 10am–8pm; Sunday 10am–2pm.

Information booths, situated in **Plaça Catalunya**, the **Port** and the **Sagrada Família**. Open daily: 9am–9pm.

Also the **"Red Jackets"** service: young people offering help and information, recognisable by their red and white uniforms. Usually found in the Gothic Quarter, La Rambla and Passeig de Gràcia.
Tourist Information Centre for Catalonia, information on the rest of Catalonia in Palau Robert (complete with leisurely garden). Passeig de Giàcia 107, tel: (93) 238 4000; www.gencat.es/probert.
General information: tel: 010. This is the Barcelona City Council's service that will provide a wealth of information, or at least tell you where to telephone. English spoken.

Consulates

Australia, Gran Via Carles III, 98, tel: (93) 330 94 96, fax: (93) 411 09 04.
Canada, Pg. de Gràcia 77, 3°, tel: (93) 215 0704.
Ireland, Gran Via Carles III, 94, tel: (93) 491 5021, fax: (93) 411 29 21.
United Kingdom, Avinguda Diagonal,

477, tel: (93) 419 9044, fax: (93) 405 24 11.
United States, Pg. Reina Elisenda, 23, tel: (93) 280 2227, fax: (93) 205 52 06.

Getting Around

On Arrival

Whether you arrive in the airport, rail or bus station, or in your own car, you probably will stand out as the vulnerable tourist, so be aware and keep your bags or car attended until you are in a hotel or *pension*. Check that your return flight is confirmed.

From the Airport

Barcelona is only 12 km (7 miles) from El Prat airport and is easily reached by train, bus or taxi.

Trains to Sants, the central station, depart every 30 minutes from 6.14am–10.44pm and take about 18 minutes. The same service from Sants to the airport operates from 5.44am–10.14pm. Approximate cost is 300 pesetas. Although advertised as the train to Sants, it continues to Plaça de Catalunya and Arc de Triomf which can be more convenient for central parts of the city.

Aerobús, an efficient, comfortable bus service, runs to Plaça Catalunya every 15 minutes on weekdays, and every 30 minutes on holidays and during the weekends stopping at strategic points en route. The best way to and from the airport. From 6am–11pm (6.30am–10.50pm at weekends). Approximate cost is 450 pesetas.

There is also a bus service (line EA) to and from Plaça d'Espanya but it is rather irregular, though the night service (EN) may be useful running from 9pm–2.40am. It leaves from Plaça d'Espanya from 9.40pm–3.15am.

To reach most central parts of Barcelona by taxi will cost from about 1,500–2,000 pesetas, plus an airport supplement and a token amount for each suitcase. To avoid misunderstandings try asking how much it will cost before getting in to the taxi. "*Cuánto vale el recorrido desde el aeropuerto hasta...* (e.g.) *Plaça de Catalunya?*". Get him to write down the answer if necessary. To be really thorough, you can check with the taxi authorities in the airport. Stickers on inside windows in English establish the rules and rates.

Porter services: Both El Prat airport and Sants railway station have a porter service, with fixed rates according to the number and weight of bags.

Iberia information: tel: (902) 400 500.

Airport: tel: (93) 298 3838.

RENFE (National and international rail services): tel: (93) 490 0202 (National), (93) 490 1122 (International).

Radio Taxi: tel: (93) 300 3811/(93) 358 1111.

Public Transport

Barcelona is a manageable city to get around, whether on foot or by public transport. The latter is efficient and good value. The only means of transport to avoid is your own: the parking problems, the threat of the police clamp or removal lorry, the wracked nerves as you struggle to adjust to local driving habits and the traffic system, the frustration at not being able to enjoy the sights you pass, all conspire to make travelling by car in this city a nightmare. Leave your car in a car park.

Public Transport, tel: 010.

By Metro

The Metro is Barcelona's underground network. It has five colour-coded lines – I, II, III, IV and V. The new line 5 (V) is equipped for wheelchairs (and prams) with lifts at every station. Trains are frequent and cheap, with a set price per journey, no matter how far you travel. It is more economical to buy a card that allows you 10 journeys (*tarjeta multi-viaje* T-2) available at any station. Trains run from 5am–11pm Monday to Thursday, 5am–1am on Friday and Saturday, and 6am–midnight on Sunday.

The train service, Ferrocarrils de la Generalitat de Catalunya (FGC), interconnects with the Metro, looks like the Metro and functions in the same way but extends beyond the inner city area to towns on the other side of Tibidabo, like San Cugat, Terrassa and Sabadell (all from Plaça de Catalunya) and to Manresa and Igualada (from Plaça d'Espanya). It is a useful service for reaching the upper parts of Barcelona and for parts of Tibidabo and the Parc de Collserola.

The Metro ticket is valid on this line within a limited area, but to travel beyond is more expensive. The FGC lines show in a darker blue on the Metro map. Within town the timetable is the same as the Metro, but beyond, it varies according to the line. Check in any of the stations or tel: 010, a useful number for information on any form of public transport.

By Bus

The bus service is good for reaching the areas the Metro doesn't, and for seeing more of Barcelona – at speed. Thanks to bus and taxi lanes, journeys can be fast, so hold on tight. Single tickets are the same price as Metro tickets and can be bought from the driver or a multiple card (*tarjeta multiviaje* T-1) of 10 journeys can be punched inside the bus; this ticket is valid for bus, Metro and urban lines of FGC and can be bought in the Metro banks or *estancs* (tobacconists). Most buses run from between 5 and 6am–10pm. There are some night services (the Nit bus), but lines vary so check on the map or at bus stops.

A more exclusive bus, the Tomb Bus, is convenient for covering the shopping area between Plaça Catalunya and the top end of Av. Diagonal (Plaça Pius XII), which is not well connected with metros. The Tibibus runs from Plaça Catalunya to Plaça del Tibidabo (on the top of the hill).

By Taxi

All Barcelona taxis are black and yellow, and show a green light when they are available for hire. There are taxi ranks at the airport, Sants station, Plaça de Catalunya and other strategic points but taxis constantly move around town and can be hailed at any street corner. Rates are standard and calculated by meter, starting at a set rate and clocking up at a rate governed by the time of day: night-times, weekends and fiestas are more expensive.

If you go beyond the metropolitan area, the rate will increase slightly. The final charge is what shows on the meter, except when supplements are due for luggage, dogs or to and from the airport. Drivers do not expect a tip though a small one is always appreciated. A sticker inside the rear window outlines (in English) rates and conditions. Taxis equipped for wheelchairs or a group (7 seats) are available. Tel: (93) 455 8946/(93) 300 1100.

By Train

The following stations currently function as described, but before planning any journey it is advisable to call RENFE (the national train network) for the latest information and ticket deals, tel: (93) 490 0202.

Sants station, Plaça Països Catalans s/n: long distance national and international trains. Some of these will also stop in Passeig de Gràcia station which is very convenient for central parts of town. Confirm beforehand that your train really does stop there.

Regional trains leave Sants for the coast just south and north of Barcelona including a direct train to Port Aventura theme park and the high-speed Euromed to Alicante with various stops in between.

Estació de França, Av. Marqués de l'Argentera: long distance national and international trains.

Plaça de Catalunya station, Plaça de Catalunya: apart from the Metro and Generalitat railways (FGC), RENFE has a station in Plaça de Catalunya. Trains to Manresa, Lleida, Vic, Puigcerdà, La Tour de Carol, Mataró (Maresme Coast) and Blanes.

Plaça d'Espanya station, Plaça d'Espanya: FGC trains to Montserrat, Igualada and Manresa.

It is advisable to purchase tickets in advance, especially at holiday times. The easiest way is by telephone 24 hours in advance (93) 490 0202. In Sants queues can be long and ticket clerks impatient and not very helpful.

Left Luggage

Left luggage lockers (*consigna*) are available in Sants railway station from 4.30am–12.30am. There is an equivalent service at Estació de França, Pg. de Gràcia and Barcelona Nord bus station. At the sea terminal on Moll Barcelona there is a left luggage office which is open 8am–1am.

By Coach

There are regular long-distance coach lines running all over Spain which leave from the Estació d'Autobusos Barcelona Nord, Ali-bei, 80 or Sants bus station. For general information on services, tel: (93) 265 6508.

Around Catalonia:

Costa Brava: Sarfa, tel: (93) 265 1158.

Costa Maresme: Casas, tel: (93) 798 1100.

Delta del Ebro: Hife, tel: (93) 322 7814.

Montserrat: Julià, tel: (93) 490 4000.

Pyrenees: Alsina Graells, tel: (93) 265 6866.

Private Transport

By Car

Cars are better left in a parking place while you travel around town. Avoid parking anywhere that is not legal, particularly entrances and private garage doors: the police tow offenders away with remarkable alacrity and charge for retrieval is heavy. Street parking, indicated by blue lines on the road and a nearby machine to buy a ticket for display in the car, is limited. Convenient car parks are in Passeig de Gràcia, Plaça de Catalunya, Plaça de la Catedral and many side streets; there are also several under construction.

Useful addresses:

Royal Automobile Club of Catalonia (RACC), Av. Diagonal 687, tel: (93) 495 5000/900 365 505 (24 hours).

24-hour repairs, workshop/towing service: Detroit, Carrer de Biscaia, 326, tel: (93) 351 1203.

Towing service, Autogruas Barcelona, tel: (93) 232 4466.

Car Hire

Avis, Casanovas, 209, tel: (93) 209 9533; (93) 478 1706 (Airport).

Eurodollar-Atesa, Balmes, 141, tel: (93) 217 4442; (93) 370 0805 (Airport).

Ital-Budget, Travessera de Gràcia, 71, tel: (93) 201 2199.

Europcar, Consell de Cent, 363, tel: (93) 488 2398; (93) 379 9051 (Airport).

Hertz, Tuset, 10, tel: (93) 217 3248; (93) 370 5811 (Airport).

Vanguard, Londres, 31, tel: (93) 439 3880.

Motorcycle Hire: Vanguard, Londres, 31, tel: (93) 439 3880.

On Foot

Walking is one of the best ways of getting around Barcelona, though there are days when the traffic fumes in the busy Eixample suggest it may not be the healthiest. However it is ideal for seeing the many details of Barcelona that cannot possibly all be charted by maps or guide books – Modernista entrances and doorways, ancient corner shops, hidden roof gardens, balconies, local characters, daily life.

Hitch-hiking is not common among young people, though it is acceptable. An organisation exists to make contact between drivers with passenger space and people willing to pay a low price for a shared journey: Barnastop, Sant Ramón, 29, tel: (93) 443 0632. Monday–Friday 11am–2pm/5pm–8pm, Saturday 6–8pm.

Maps

The Tourist Board issues a good general map of the city (*plano de la ciudad*). A transport map is also available from Metro stations. The *Guia Urbana*, the taxi drivers' bible, is the most comprehensive map of the city.

Where To Stay

Hotels

Barcelona has more than 400 hotels, offering a wide range of accommodation from the humble *pension* to 5-star luxury. Take care when choosing a *pension*: it could have all the charms and comforts of staying with a local family or it could equally well be the local brothel.

Under new regulations for the classifications of establishments in Catalonia *hostales, hostal-residencias, casas de huespedes* (CH – Guest Houses) and *fondas* should all be re-categorised either as hotels or as *pensions*. It will probably take some time to enforce the new categories so be prepared to find the old names above the door – and in this listing.

The categorisation is:

Hotels (one star to five star) – a bathroom in every room is obligatory.

Pensions: One star – 15 percent of rooms with bath. Two star – 25 percent of rooms with bath.

The following selection is categorised according to price based on the cost of a double room with bath. Luxury: from around 15,000 pesetas to more than 30,000; moderate: from 8,000 pesetas to around 15,000; economy: below 8,000 pesetas. All those mentioned are hotels unless specified otherwise. Remember that a flight and hotel package often works out cheaper. If you are planning to stay a while, find out what packages are on offer from your home country.

LUXURY

Arts, Pg. de la Marina, 19, tel: (93) 221 1000; fax: (93) 221 1070. The hotel with the highest profile in town, it is one of the two towers that mark the entrance to the Olympic Village, on the sea front. Rooms with a view.

Avenida Palace, Gran Vía, 605–607, tel: (93) 301 9600; fax: (93) 318 1234. Classic old-world gilt and chandeliers at new world prices. Comfortable, good service. Request one of the rooms that still has original fittings, on fourth floor upwards for good city views.

Colón, Avinguda Catedral, 7, tel: (93) 301 1404; fax: (93) 317 2915. A classic, in the centre of the *barri Gótic*. Bedrooms can be disappointing after the comfort of the ground floor. Request room facing Cathedral.

Claris, Pau Claris, 150, tel: (93) 487 6262; fax: (93) 487 8736. Well positioned in the middle of the Eixample, its striking interior was built behind the original building's facade.

Comtes de Barcelona, Passeig de Gràcia, 75, tel: (93) 488 2200; fax: (93) 488 0614. Contemporary elegance in a Modernist building.

Ducs de Bergara, Carrer de Bergara, 11, tel: (93) 301 5151; fax: (93) 317 3442. Very attractive hotel in a typical Eixample building from the turn of the century, with some original features well preserved. Intimate atmosphere. A rare alternative to impersonal chain hotels.

Husa Palace, Gran Vía, 668, tel: (93) 318 5200; fax: (93) 318 0148. Luxury maybe, but really exorbitant even for business accounts. Splendid entrance hall and lobby where tea can be taken. Dalí had a permanent suite here.

Le Meridien Barcelona, Rambla, 111, tel: (93) 318 6200; fax: (93) 301 7776. A large hotel well renovated in keeping with the refurbishing of Barcelona, it is a favourite with touring rock stars.

Regente, Rambla de Catalunya, 76, tel: (93) 487 5989; fax: (93) 487 3227. Pleasant hotel in excellent position. Some attractive original features have survived amid the standard hotel furnishings. Rooftop swimming pool.

Rivoli Rambla, Rambla, 128, tel: (93) 302 6643; fax: (93) 317 5053. A renovated bank. Behind its striking facade is a modern hotel with features designed by some of Barcelona's leading talent.

MODERATE

Aparthotel Bonanova, Carrer de Bisbe Sevilla, 7, tel: (93) 418 1661; fax: (93) 418 4497. In a quiet residential area in the upper part of Barcelona. For those who prefer independence. Rooms equipped with kitchen/dining areas. Reasonably priced. Ask for a room with terrace.

España, Carrer de Sant Pau, 9, tel: (93) 318 1758; fax: (93) 317 1134. Magnificent Modernist decor on the ground floor by Domènech i Montaner is refreshingly mixed with kitsch and a Fifties bar. Rooms modernised. Popular among American intellectuals. Visit It at least the set lunch is good value and the wonderful surroundings worth every peseta.

Granvia, Gran Vía, 642, tel: (93) 318 1900; fax: (93) 318 9997. Faded baroque splendour which has its charms. Well situated near Passeig de Gràcia. Interior rooms are preferable to avoid Gran Vía traffic.

Nouvel, Carrer Santa Anna, 20, tel: (93) 301 8274; fax: (93) 301 8370. Attractive old hotel in pedestrian street off the Ramblas.

Oriente, Rambla, 45, tel: (93) 302 2558; fax: (93) 412 3819. One of Barcelona's best known hotels. Not what it was despite the price increases but still full of character.

Rialto, Carrer de Ferran, 42, tel: (93) 318 5212; fax: (93) 318 5312. Modernised and pleasant in this bustling street just off Plaça Sant Jaume.

Regina, Carrer de Bergara, 4, tel: (93) 301 3232; fax: (93) 318 2326. Reasonable-standard hotel in good position near Plaça de Catalunya.

Sant Agustí, Plaça Sant Agustí, 3, tel: (93) 318 1658; fax: (93) 317 2928. Comfortable and clean, overlooking quiet square. Well worth paying 2,000 pesetas more for one of their "de luxe" rooms on the fourth floor.

Suizo, Plaça de l'Angel, 12, tel: (93) 310 6108; fax: (93) 310 4081. Pleasant, homely, comfortable in a good position in the *barri* Gótic. Request room on Baixada Llibreteria for an attractive outlook and more peace.

ECONOMY

Hostal Palacios, Gran Vía, 629 bis, tel: (93) 301 3792. (*Pensión*) Convenient, pleasant *pensión*.

Residencia Windsor, Rambla de Catalunya, 84, tel: (93) 215 1198. A gem, impeccably clean, light and airy in contrast to the usual drab, sad *hostales*. Essential to book in advance and request a room looking on to Rambla de Catalunya. Excellent position near Diagonal.

Jardí, Plaça Sant Josep Oriol 1/Plaça del Pi, tel: (93) 301 5900. (*Pensión*) Fairly basic but clean and very well situated overlooking two of the most attractive squares in the *barri* Gótic. Extremely popular so book in advance if possible.

Peninsular, Carrer de Sant Pau, 34, tel: (93) 302 3138; fax: (93) 412 3699. Fairly basic but comfortable, with attractive Art Nouveau touches. The *barri* Gótic is full of *pensiones* but choose them with care: the streets between Carrer de Ferran and Plaça de Catalunya are better than those nearer the port. Several reasonable places are in Carrer de Carme, Portaferrissa and Santa Anna. For those who prefer to visit the *barri* Gótic by day and sleep in another part of town try:

Hostal Ciudad Condal, Carrer de Mallorca, 255, tel: (93) 215 1040. (*Pensión*)

Hostal Felipe II, Carrer de Mallorca, 329, tel: (93) 258 7758. (*Pensión*)

Camp Sites

There are 300 camp sites in Catalonia, 70 percent of the total number in Spain. Twelve of these are within easy reach of Barcelona. Most are south of

the city, near the stretch of beach which begins at the end of the airport tarmac and runs through Viladecans, Gavá and Castelldefels. The road into Barcelona is notoriously busy and dangerous, the beaches and sea are crowded and of dubious cleanliness, but the air provides a refreshing change from the city.

In Barcelona:

El Toro Bravo, (1,200 sites). Autovía de Castelldefels, Km 11, Viladecans, tel: (93) 637 3462.

At Km 12 and Km 12.5 on the same road are:

Filipinas, (1,063 sites), tel: (93) 658 2895.

La Ballena Alegre, (1,500 sites), tel: (93) 658 0504.

Also on the same road, but in Gavá, at Km 13.2 and Km 15 are:

Tres Estrellas, (407 sites), tel: (93) 633 0637.

La Tortuga Ligera, (750 sites), tel: (93) 633 0642.

Just along the road in Castelldefels, the most popular of these resorts, is the **Estrella de Mar** (525 sites), tel: (93) 633 0784.

North of Barcelona:

Masnou, (120 sites) Camilo Fabra, 33, tel: (93) 555 1503.

Eating Out

Catalan Food

Eating is an important part of Catalan culture, something to be taken seriously and enjoyed to the full. The traditional gathering together of the family for Sunday and feast day lunches is an ancient ritual, providing an opportunity to eat well and converse long into dinner time. On Sunday mornings the *pastelerias* are full of freshly cologned fathers and sons buying indulgent pastries for dessert, then between 2pm and 5pm a sacred quiet descends over the city. Even on working days most shops and offices close during this time while lunch is seriously observed. The Catalans have just cause to preserve the tradition: real Catalan cooking is delicious and nutritious and considered, along with the Basque, the best in Spain. It is certainly part of the experience of visiting this country which should not be missed.

Catalan food is said to embody the key elements of Catalonia, having evolved from using the freshly available produce of the Mediterranean sea, the fertile plains and the mountains. It is the pride of Catalans that their country can offer miles of rugged coastline and sheltered beaches, as well as awesome mountain ranges and rich valleys, all within easy access of each other. Similarly the cooking combines *mar i montanya* (sea and mountains) which makes for strange sounding marriages on the menu, though delicious in the tasting, such as meat balls with cuttlefish, or chicken with shellfish.

If anything Catalan gastronomy can err on the side of richness: it has all the goodness of Mediterranean cooking which is increasingly being considered as one of the healthiest, based on olive oil and fresh vegetables. Its strong flavour is due to abundant use of garlic and sauces made with almonds and cognac.

A rich meal can be well balanced by the omnipresent fresh salad and simple, but often the most delicious, grilled fish or meat; the best is *a la parrillada*, food grilled over charcoal. Eaten with *allioli* (a Catalan garlic sauce, not to be missed) and *pa amb tomàquet* (bread or toast dressed with tomato and olive oil) this is one of the most typical Catalan meals.

It is worth adapting to local meal times during your stay, so as to eat when food is at its freshest.

Breakfast: coffee or milk with a sweet cake or croissant first thing in the morning, followed by a mid-morning break of a hearty sandwich often with beer or wine.

The *Aperitivo*: an aperitif before lunch, around 1pm, of a *vermut* (usually red vermouth, often with soda) and olives, or some other *tapa* (snack).

Lunch: peak time is 2pm lingering on to 4pm or later at weekends. After 3.30pm there is a danger of not being served. Lunch is the main meal of the day and the best time to find freshly cooked food and the most economical meals. Every restaurant has a *menú del día* (set menu), offering a choice of starters (soup, salad, vegetables), a main course of meat or fish, a dessert (flan, yogurt, tinned peaches or fresh fruit) and wine, beer or a soft drink. Standard and price vary according to the establishment, but it is always good value. For around 1,000 pesetas you can have an excellent meal. If the *menú del día* is not in immediate evidence, ask for one: "*hay menú?*". Some restaurants may try and withhold it from rich-looking tourists.

***Merienda*:** a kind of afternoon tea, from 5–7pm, consisting of milky coffee or hot chocolate and sticky cakes and often a large plate of cream eaten just on its own. For a classic *merienda* try the cafés around the Plaça del Pi, especially in Carrer Petritxol.

Dinner: at home this is usually a light meal, often *tortilla*, a Spanish omelette, around 10pm. Restaurants do not usually have a set menu at night, so eating out can be more expensive than at lunch time.

***Tapas*:** if you have had a good lunch, the evening is the ideal time to "do *tapas*" i.e. to visit several bars having a glass of wine and a snack in each. Only foreigners eat *tapas* at lunch time, and it can prove to be a much more expensive way of eating.

What To Eat

The French saying *On connait les gens à table* is as valid here as anywhere in the world: the *barcelonéses* are what they eat. On the white tablecloths of the city are laid the very best produce from the sea, the mountains, the valleys and the plains. From the mountainous regions during the autumn months come the succulent *setas* (wild mushrooms), cooked in elaborate sauces or braised with a little garlic and parsley. Cured and smoked meats are another speciality of the Catalan cuisine: *botifarra* (a tasty sausage), *fuet*, Vic sausages and so on.

The *escudella i carn d'olla* is a Catalan classic, a wholesome soup followed by the meat and vegetables cooked in it. A dish such as *pan tomàquet*, slices of country bread rubbed with tomatoes and flavoured with a dash of home-grown olive oil, is a typical speciality that bridges all social classes. And, of course, no self-respecting *barcelonés* would dream of finishing a meal without a flan dessert topped with burnt sugar called *crema catalana*.

In Barcelona the number of pastry shops per square metre must rank among the world's highest. For each feast day and festival there is a corresponding traditional sweetmeat: *Bunyols* during Lent, *Las Monas* for Easter, *Panellets* (marzipans) for All Saints. Throughout the long summer months the *barcelonéses* celebrate their numerous local festivals with an abundance of fireworks, champagne and *cocas* (pastries covered in sugar, crystallised fruits and pine nuts).

The best menus vary according to what is in season. These will be singled out under "*Platos del Día*" or "*Recomendaciones*", or the head waiter will advise. Following is a list of some typical Catalan dishes:

Starters

Escalivada: salad made of cooked peppers and aubergines.

Esqueixada: salad of raw salted cod, onions and peppers.

Amanida Catalana: a mixed salad with cold meat/sausage added. Can be dull.

Xatò: salad of *frisée* lettuce with tuna, anchovies and a romesco sauce. Speciality of Sitges.

Bolets: generic name for the various wild mushrooms in season in the Autumn. *Rovelló* is one of the best, especially just grilled with garlic and parsley. Often used in meat dishes at this time of the year.

Espinacs a la Catalana: spinach cooked with raisins and pine nuts.

Faves a la Catalana: small broad beans stewed with herbs and pork and sausage meats. Best in spring.

Escudella: the most traditional Catalan soup, usually followed by the *carn d'olla*, i.e. the meat and vegetables which have been cooked in the soup. A Christmas dish though formerly staple diet of every Catalan household.

Canelons: another Catalan tradition despite their Italian associations.

Calçots: spring onions cooked on a charcoal grill and served with a sauce. Only in season.

Arrós negre: one of the many traditional rice dishes. Black rice with squid, cooked in the squid's ink.

Fideus: an excellent and lesser known variation on paella, in which noodles replace the rice making a moister dish. A good, traditional paella is increasingly difficult to find.

Main courses

Botifarra amb mongetes: the local, very tasty, sausage served with haricot beans.

Estofat: stews, made from beef or older veal, usually have a rich, succulent sauce.

Oca amb naps: goose with turnip.

Conill: rabbit, grilled and served with allioli, or stewed.

Xai: lamb. Cutlets (*costelletes*) are especially good in Catalonia.

Fricandó: classic stew with *moixernons*, a small, delicate wild mushroom.

Bacallà: salted cod can be served in many ways: *a la llauna* – with garlic, parsley and tomato; *amb xamfaina* – with a sauce of tomato, pepper and aubergine. This sauce often served with meat.

Suquet: a seafood stew.

Fish and shellfish should not be missed in Barcelona. Often served in rich sauces, the simplest and perhaps best way is grilled or done in the oven, *al forn*.

Desserts

Crema catalana: an essential during your stay, a cinnamon flavoured custard with a burnt caramel top.

Mel i mató: a curd cheese with honey.

Postre de músic: roasted nuts and dried fruits usually served with a cold glass of moscatel.

Apart from these classic *postres*, the usual run of commercial ice-creams, sorbets and *macedonia* (fruit salad) are always available, as well as fresh fruit.

Tapas

The best way to choose *tapas* is to look and point, so you can be sure to only select the freshest. Ham, spicy cold meats and cheese eaten with *pa amb tomaquet* are often the best bet. *Tapas* tend to be more Spanish than Catalan in origin, so this selection is given here in Castilian rather than Catalan.

Jamon serrano: cured ham. *Jabugo* is the best.

Queso: cheese. Try *manchego seco* for a strong flavour, *cabrales*, a potent blue cheese from Asturias in vine leaves or *cabra*, goat cheese.

Salchichón, chorizo: spicy sausages.

Anchoas: anchovies.

Boquerones: small, pickled fish.

Berberechos: cockles; normally out of a tin but delicious with an aperitivo.

Tortilla: Spanish style omelettes. *Española* (potatoes and onions); *espinacas* (spinach); *payés* (mixed vegetables); *ajos tiernos* (young, tender garlic). *Francesa* is the classic French omelette made without a filling.

Patatas bravas: fried potatoes served with a hot spicy sauce, or garlic mayonnaise.

Ensaladilla: "Russian" salad, with potatoes, vegetables and mayonnaise.

Pescaditos: small fried fish.

Pulpo: octopus, a speciality from Galicia.

Where To Eat

In a short holiday there are not enough meal times to visit all the restaurants that should be visited in Barcelona. The following have been selected for their good food combined with atmosphere or pleasant location. Nearly all serve Catalan food and many other regional dishes. At lunch-time try any corner bar with a reasonable looking *menu del día*.

The following selection is divided into "prime", "moderate" and "economical" categories on a financial basis. Prime will cost a minimum of 3,000–4,000 pesetas a head, moderate a minimum of 2,000 pesetas and economical around 1,000 pesetas. Many establishments close on a Sunday evening/Monday and in August.

Prime

A Contraluz, Carrer Milanesat, 19, tel: (93) 203 0658. In a quiet street in the residential Tres Torres area, this house and garden are a quiet, relaxing place for lunch or dinner. A refreshing change from down-town bustle. Try their reasonably-priced Menu del Día at lunch time. (En route to the Museu-Monestir de Pedralbes.)

Agua, Pg. Marítim, 30, tel: (93) 225 1272. About as near as you'll get to eating on the beach in 90s Barcelona, this is the latest place to eat fish.

Botafumeiro, Carrer de Gran de Gràcia, 81, tel: (93) 218 4230. This is a Galician restaurant but it is also one of the best places to eat seafood in Barcelona. Oysters at the bar.

Can Majó, Carrer d'Almirall Aixada, 23, tel: (93) 221 5818. One of the best and most established of the Barceloneta fish restaurants, and one of the few places you can be sure of a good paella.

Casa Leopoldo, Carrer de Sant Rafael, 24, tel: (93) 441 3014. Worth hunting down in the narrow streets of the *barri Xines*, a family-run Barcelona classic. Favourite of artists and intellectuals. Excellent fish.

Jaume de Provença, Carrer de Provença, 88, tel: (93) 430 0029. Classic Catalan and international cooking

La Venta, Plaça Doctor Andreu, tel: (93) 212 6455. Attractively decorated building and leafy terrace at the foot of the funicular to Tibidabo. Perfect for spring-time lunches or summer nights.

La Vaqueria, Carrer Deu i Mata, 139–141, tel: (93) 419 0735. A place to be seen, especially for a certain bejewelled section of Barcelona society who will later be dancing in the trendy night club Up and Down. Two interior decorators from the same set have given a beautiful, dream-like quality to this old cowshed.

Passadís de'n Pep, Pla de Palau, 2, tel: (93) 310 1021. For people "in the know", the kind of place you will walk past if you are not. Excellent seafood.

Talaia, Carrer Marina, 16, tel: (93) 221 9090. A more recent addition to the Olympic Port, with more guarantee of eating well. A high standard of creative cooking, specialising in fish.

Tragaluz, Pge. Concepció, 5, tel: (93) 487 0196. Situated in a charming passageway off Pg. de Gràcia, it is a fine example of 1990s Barcelona design, and unlike many trendy places actually has excellent food. The vast skylight, which lends its name to the restaurant, gives the impression of eating on a light, airy terrace. One of those Barcelona spots where a visit to the Ladies/Gents is essential.

Moderate

Agut, Carrer de Gignás, 16, tel: (93) 315 1709.

Bilbao, Carrer de Perill, 33, tel: (93) 458 9624. Jolly bustle in Gràcia. Especially good at lunchtime.

Café de l'Academia, Carrer de Lladó, 1, tel: (93) 315 0026. Nouvelle Catalan cooking, well presented. Stylish, modernised medieval building in an attractive square in the *barri* Gòtic, with outdoor tables in the summer. Good value.

Carballeira, Carrer de Reina Cristina, 3, tel: (93) 310 1006. Excellent Galician fish. At lunch-time on Sundays try a simple *tapa* at the bar of *arroz a banda*, delicious rice cooked in fish stock. Accompany it with a glass of Ribeira, Galician white wine; try the cloudy one, *turbio*.

The following venues fall into a "classic" category, as white table-clothed, traditional, bustling Catalan restaurants with dignified service. They never change and are always fun, good food and value:

El Caballito Blanco, Carrer de Mallorca, 196, tel: (93) 453 1033.

Restaurant Ponsa, Carrer d'Enric Granados, 89, tel: (93) 453 1037.

Senyor Parellada, Carrer d'Argentería, 37, tel: (93) 310 5094. Unusual and classic Catalan dishes in a sophisticated, very pleasant environment. Don't be talked into more than you want by the over-keen Maitre d'.

Set Portes, Passeig Isabel II, 14, tel: (93) 319 3033. Over 150 years old and recently sympathetically restored, recapturing the original atmosphere. Another classic, popular for family Sunday lunches. Specialises in rice dishes, one for each day of the week. Also has the advantage of remaining open through the afternoon and evening until 1am.

Economical

The following are especially good (and economical) at lunch-time.

Casa Joana, Major de Sarriá, 59. Good value for this up-market part of town.

Can Tripas, Carrer de Sagués, 16. Cheap, cheerful and crowded: a paradox amid the elegant shops of the Diagonal/Plaça Francesc Macià area.

Egipte, Carrer de Jerusalén, 3, tel: 317 7480. Just behind the Boqueria market, a popular, lively place that grew from being a small market restaurant into several well decorated floors and two annexes.

Kasparo, Pl. Vicenç Martorell. Charming terrace bar in secluded square just off Ramblas. Delicious and cosmopolitan light snacks. Play area in square for kids.

Café La Ribera, Plaça Olles, (behind Passeig del Born). Friendly, charming owner creates the atmosphere. Excellent food presented with more style than many restaurants, for half the price.

La Cassola, Carrer de Sant Sever, 3, tel: (93) 318 1580. Family run. Good home-made Catalan food.

Rodrigo, Carrer d'Argentería. Another endearing family-run busy restaurant, popular with foreign language teachers. Delicious food.

Romesco, Carrer de l'Arc de Sant Agustí. The dazzling fluorescent lighting deters no-one. Popular prices for good food. Famous for its "*arroz a la cubana*".

Also very good value are the Regional Centres, which are clubs for people from different regions of Spain, open to the public at midday. Try **Hogar Extremeño** (Extremadura) at the bottom of Avinguda Portal de l'Angel, or **Centro Murciano** (Murcia) in Carrer de Portaferrissa.

World Cuisine

AMERICAN

From Hard Rock Café in Plaça Catalunya to Planet Hollywood in the Olympic Village, American chains and fast food outlets are invading Barcelona.

JAPANESE

Koyuki, Carrer de Córcega, 242, tel: (93) 237 8490. As the Japanese population of Barcelona increases so does the number of restaurants. This is one of the simplest but best, less expensive than most and frequented by comic-reading Japanese.

MOROCCAN

La Rosa del Desierto, Plaça Narcís Oller 7, tel: (93) 237 4590. Pioneers of Moroccan cooking in Barcelona. Good couscous.

PAKISTANI

Shalimar, Carrer de Carme. Above average (for Barcelona) Pakistani and Indian cooking, at a reasonable price.

PIZZAS

La Pizza Nostra, Montcada, 29. Pizzas with an Argentinian influence. Handy for Picasso museum.

SYRIAN

Xix Kebab, Carrer de Córcega 193, tel: (93) 321 8210. Soothing atmosphere and delicate, very tasty food.

TAPAS

Available nearly everywhere but to be chosen with care. Recent additions to Barcelona are several Basque bars, famed for their prowess in tapas and good wine. Also:

Bar Roble, Carrer de Lluís Antúnez, 7, tel: (93) 218 7387. Also well-known for paella on Thursday lunch, but you must book.

El Raval, Carrer de Doctor Dou. A bar that serves pâtés, cheese and salads. Ideal for after concerts or theatre. Frequented by artists and actors.

Carrer de Mercè behind Passeig de Colom lined with *tapas* bars: don't miss "*jamon canario*" (ham on the bone) in the corner bar.

José Luis, Avinguda Diagonal, 520. For those who want *tapas* without roughing it. Sophisticated snacks at elevated prices – beware the bill.

Montesquieu, Carrer de Mandri, 56. Good seafood.

Mundial Bar, Plaça Sant Agustí Vell 1. Especially good for shellfish.

Sol Soler, Plaça del Sol. Good alternative *tapas*. Relaxed atmosphere in evening.

Xampanyet, Carrer de Montcada, near Passeig del Born. Ceramic-tiled pretty bar that serves a fizzy white wine of the same name. Perfect for an aperitif with anchovies.

VEGETARIAN

Biocenter, Carrer de Pintor Fortuny, 25. Delicious salads with a difference – difficult to find in Barcelona. Now open in the evenings.

Comme-Bio, Gran Vía, 603. Soothing surroundings reminiscent of the Avenida Palace Hotel next door. A relief from the usual vegetarian pine.

Drinking Notes

Despite the proliferation of bars and drink available at reasonable prices, there is little evidence of drunkenness in public places. Such excess is popularly associated with tourists from Northern Europe overcome by the accessibility of alcohol in Spain, though hopefully that image is becoming a cliché of the Costas of the past. First-time visitors to Spain should be aware that measures of spirits are larger than in most other countries. Also, it is important to specify the brand when asking for a drink in a bar, to avoid rough imitations. Beware the bottles that look remarkably similar to your own favourite brand.

Beer is served in bottles of a fifth (*un quinto*), a half litre (*una mediana*) or draught from the tap; for the latter ask for "*una caña*". When ordering water, soft drinks or wine you will often be asked if you want it "*fresco o natural?*", chilled or room temperature. Red wine is usually served "*fresco*" during the summer unless you specify "*natural*".

Sangria can be dangerously refreshing; often made from cheap wine, cheap brandy and an excess of sugar, and drunk under a hot sun it can take its toll. Best avoided.

Wine is regarded as a drink to accompany meals not to be continued late into the night. Table wine is often drunk with "*gaseosa*", a light lemonade, at lunch time. There are a lot more wines to Spain than the Riojas which have put the country on the food and wine map. Catalonia is the second largest producer of wines in Spain, so make the most of the range of local wines on offer. The official mark of quality is D.O. (Denominacion de Origen). The main Catalan regions are:

Penedés: The most important and internationally famed area, just to the west of Barcelona and easily visited. Known for its *cava* (champagne-style sparkling wine) and white wines, but also produces some good reds and rosés. Try any of the following producers: Torres (Gran Coronas or Gran Viña Sol and Viña Esmeralda), Masia Bach, Marqués de Monistrol (especially whites), René Barbier, Cavas Hill.

Alella: A few miles north of Barcelona, this region is best for its whites, Alella Marfil and Marqués de Alella.

Empordà–Costa Brava: A region near the French border in the northeast. Perelada wines are good. Blanc Pescador is a refreshing, reasonably priced white that slips down easily at lunch-time.

Costers del Segre: In the province of Lleida. The company Raimat produces excellent wines that are often overlooked. Try their Clos Abadía and Cabernet Sauvignon, Clos Casal and Chardonnay.

Priorat: Quite heavy reds. Main producers are Scala Dei, De Muller and Priorat Unió.

Cava

Another pride of Catalonia, *cava* is the sparkling wine made by the *méthode champenoise*. Produced in the Penedès region for over 100 years it has now gained international recognition, especially in the United States where certain brands have gained popularity over French champagnes. In Catalan homes it is generally drunk at festive occasions and with Sunday lunch, usually to accompany sticky cakes at dessert.

Codorniú and Freixenet are the most established labels but other well regarded producers are Conde Caralt, Juve i Camps, Segura Viudas and Marqués de Monistrol. Try "*brut*" and "*brut nature*" for the best quality. A visit to the cellars of various producers in Sant Sadurní d'Anoia, a small town near Vilafranca del Penedés, which is the centre of *cava* country is a pleasant excursion. Codorniú has impressive modernist buildings designed by Puig i Cadafalch and along with Freixenet offer organised tours. Call to arrange visits: Codorniú tel: (93) 818 3232. Freixenet tel: (93) 818 3200.

Keen *cava* drinkers who cannot make it to Sant Sadurní could visit Xampany, Carrer de València 200, in Barcelona; this specialist shop sells over 100 different *cavas* and offers tastings.

Attractions

City Tours & Day Trips

Barcelona is densely built between the hill of Tibidabo and the sea and bordered by Montjuïc to the south. It is worth making a trip up either hill or over the port in the cable-car for a good view and instant orientation of the city's layout. Avoid misty or heavily polluted days.

A convenient way of getting an overall idea of the city is to catch the Tourist Bus (Barcelona Bus Turistic), which at a reasonable price follows a circuit that takes in the most interesting parts of the city. You can select a northern route or southern, get on and off freely to visit the attractions that interest you, and then resume the journey when you are ready. It also offers discounts on entrance charges. The bus comes by frequently, the first leaving Pl. Catalunya at 9am. Operates from March to early January. The fleet includes buses equipped for wheelchairs and open-air double deckers.

Tibidabo

The most enjoyable way up the hill is the Tramvia Blau (Blue Tram), which runs from the foot of Avinguda Tibidabo (FGC station Av. Tibidabo) to the Funicular Railway which continues to the summit. The services interconnect, running frequently every day 7am–9.35pm and later at weekends and in the summer, according to the opening hours of the amusement park at the top.

While waiting for the tram note "La Rotonda", a former hotel turned hospital. There are also some magnificent modernist *torres* (villas) on the route, where the rich Barcelonans used to summer, now mostly converted into flats or offices.

The amusement park on the summit comprises fairground attractions, a museum of automata (some from the early 19th century), a lookout tower and restaurants. A good spot for a drink with a view on a balmy summer evening. An unexceptional church at the entrance, the Sagrat Cor Temple, is popular for weddings.

Its opening times vary according to the time of year, so the safest bet is to call beforehand, tel: (93) 211 7942 or check in the daily press.

Entrance fee: "*De paseo*" covers the entrance charge and six attractions, including the famous "*Avion Tibiair*" and the museum; "*pase libre*", just over three times as much, gives access to all the attractions. Reductions are available for half-days, groups, very young and old.

An alternative excursion, if you can't face the fairground at the top, is to take the tram to the funicular station but then walk up through the gardens as far as Carretera de les Aigües, a rough road that skirts the mountains for several miles: the view is excellent and the pine-scented air is the perfect antidote to Barcelona. (This road can

237

also be reached from FGC station Peu del Funicular.) Returning to the tram pause for a drink in the Merbeye or Mirablau bars, or treat yourself to a meal on the terrace of La Venta, good food in very charming surroundings.

Torre de Collserola: Another legacy of the Olympic Games, this communications tower designed by Norman Foster, has changed the Tibidabo skyline. A transparent lift will take you up to a glassed-in viewing platform at a giddy height of 560 m above sea level. Transport is provided from the top funicular station, or from the car park, which can be reached from the road to Vallvidrera. Entrance fee.

Montjuïc

There is something for everyone on Montjuïc: good views from the castle, museums, a fairground, Poble Espanyol (the "Spanish village"), the Olympic complex, sports facilities, and walks or bicycle rides through the gardens.

You can get to Montjuïc by cable car from the port, by the Metro to Plaça d'Espanya or Paral.lel, by bus to Plaça d'Espanya (Nos. 9, 27, 50) or Palau dels Esports (No. 55). A bus from Plaça d'Espanya (No. 61) to Avinguda Miramar covers key areas of the hill. An alternative is to take the funicular from Paral.lel Metro station to the amusement park, from where there is a cable car to the castle and military museum. One of the best ways to get to the Olympic complex is by escalator: a series of escalators go from Av.Maria Cristina up past the Palau Nacional to the stadium.

Poble Espanyol: Recently refurbished and injected with new life it can be fun, but remains a tourist showcase and seems to lack a genuine heart. There is plenty on offer: daily entertainments recreating village fiestas in the main square and streets, an audio-visual on Barcelona and shops selling crafts. There are bars and restaurants of every type: for cocktails, *tapas*, fruit juices or even sherry and olives in an Andalusian *patio* (though beware of being talked into the most expensive item on the menu here; not much sign of the warm Andalusian spirit in this *patio*). The village has bars with live music, jazz, and floor shows. There are restaurants which offer regional dishes, Mediterranean food, pizzas or

tea and cakes. Naps, a vegetarian restaurant, has refreshingly different salads. The Tablao de Carmen offers a set dinner and flamenco show: both are good, but try and go in a crowd or on a busy night for greater atmosphere.

Village opening times: daily from 9am. Closing time varies according to day of week (4am on Friday and Saturday). Entrance fee. For more information tel: (93) 325 7866.

Olympic complex: The most important of the city's four Olympic locations, Montjuïc has the stadium (built within the 1929 stadium), the Palau Sant Jordi for indoor events, the Picornell swimming pools and the diving pool. The stadium can be visited from 10am–6pm every day and the esplanade and Palau Sant Jordi at weekends, except when events are taking place. For guided tours of both, tel: (93) 426 2089.

The Galeria Olímpica, at the south gate of stadium (tel: (93) 426 0660), is an exhibition space and photo and video library where you can find everything you could possibly want to know about the 1992 Games.

Port and Waterfront

The new 5 km (3-mile) waterfront is made up of the commercial port (the third most important in the Mediterranean); the Port Vell (the old port), landscaped and opened up, with a new marina, walkways, an Imax cinema (180° screen) and Maremagnum, a commercial centre with shops, bars and restaurants; Barceloneta with seafood restaurants and beaches; the Olympic Village and Port, and the newly landscaped beaches beyond. It provides a range of activities, though more than anything a fresh, open space for walking and getting a sense of the Mediterranean. Some of the key points are:

Cable car: Another relic of the 1929 exhibition and still going strong. For a spectacular view catch it at any of the three stations – Barceloneta, Moll de Barcelona or Miramar on Montjuïc. It runs daily except Mondays from noon–5.45pm.

Columbus monument: This monument to the navigator at the foot of the Ramblas is one of the landmarks of Barcelona. For a fine aerial view of the city take the lift which runs inside the

column. From 10am–2pm and 3.30–7pm and from 10am–7pm on Sundays and holidays in the winter; closed: Monday; from 9am–9pm daily in the summer (June–September).

Golondrinas: For a trip round the harbour, or to the Olympic port take one of these pretty boats moored near the Columbus monument. Every 30 minutes from 11am untill dusk, tel: 442 3106.

Escua: A boat from the Portal de la Pau to the Olympic Port. The ticket price includes trip, guide and refreshment. Monday to Friday and weekends in the winter: 11am, 1pm and 4pm. Weekends in July and August have an extra trip at 6pm.

Bicycle hire: To get around the port and beaches the healthy way, hire bicycles, tricycles or tandems opposite the Parc de la Ciutadella in Passeig de Picasso. (See *Sport* for details).

Olympic village: These apartment blocks and commercial buildings, designed by internationally famed architects, are gradually becoming occupied, turning it into a real neighbourhood. The Port, where the Olympic sailing events took place, is lined with restaurants and bars which are as popular for open-air lunches as late-night clubbing. The beaches, with tons of imported sand, are overwhelmingly crowded on summer weekends, but can be pleasant at off-peak hours. Well connected by metro and bus, the area is worth visiting.

Parc de la Ciutadella

A real family park with a happy atmosphere. On Sunday morning the park is full of families parading before going off to large lunches. Apart from the Museum of Modern Art and the Zoological Museum housed in an interesting old building, look out for the Catalan Parliament building in the former Governor's Palace, the Umbracle with its tropical vegetation and the Hivernacle, where concerts and exhibitions are often held. The concerts are particularly enjoyable on a summer night. Boats can be hired on the lake.

The zoo is in Ciutadella park. Its main claim to fame is "Snowflake", the white gorrilla (the only albino gorrilla in captivity). Open: 10am–5pm and in the summer 9.30am–7.30pm.

Countryside Day Tours

PARC DE COLLSEROLA

Collserola is a natural park area formed by the forested hills which lie between Barcelona and Sant Cugat (the hill of Tibidabo and beyond). An excellent leaflet available at tourist offices shows the walks, tracks, picnic spots etc., and gives names and addresses of riding centres, restaurants and other places of interest. The whole area is easily reached from Barcelona (FGC from Plaça de Catalunya) but feels like "real" country.

For more information: Patronat del Parc de Collserola, Ctra de l'Església, 92, tel: (93) 280 35 52. An information centre is open from 9.30–3pm daily (FGC station Baixador de Vallvidrera and a walk up through the woods).

MONTSERRAT

The sacred centre of Catalonia, the mountain and monastery of Montserrat is where the Black Virgin, patron saint of Catalonia, is worshipped. Montserrat is within easy reach of Barcelona by car, by train from Plaça d' Espanya or by organised excursion. Daily visits leave Barcelona at 9am. The Montserrat choir sings at 1pm and 6.45pm.

For excursions contact: Julià Tours: Ronda Universitat, 5, tel: (93) 301 7775/317 6454. Pullmantur: Gran Via, 635, tel: (93) 317 1297.

WINE COUNTRY

Vilafranca del Penedès and Sant Sadurní d'Anoia are in the heart of the most important wine region of Catalonia and make a pleasant trip from Barcelona. In Vilafranca the Wine Museum is open every day except Monday, and in Sant Sadurní the cellars of *cava* producers Freixenet and Codorníu can be visited. (See *Eating Out* section for details and Tourist Office, Vilafranca, tel: (93) 892 0358.)

SPAS

There are many different spas in Catalonia, offering diverse treatments. Some are quite near Barcelona. For details contact: Associació Balneària, Balmes, 191, tel: (93) 218 3699.

TOUR GUIDES

For professional tourist guides/interpreters to accompany groups contact: the Professional Association of Barcelona Tour Guides, tel: (93) 319 8416; the Barcelona Guide Bureau, tel: (93) 268 2422; City Guides, tel: (93) 412 0674.

Cultural

The combination of Catalonia's rich cultural heritage and the dynamism of contemporary movements makes Barcelona one of Europe's cultural capitals. In fact it is bidding to become European City of Culture in 2004, part of an ambitious scheme backed by UNESCO to hold a Universal Forum of Cultures in and around the city, and across the world by Internet. Apart from its architecture and 46 museums, there is a busy calendar of music and arts festivals, visiting exhibitions and constant activity in design, theatre and the arts in general, to say nothing of daily performances from street artists in the Ramblas and small squares of the *barri* Gòtic.

Whatever time of year you visit, there will be some cultural activity. Posters, banners, the daily and weekly press all herald what's on. The City Council has a Cultural Information Centre in the Palau de la Virreina, Rambla, 99, which is very helpful and has leaflets and information on nearly all cultural activities. It also sells tickets. The Information Centre in Plaça Catalunya sells tickets at half-price on the day of a performance. Also two of the savings banks have an efficient system for ticket sales: Tel-Entrada of the Caixa de Catalunya tel: 902 101 212 and Servicaixa of "La Caixa" in most branches of the bank.

Museums

Apart from the permanent collections, check what itinerant exhibitions are in town, particularly in the Museu Picasso, Fundació Joan Miró and Fundació Tàpies, as well as the cultural and exhibition centres that are listed below.

Except where specified below most museums are closed on Monday, lunch-times, and Sunday and holiday afternoons. Check before if possible in the local press.

Museu Arqueològic, Passeig Santa Madrona, Montjuïc, tel: (93) 423 2149. Open: Tuesday–Saturday 9.30am–1.30pm and 4–7pm, Sunday 10am–2pm. Archaeological discoveries from the first inhabitants of Catalonia and the rest of the Iberian Peninsula.

Museu Barbier-Mueller d'art precolombí, Montcada, 14, tel: (93) 319 7603. Open: Tuesday–Saturday and public holidays 10am–8pm, Sunday 10am–3pm. This magnificent collection of pre-Colombian art was given to Barcelona from the Barbier-Mueller Museum in Geneva. Some fascinating and unique pieces from prehispanic America.

Museu Diocesà, Pla de la Seu, 7, tel: (93) 315 2213. Open: Tuesday–Saturday 11am–2pm and 5–8pm, Sunday 11am–2pm. Religious art housed in a strikingly beautiful Gothic building with Renaissance additions, right by the cathedral.

Museu Etnològic, Passeig Santa Madrona, Montjuïc, tel: (93) 424 6402. Open: Tuesday–Sunday 10am–2pm, Wednesday/Thursday until 7pm. Ethnographical items from all over the world, especially Latin America, the Philippines and New Guinea.

Museu d' Història de Catalunya, Plaça Pau Vila, tel: (93) 225 4700. Open: Tuesday–Thursday 10am–7pm, Friday and Saturday 10am–8pm, Sunday 10am–2.30pm. An interactive tour through the history of Catalonia, it works well as a generic history museum. In the impressive Palau de Mar, a restored warehouse in the port. Entertaining for the whole family.

Museu Nacional d'Art de Catalunya (MNAC), Palau Nacional, Montjuïc, tel: (93) 423 7199. Still undergoing major renovation work, this rather forbidding building that overlooks the fountains of Montjuïc houses an impressive collection of Catalan Romanesque art. Many of the frescoes were painstakingly salvaged from remote churches in the Pyrenees and brought down the mountain-side by donkey at the beginning of the century. It also houses a collection of Gothic art, some baroque and Renaissance pieces and has a temporary exhibition space.

Institut Jardí Botànic, Avinguda Montanyans, Montjuïc, tel: (93) 325 8050. Call to arrange visit.

Fundació Joan Miró, Plaça de Neptú, Montjuïc, tel: (93) 329 1908. Open: Tuesday–Saturday 11am–7pm, Thursday 11am–9.30pm, Sunday 10.30am–2.30pm. Cafeteria, restaurant and bookshop. One of the largest collections of Miró's work in the world, including paintings, drawings, sculptures, tapestries and the complete graphic work, well exhibited in this building especially designed by the artist's contemporary Sert. Regular exhibitions of contemporary art.

Museu Militar, Montjuïc Castle, tel: (93) 329 8613. Most impressive for its view over the port.

Museu Marítim, Av. Drassanes, 1, tel: (93) 301 1831. Open: Tuesday–Sunday from 10am–7pm. Housed in well-preserved 14th-century royal shipyards worth seeing in themselves, this maritime museum has an interesting collection of models, navigational instruments, figureheads, drawings and replicas. A scale model of the galleon used by Don Juan de Austria in the Battle of Lepanto is now part of an exciting interactive space "La Gran Aventura del Mar" charting Catalonia's sea-faring history. A haven for boat enthusiasts of all ages.

Museu de Cera, Passatge de la Banca, 7, tel: (93) 317 2649. Open: Monday–Friday 10am–1.30pm and 4–7.30pm, Saturday and Sunday 10am–1.30pm and 4.30–8pm. The Wax Museum near the end of the Ramblas. Not exactly a Madame Tussauds, but an option for entertaining children.

Museu d'Història de la Ciutat, Plaça del Rei, tel: (93) 315 1111. Open: Tuesday–Saturday 10am–2pm and 4–8pm (10am–8pm in summer), Sunday 10am–2pm. The museum of the city's history, including archaeological remains in the cellars and adjoining streets.

Museu Frederic Marès, Plaça Sant Iu, tel: (93) 310 5800. Open: Tuesday–Saturday 10am–5pm, Sunday 10am–2pm. Displays of sculpture, from Roman to baroque, and an interesting portrayal of daily life from the 15th to 20th centuries. Charming café in its patio in summer.

Museu de la Catedral, Cathedral Cloister, tel: (93) 310 2580. Open: Monday–Saturday 11am–1pm. Cathedral treasures.

Museu Picasso, Carrer de Montcada, 15–19, tel: (93) 319 6310. Open: Tuesday–Saturday and public holidays 10am–8pm, Sunday 10am–3pm. Essential on any itinerary of Barcelona's museums. The museum has an absorbing collection of Picasso's early work, his sketches in school books, a masterly portrait of his mother accomplished when he was 16, his early days in Barcelona and Paris, but it is limited on the later periods apart from the series *Las Meninas*. Housed in the magnificent Gothic palaces of Berenguer Aguilar, and the barons Castellet and Meca, this museum is the answer to the clichéd "My three-year-old could do that!". Unfortunately, it offers poor support in foreign languages; for details buy the catalogue in the bookshop, though the arrows and dates provide a chronological guide. Visit at lunch-time to avoid queues. Attractive cafeteria.

Museu Tèxtil i de la Indumentària, Carrer de Montcada 12–14, tel: (93) 310 4516. Open: Tuesday–Saturday and public holidays 10am–8pm, Sunday 10am–3pm. The Textile and Clothing Museum is housed in yet another elegant palace. It is worth visiting if you are interested in period costume, but limited on textiles and documentation. Occasional visiting exhibitions. Excellent shop with inspired gift ideas and pleasant café.

Museu d'Art Modern (MNAC), Parc de la Ciutadella, Plaça d'Armes, tel: (93) 319 5728. Open: Tuesday–Saturday 10am–7pm, Sunday 10am–2.30pm. This large collection of mostly Catalan 19th and 20th-century paintings, drawings sculpture and decorative art is currently in the former Ciutadella Palace, a perfect setting that makes a soothing excursion. Little really contemporary art, but a good collection of Fortuny, Nonell, Casas, Rusiñol and Sert from around the turn of the century. Worth visiting. Soon to be relocated to the Palau Nacional (MNAC) on Montjuïc.

Museu de Geologia, Parc de la Ciutadella, tel: (93) 319 6895. Open: Tuesday–Sunday 10am–2pm.

Museu de Zoologia, Parc de la Ciutadella, tel: (93) 319 6912. Open: Tuesday–Sunday 10am–2pm. Zoological collection well presented in this Domènech i Montaner building originally the restaurant in the 1888 universal exhibition.

Museu de la Ciència, Carrer de Teodor Roviralta, 55, tel: (93) 212 6050. Open: Tuesday–Sunday 10am–8pm. The Science Museum at the "top end" of Barcelona near Av. Tibidabo station, providing an opportunity to see another part of Barcelona. Funded by the benevolent and wealthy bank "la Caixa", it is a new generation science museum with fascinating hands-on exhibits, creative temporary exhibitions and a special area for 3–6 year olds. Guaranteed to entice the whole family.

Museu-Monestir de Pedralbes, Baixada Monestir, 9, tel: (93) 203 9282. Open: Tuesday–Sunday 10am–2pm. This is the perfect antidote to several days of intense living in the centre of Barcelona. The 14th century three-tiered cloisters of the Monastery of Pedralbes still occupied by Clarista nuns, are pure serenity. They contain some remarkable paintings by the Catalan Ferrer Bassa, a leading Italo-Gothic artist in the 14th-century. The museum, a glimpse into monastic life, makes the visit even more worthwhile.

Fundación Colección Thyssen-Bornemisza, housed in the Monastery of Pedralbes, it has the same opening hours. When the Baron donated part of his invaluable collection to Spain, this section was destined for Barcelona. It consists of 13th to 18th century Italian and German works. The greater part of the collection is kept in Madrid.

Museu de la Música, Diagonal, 373, tel: (93) 416 1157. Open: Tuesday–Sunday 10am–2pm, Wednesday 5–8pm (in winter). This collection of musical instruments from the 16th to the 20th centuries is housed in the modernist building "Casa Quadras" designed by Puig i Cadafalch, but destined to be re-housed in the new Auditorium (Glories).

Casa-Museu Gaudí, Park Güell, Carrer Olot, tel: (93) 284 6446. Open: October–April 10am–2pm and 4–7pm from May to September. Closed on Saturday. House within the park where Gaudí lived from 1905 to 1925, displaying furniture he designed, drawings and projects.

Museu Verdaguer, Vil.la Joana, Vallvidrera, tel: (93) 204 7805. Open: Tuesday–Sunday 10am–2pm. The Catalan poet Jacint Verdaguer lived and died here. The museum is a collection of his personal belongings. In the woods of the Collserola Park reached by FGC train to Baixador de Vallvidrera.

Palau Reial de Pedralbes, Diagonal, 686, tel: (93) 280 1621. Open: Tuesday–Sunday 10am–3pm. Often closed for official receptions, so check before visiting. Standing in elegant, spacious gardens, the palace was built in the 1920s for King Alfonso XIII. It contains the *Ceramic Museum*, Spanish pottery from the 12th–19th centuries and some contemporary work and the Museum of Decorative Arts.

Museu d'Art Contemporani de Barcelona, Plaça dels Angels, tel: (93) 412 08 10. Open: Tuesday to Friday noon–8pm, Saturday 10am–8pm, Sunday 10am–3pm. This new museum of contemporary art, designed by the American architect Richard Meier, houses a permanent collection of Catalan, Spanish and international work dating from the post-war period. There are temporary exhibitions and other activities, with special attention on photography, video and graphic work. The whole complex and its surrounding historical buildings make it an interesting new, cultural centre in Barcelona.

Fundació Tàpies, Aragó, 255, tel: (93) 487 0315. Open: Tuesday–Sunday 11am–8pm. A permanent collection of the work of Antoni Tàpies, Barcelona's most internationally renowned contemporary artist, housed in a Modernist building strikingly converted inside and out. Look out for the Tàpies sculpture on the roof. Interesting temporary exhibitions of contemporary artists.

Galeria Olímpica, (See under *Attractions*: Montjuïc)

Museu del Futbol Club Barcelona, FC Barcelona Stadium, tel: (93) 496 3608. Call to check opening times. For football fans of all ages, everything you could wish to know about Barça, including a view of the stadium from the president's box.

Exhibition Centres

The following centres regularly hold good temporary exhibitions of visual arts. Consult local press for details:

Centre d'Art Santa Monica, Rambla Sta. Monica, 7, tel: (93) 412 2279.

Centre de Cultura Contemporània de Barcelona (CCCB), Carrer Montalegre, 5, tel: (93) 412 0781. Seminars and a range of activities as well as exhibitions of contemporary art.

Centre Cultural de la Fundació "la Caixa", Passeig Sant Joan, 108, tel: (93) 458 8907.

Fundació Caixa de Catalunya in La Pedrera, Provença 261, tel: (93) 484 5979.

Palau de la Virreina, Rambla 99, tel: (93) 301 7775. Also cultural information centre.

Palau Robert, Passeig de Gràcia, 107. Also tourist information on Catalonia and a small, attractive public garden.

Art Galleries

Galleries tend to be congregated into specific areas of the city: the first is Passeig de Gràcia/Rambla de Catalunya and interconnecting streets (notably Consell de Cent); the second is the old town, classical around Plaça San Josep Oriol and contemporary near the Born and in El Raval district near the MACBA; and thirdly the streets behind Plaça Francesc Macià. Opening hours are usually 10.30am–1.30pm and 4.30–8.30pm Tuesday–Saturday.

Among the most interesting are:

Ambit, Consell de Cent, 282.

Carles Taché, Consell de Cent 290.

D Barcelona, Diagonal, 367.

Eude, Consell de Cent, 278.

Joan Prats, Rambla de Catalunya, 54.

Kreisler, Valencia, 262.

Subex, Mallorca, 253.

Carles Poy, Doctor Dou, 10.

Galeria 4RT, Boters, 4.

Maeght, Montcada, 25.

Metrònom, Fusina, 9.

Sala Pares, Petritxol, 5–8. The oldest gallery in Barcelona.

Sala Artur Ramon, Palla, 23.

Fernando Alcolea, Plaça Sant Gregori Taumaturg, 7.

Music

CLASSICAL MUSIC

A busy season of concerts by the Orquestra Sinfónica de Barcelona i Nacional de Catalunya (OBC) and visiting orchestras and soloists runs from September to early July, complemented by festivals such as the Festival de Música Antiga and various international music festivals outside Barcelona in July and August. Barcelona's different Arts Festivals also include classical music. Notable among the many festivals is one for 20th-century music in October and the Festival de Guitarra de Barcelona in April and May (Tel: 902 101 212). The main locations are:

Auditori Municipal, Pl.de les Arts, a

new, huge music auditorium being constructed in the Plaça de les Glories complex. Completed in 1998.

Centre Cultural de la Fundació "la Caixa", Passeig de Sant Joan, 108, tel: (93) 458 8907.

Palau de la Música Catalana, Carrer Sant Francesc de Paula, 2, tel: (93) 268 1000. If you have an opportunity to go to a concert in this extravagant Modernist concert hall by Domènech i Montaner, go – whatever the programme.

CONTEMPORARY MUSIC

Fundació Miró, Montjuïc, tel: (93) 329 1908. The gallery hosts a season of 20th-century music, with particular emphasis on Catalan composers.

Nick Havanna, Rosselló, 208, tel: 2(93) 215 6591. Known more for late night drinking, this trendy bar also holds a season of 20th-century music.

CCCB, Montalegre, tel: (93) 412 0781.

JAZZ

The Terrassa Jazz Festival in the spring and the Barcelona International Jazz Festival in the autumn gather together some leading names. In addition there are regular jazz and blues sessions in an ever-increasing number of venues. To name a few:

Barcelona Pipa Club, Plaça Reial, 3.

Bikini, Deu i Mata, 105, plus other music.

Harlem Jazz Club, Carrer de Comtessa de Sobradiel, 8.

Jamboree Jazz and Dance Club, Plaça Reial, 17.

Jazz Matazz, Passatge Domingo.

La Boite Mas í Mas, Diagonal, 477.

La Cova del Drac, Vallmajor, 33.

ROCK/POP

Barcelona is now on the itinerary of most major international tours. Booking for these is usually through banks and music shops, notably in Carrer de Tallers, just off the Ramblas. On a smaller scale, some interesting offbeat musicians and eternal old timers often pass through. Check the listings. Some key venues:

Garatge Club, Pallars, 195.

Otto Zutz, Lincoln, 15

Sala Apolo, Nou de la Rambla, 113.

Tarantos, Plaça Reial. Specialises in flamenco.

Zeleste, Carrer d'Almogàvers, 122.

SALSA
Antilla Cosmopolitan, Muntaner, 244.

CELTIC
Irish pubs are multiplying and nearly all have live music sessions. Check the local listings.

OPERA & BALLET
The Gran Teatre del Liceu, Barcelona's opera house, is scheduled to re-open in 1999 after its devastating fire. Meanwhile a reduced programme of opera in concert form and ballet is taking place in other venues, such as the Palau Sant Jordi, the Teatre Victòria and the Palau de la Música Catalana.
Gran Teatre del Liceu, Rambla, 61, tel: (93) 485 9913/902 332 211 (tickets).

CONTEMPORARY DANCE
The Barcelona Contemporary Ballet has a short season, supplemented throughout the year by visiting groups. Dance is an important part of the Mercat de les Flors programme. Also at Teatre de l'Institut, Carrer de Sant Pere Més Baix 7, tel: (93) 268 2078 and L'Espai, Trav. de Gràcia, 63, tel: (93) 414 3133.

Theatres
Catalonia has a long tradition of theatrical talent from Margarita Xirgu, actress and Lorca's collaborator, to Nuria Espert, internationally renowned for her performances and directing. Outstanding amongst contemporary talent are Josep Maria Flotats and the refreshingly satirical Albert Boadellas with his brilliant company Els Joglars. The notorious La Fura dels Baus is an avant-garde company who can make theatre-going an uncomfortable but worthwhile experience. On a lighter level, and sometimes to be found in the streets of Barcelona, are La Cubana – satirical and fun. Naturally productions are in Catalan, but for true enthusiasts the theatrical experience should compensate for language problems. Occasionally some Spanish theatre is performed. The main theatres are:
Malic, Carrer de Fussina, 3, tel: (93) 310 7035. Predominantly a puppet theatre: a tiny space that holds grand productions.
Mercat de les Flors, Carrer de Lleida, 59, tel: (93) 318 8599. This is the

former flower market converted into two theatrical areas. Its dome was painted by Miquel Barceló. It has a very active programme with many visiting groups and unusual productions.
Poliorama, Rambla, 115, tel: (93) 318 8181.
Romea, Carrer de Hospital, 51, tel: (93) 310 5504.
Teatre Lliure, Carrer de Montseny, 47, tel: (93) 218 9251. Good contemporary productions from the theatre's own company.
Teatre Nacional de Catalunya, Plaça de les Arts, tel: (93) 246 0041. Located next to the new auditorium near Plaça de les Glories, Catalonia's National Theatre's programme seems constantly overshadowed by political wranglings.

Movies
Barcelona has a great cinema-going tradition. Thanks to an increasing number of cinemas which specialise in "*version original*" (VO in the daily listings) foreign films that have not been dubbed are widely available. The main ones are listed. Most sessions begin around 4pm and the last and most popular one is around 10.30pm, with some late-night shows at weekends.
Alexis, Rambla de Catalunya, 90.
Arkadin, Travessera de Gràcia, 103. (Tiny, get there early.)
Casablanca, Passeig de Gràcia, 115.
Icària-Yelmo, Salvador Espriu, 61. 15 screens.
Maldà, Carrer del Pi, 5.
Renoir-Les Corts, Eugeni d'Ors, 12. 6 screens.
Rex, Gran Vía, 463.
Verdi, Carrer de Verdi, 32. (Nine screens. Always has something interesting.)
The Filmoteca de la Generalitat de Catalunya in Av.Sarrià, 33, is a film theatre showing less commercial films and retrospectives.

Festivals
The Grec Festival, held from late June until early August, the Grec is Barcelona's summer festival, bringing together a high standard of national and international talent in theatre, music and dance. Performances take place all over the city, but one of the most impressive and appealing venues on a summer night is the Grec Theatre itself on Montjuïc: an outdoor amphitheatre.

For information and booking: Palau de la Virreina, Rambla, 99, tel: (93) 301 7775 or the city council information service, tel: 010.
The **Sitges Festival Internacional de Cinema de Catalunya** is a well established annual event every October, tel: (93) 415 3938.

Nightlife
The first thing to understand about nightlife in Barcelona is that night means night, and nothing really gets going until after 1am. For an authentic Barcelona night out, start to think about cocktails around 9pm and dinner, at a leisurely pace, from 10-ish. This way you will be all set to begin the *juerga* (fun/wild time) by 1am with enough energy to keep going until at least 4 in the morning. Then it's time to think about going to an "Afters" bar (until past breakfast time). This demanding schedule is usually practised from Thursday to Saturday – though the hardy are out playing any day of the week and still miraculously make it to their offices at 9am.

Bars
Of the trendy bars which are regularly featured in international design magazines, the "in" place changes every few months when yet another one opens and becomes the bar where anybody who thinks they are anybody goes. Some are just for drinking and socialising (and being seen) and some are for drinking and dancing (and being seen). This selection is loosely divided into pre-dinner and post-dinner bars, the former including some classics which never go out of fashion and those which are pleasant at any time of day; the latter includes discos and bars which only open from 8pm at the earliest.

PRE-DINNER BARS
Bar Pastis, Carrer de Santa Mònica, 4. More than 40 years old this small corner of Marseilles at the bottom of the Ramblas offering *pastis* to the strains of Brel and Piaf, is a welcome alternative to the high design and high tech of bars elsewhere.
Berimbau, Passeig del Born, 17. Brazilian bar with stunning *caipirinhas* – the Brazilian cocktail you will never forget.

Boadas, Carrer de Tallers, 1. A classic Barcelona cocktail bar. The cartooned figure of the original owner watches from highly polished walls while his elegant daughter mixes the snappiest Martinis and her waiters attend your every need. Their *mojito*, Hemingway's Cuban favourite, is highly recommended.

Café del Sol, Plaça del Sol. Terrace on the square. A good start to an evening in the Gràcia district, with its many alternative bars and restaurants.

Dry Martini, Carrer d'Aribau, 162. A sophisticated cocktail bar that serves excellent Martinis to a middle-class clientele.

Gimlet, Carrer de Santaló, 46. Slick, modern design. Good for post-dinner.

Mirablau, at the foot of the Tibidabo funicular, with a spectacular view over Barcelona day and night.

Snooker Club, Carrer de Roger de Lluria, 42. Elegant, modern snooker club for a cool cocktail or an after-dinner drink.

Velódrom, Carrer de Muntaner, 213. An old bar in the middle of the Eixample with high, nicotine-stained ceilings, peeling paint and fluorescent lighting, but which never loses its charm or popularity.

There is also a plethora of popular bars on the Moll de la Fusta, the Port Vell, Maremagnum and the Olympic Port, many with music. Ideal for post-dinner, too.

PUBS

Having great success amongst ex-pats and Catalans alike is the new wave of pubs, which are a far cry from the old clichéd "English Pub" of the past, and much more authentic. For example:

The Clansman, Vigatans, 13. Scottish pub with the malts to prove it.

Flann O'Brien's, Casanova, 264. An Irish pub, of course.

The Quiet Man, Marquès de Barberà, 11. An Irish pub selling draught Guinness. Good atmosphere. Live music.

POST-DINNER

La Fira, Carrer de Provença, 171. Fun bar with the atmosphere and bustle of the fairground; fascinating old automatons on display.

Nick Havanna, Carrer de Rosselló, 208. Famed for its design and in-crowd. Several years on and still a leader.

Satanassa, Carrer d'Aribau, 27. One of the wildest.

Torres de Avila, Poble Espanyol. An extravaganza created by designers Arribas and Mariscal (of Olympic mascot fame), which is an expensive place to drink, but well worth one visit to check out Barcelona '90s design at its zenith.

Universal, Carrer de Marià Cubí, 184. Striking decor on three floors. An essential stop on the nocturnal tour.

Velvet, Carrer de Balmes, 161.

Discos

Check with the local press because they change from month to month, but some classics that remain are:

Distrito Distinto, Avinguda Meridiana, 104.

Fibra Optica, Beethoven, 9.

Karma, Plaça Reial, 10. A real crush of a disco.

KGB, Carrer d'Alegre de Dalt, 55.

Up & Down, Carrer de Numancia, 179. One of the most famous nightspots of Barcelona, its members are somewhere between the jet set and *Dallas*. With the required amount of lip-gloss or jewellery you'll pass. Sevillanas on Wednesday.

Otto Zutz, Carrer de Lincoln, 15. One of the first designer-discos. Best after 2am. Live music occasionally.

Tablaos

A "Tablao" is a bar/restaurant that has a flamenco show. Strictly not Catalan, though recently this import from Andalusia has become popular among Catalans to the point of being trendy. It is advisable beforehand to confirm the times of the shows and whether dinner is obligatory or not.

El Patio Andaluz, Carrer d'Aribau, 242, tel: (93) 209 3378.

El Tablao de Carmen, Poble Espanyol, tel: (93) 325 6895. A good authentic show and reasonable dinner.

Los Tarantos, Plaça Reial, 17, tel: (93) 318 3067. Stylishly refurbished. Good shows.

Music Halls/Cabarets

Barcelona has a long and colourful tradition of show business, centred on the area known as the Paral.lel. The shows, the surrounding bars, the characters involved, all provide a sharp contrast to the high design and yuppiedom of the Eixample and upper parts of town. Sadly, with reducing demand, theatres are in decline; the most famous, **El Molino**, has been forced to shut. However, for a global view of Barcelona check in listings what's on and try a show. An alternative is:

Bodega Bohemia, Carrer de Lancaster, 2, tel: 302 5081. Unique, one of Barcelona's treasures. Retired cabaret artistes entertain the audience and themselves.

Dance Halls

Cibeles, Córsega, 363.

La Paloma, Carrer de Tigre, 27, tel: (93) 301 6897. Another Barcelona classic. Orchestra Thursday–Sunday. Sessions 6–9.30pm and 11.30pm–3.30am.

Sala Apolo, Carrer Nou de la Rambla, 113, tel: (93) 441 4001. Open: weekends until daylight.

Casinos

Casino Castell de Perelada, Perelada, tel: (972) 53 8125. In the province of Girona, only 13 miles (20 km) from the French border.

Gran Casino de Barcelona, Sant Pere de Ribes, tel: (93) 893 3666. About 30 miles (42 km) out of Barcelona in the hills behind Sitges.

The Gay Scene

The gay scene is low-key, though reasonably thriving in Barcelona. It is discreet rather than ostentatious, but well tolerated. Nearby Sitges (half an hour south of the city on the coast) is a real mecca for gays, particularly in the summer months and well worth a visit. The drag parade during Carnival in February is renowned.

For advice and information on the latest venues, any of the following are really friendly and helpful:

Casal Lambda, Ample 5. From 7pm onwards. A cultural centre.

Coordinadora d'Iniciatives Gais, Carolinas 13, tel: (93) 237 0869.

Info Gai, La Paloma, 12, tel: (93) 318 1666.

Sextienda, Rauric 11, tel: (93) 318 8676.

Also worth a try is:

Metro, Sepúlveda 185, is latest bar/disco, for men and women. Best after 1.30am.

Shopping

If you can't face trudging home with virgin olive oil, or fear your holiday budget will disappear if you venture into leather at Loewe, it is still worth seeing the spectacle of the food markets and doing some serious window shopping while in Barcelona.

Shopping Areas

Apart from the specific areas mentioned, in the section "What To Buy", the entire length of Passeig de Gràcia and Rambla de Catalunya and the interconnecting streets provide enjoyable shopping, as does the barri Gòtic, and the Avinguda Diagonal, from the top of Rambla de Catalunya up to the roundabout which forms Plaça Francesc Macià (still often referred to as Calvo Sotelo). The streets behind this Plaça, Pau Casals, Mestre Nicolau and Bori i Fontesta are good for fashion, but expensive.

The upper parts of town have their own local district atmosphere and make a refreshing change from the Eixample and barri Gòtic. Try Carrer de Muntaner, around its Metro station and upwards: interesting shops and bars, one of the best shoe shops in town, Las Maravillas (No. 356), and good wines by the glass to accompany delicate snacks in the Tivoli (No. 361).

The largest department store in Barcelona is El Corte Inglés, with a huge branch in Plaça de Catalunya and others in Avinguda Diagonal and Portal de l'Angel. Open: Monday–Saturday 10am–9.30pm.

Main shopping malls:

Bulevard Rosa (3 locations), Passeig de Gràcia, 55; Diagonal, 474; Diagonal, 609-615.

El Triangle. A large development in Plaça Catalunya which caused the demise of the famous Zurich café-bar. Due open late 1998.

Galeries Maldà, Carrer de Portaferrissa, 22.

La Avenida, Rambla de Catalunya, 121.

Useful for its opening hours, including Sunday, is:

VIP'S, Rambla de Catalunya, 7. Open 9am–1.30am and until 3am on Friday and Saturday.

There has been an epidemic of vast shopping centres recently; on the whole soulless but useful, with branches of the main chains. The main ones within the city are:

Barcelona Glòries, Plaça de les Glòries. Probably the largest in Catalonia, complete with hypermarket.

L'Illa, Av.Diagonal, 545. Its claim to fame is Barcelona's first Marks & Spencer and **FNAC** (books and discs).

Shopping Hours

Most shops open between 9 and 10am and close religiously for lunch between 1 and 2pm, opening again between 4 and 5pm until 8pm. Many clothes and food shops close at 8.30 or 9pm. The large department stores and some of the shopping galleries remain open through lunch-time. In the summer many shops will close on Saturday afternoons. A new system of late-opening on Thursdays (10pm) is to be introduced in 1998.

Markets

There are covered markets in every district of the city selling fruit, vegetables, meat and fish. A trip to Barcelona would be incomplete without visiting at least one of them. Markets open every day except Sunday from early in the morning until around 3pm. Avoid Mondays; the selection is poor because the central wholesale market does not open on a Monday.

The largest and most colourful market is the Boqueria on the Ramblas, which stays open until 8pm Monday–Saturday. The most exotic and expensive fare is in the entrance; the bargains are to be found exploring the maze of stalls behind.

Book and Antique Fairs are held with great regularity in Barcelona: look out for posters or announcements in the press.

Coin, video games and book market, Mercat Sant Antoni. Sunday 9am–2pm. Attractive market building on the junction of Carrer de Tamarit/Comte d'Urgell.

Coin and stamp market, Plaça Reial. Sunday 9am–2.30pm.

Els Encants, Plaça de les Glòries. A genuine flea market. Some expensive antiques, some old clothes, and a lot of trash, but in among it all bargains can still be found. Very hot in the summer; early morning is better for bargains and comfort. Open: Monday, Wednesday, Friday and Saturday 8am–7pm (winter) and until 8pm (summer).

Mercat de Concepció (on Carrer de Valencia, between Carrer de Bruc and Carrer de Girona) is worth a visit: a fine example of a district market, recently renovated as Barcelona knows best – mixing new design with old.

Mercat Gòtic d'Antiguitats, Av. Catedral. Antique market every Thursday. Some interesting collections.

Moll de Drassanes. Weekend antiques market, by the sea.

What To Buy

As Europe rapidly becomes one entity and most goods are available in most countries, the bargain which cannot be found back home is a rarity. However, in certain products the choice is much wider and anything bought abroad always has good sentimental value once the holiday is over.

Leather. It is questionable whether leather garments are still worth buying in Spain, except perhaps at the top end of the market, where design and quality are outstanding. But shoes, handbags and suitcases are worth considering. The best in clothes, bags and accessories is Loewe; its shop in Casa Lleó Morera (Passeig de Gràcia, 35) is an experience in itself. There are many cheaper shops specialising in leather, particularly in and around the Ramblas and Portal de l'Angel, where you can also find shops in strange first-floor surroundings selling at factory prices; here there are bargains if you are not too worried about style.

Shoes are good value. Look out for Catalan and Spanish designers such as Yanko, Farrutx (sophisticated elegance), Lotusse (contemporary classical and very well made), Camper (trendy). The best areas for shoes and bags are Portal de l'Angel, Rambla de Catalunya, Passeig de Gràcia, Diagonal and the shopping malls.

Fashion. If you can afford the investment, a snappy little outfit from one of the latest Catalan or Spanish designers will set you aside from the crowd. Choose from Toni Miró (his shops called "Groc" are in Rambla de Catalunya, Carrer de Muntaner and Carrer Consell de Cent), Adolfo Dominguez (Passeig de Gràcia), Roser Mercé, Purificación Garcia, Jordi Cuesta, Sybilla, Joan Tomas, David Valls. For the best selection of designer labels (Spanish and International) visit the small, friendly shop Jean Pierre Bua, Av. Diagonal 469.

Lesser known designers at more approachable prices can be found in boutiques in the malls, and around Passeig de Gràcia, Rambla de Catalunya, etc. For cheap and cheerful clothes and accessories try Carrer de Portaferrisa and adjoining streets, including the malls. Gralla Hall in Portaferrisa has boutiques with more off-beat, individual designs.

Design. Much of Barcelona's current image rests upon its fame in design. To have an idea of how trendy Barcelonans decorate their homes, don't miss Vinçon (Passeig de Gràcia, 96), especially its first floor. Or Pilma, just around the corner in Avinguda Diagonal. On a smaller scale, Dos i Una (Carrer de Rosselló, 275) has David Valls socks, Mariscal earrings and gimmicks to help solve gift problems. Dom (Passeig de Gràcia and Petritxol) has inexpensive fun design.

TRADITIONAL CRAFTS

Many traditional crafts still exist in Barcelona, as do the small shops specialising in them. Whether you are looking for lace, embroidery, feathers, fans, gloves, hats, musical instruments, glass, religious artefacts, or whether you want to commission a guitar, walking stick, glass eye or lightning conductor, you can be sure that somewhere in Barcelona there is someone who specialises in it, particularly in the *barri* Gòtic, around the Born or on the streets Hospital and Carme. Most of these establishments are over 100 years old.

Alpargatas. These are the classic rope-soled canvas shoes (espadrilles). For an infinite variety of design, colour, size and to see them being made, go to La Manual Alpargetera, just off Carrer de Ferran (Carrer d'Avinyó, 7).

For really original footwear, sturdy leather boots, Mallorcan sandals or rustic shoes from different regions in Spain, visit Calzados E.Solé (Carrer d'Ample, 7).

Antiques and books. There are many elegant and expensive antique shops in the Eixample and the *barri* Gòtic, notably the streets Banys Nous and Palla. Prints and antique books are also a feature of Barcelona, particularly in the labyrinth of pretty streets around the Cathedral: visit

Librería Violán just off the Plaça del Rei for its unusual books, prints and striking Deco Posters.

Candles. From religious to decorative, candles are quite a speciality of Barcelona. Visit the shops near the cathedral, especially Cereria Subirá (Baixada Llibreteria, 7) founded in 1762.

Ceramics, from earthenware cooking pots to elegant dishes or hand-painted tiles, the ceramics of Catalonia and other regions of Spain can be found all over the city, particularly in the *barri* Gòtic, at Molsa in Plaça Sant Josep Oriol (who also have some antique pots), La Caixa de Fang in Freneria and La Roda in Carrer de Call. Traditional ironmongers usually have a good collection of the classic brown-earthenware pots at non-tourist prices, as well as wonderful cooking utensils.

Lladró porcelain remains popular and collectable. Several shops specialise in it and will dispatch abroad. Garciá (La Rambla, 4) boasts of a large collection at near factory prices. Department stores also stock Lladró.

Food and drink. A taste of Spain back home always extends the holiday. Olives marinated in garlic direct from the market, sausages (*chorizo*, *sobrasada*), ham (*jamon serrano* is the best), cheese (Manchego, Mahon, Idiazabal), nuts, dried fruit, handmade chocolates, are all easy to carry. Virgin olive oil, wine, *cava*, and moscatel are less portable, but probably worth the effort. Buy from the markets or *colmados* (grocer's shops, on street corners in every district of the city).

Specialists in *turrón* (sticky nougat-type delicacy eaten mostly at Christmas) are Planelles Donat in Portal de l'Angel and Cucurulla. For chocolates try Fargas, a decorative old shop (corner of Carrer del Pi and Cucurulla) or the famous chocolate "sculptor" Antoni Escribà who has a beautiful Modernist shop on La Rambla, 83.

Serious purchasers of *cava* should visit Xampany (Carrer de Valencia, 200), an attractive shop brimming over with more than 100 different types of *cava*, essential accessories and memorabilia.

Wickerwork. A rustic chair may not be very manageable on a charter flight, but baskets, mats etc. are easy to carry and are appreciated as presents. There is a wide choice on

the corner of Carrer de Banys Nous and Carrer Ave Maria.

EXPORT PROCEDURES

Under current laws anyone resident outside the European Union is exempt from IVA (Value Added Tax) on individual purchases worth more that 15,000 pesetas. The IVA rate is 6 or 16 percent, according to the goods. The relevant forms to fill in for Customs on leaving and on entering one's own country will be provided by the store. Ask for details at the time of purchase. Note that the goods may be subjected to an even higher tax on return home. Large stores such as El Corte Inglés have a packing/despatch service.

Sports

The city council has been very active in providing sports facilities to the community. Some are the legacy of the Olympic Games.

Can Caralleu, Carrer Esports, s/n. tel: (93) 204 6905. (Bus 94 from Tres Torres/Via Augusta). A sports centre in a pretty location on the hill of Tibidabo which offers tennis courts, fronton, volley ball and two swimming pools. Indoor facilities: open to public Monday–Friday 8–10am and 2–3.30pm, Sunday 10am–1pm. Outdoor facilities open: mid-June to mid-September 10am–5pm. Tennis courts available from 8am–11pm.

Participant Sports

BOWLING

AMFF, Carrer de Sabino de Arana, 6, tel: (93) 330 5048. Open: 11am–2am Monday–Saturday.

Pedralbes Bowling, Avinguda Doctor Marañón, 11, tel: (93) 333 0352. Open: 10am–2am, and until 4am on Friday/Saturday.

CYCLING

Cycling is becoming more popular in Barcelona, backed by the City Council which issues a guide/map. Available in tourist offices it shows suggested routes and bike lanes, and advises on taking bicycles on public transport etc.

Barcelona by Bicycle, tel: (93) 268 2105. Accompanied cycling tours of the Old Town, including a meal.

Bicitram, Passeig de Picasso, tel: (93) 792 2841. Bicycles, tandems, and

child seats for rent, near Parc de la Ciutadella. Open: weekends and holidays 10am–dusk. Easy access to park, port, beach at Barcelona.
Also in Olympic Village: Avinguda Icaria, 180.

GOLF

Many new courses are being built all over Catalonia. To play it is essential to prove membership of a recognised club: weekend fees are usually double the weekday fee. For the moment three courses within easy reach of Barcelona are:
Sant Cugat, Sant Cugat del Vallès, tel: (93) 674 3908. Bar, restaurant, swimming pool. Hire of clubs and trolleys. Closed: Monday.
Terramar, Sitges, tel: (93) 894 0580. Hire of clubs and trolleys. Open all year.
El Prat, El Prat de Llobregat, tel: (93) 379 0278. A premier course, often host to international competitions. Hire of clubs and trolleys.

HORSE RIDING

El Ecuestre, Carrer de Ciutat de Balaguer, 68, tel: (93) 417 3039. Saturday and Sunday: individual classes, and two-hour excursions on Tibidabo.
Hípica Sant Cugat, Finca La Palleria, Av. Corts Catalanes, Sant Cugat, tel: (93) 674 0006. Bus from Sant Cugat to Cerdanyola will drop you off. Excursions from one hour to the whole day in the Collserola hills.

SKIING

During the season many cheap weekend excursions are available in the Pyrenean resorts, with transport from Barcelona. Most travel agencies have information.

SWIMMING POOLS

Banys Sant Sebastià, Plaça del Mar, tel: (93) 221 0010. Large indoor pool overlooking sea and outdoor pool. Well equipped.
Parc de la Creueta del Coll, Mare de Deu del Coll, 87, tel: (93) 211 3599. Large outdoor pool/lake, in one of Barcelona's new urban parks complete with Eduardo Chillida sculpture. Boats can be hired in the winter. Swimming: June to end of August Monday–Friday 10am–4pm, Sunday and holidays 10am–7pm. Ideal for small children.
Piscinas Bernat Picornell, Av.de

l'Estadi, 30–40, tel: (93) 423 4041. Renovated for the Games. Now open to the public.
Piscina Municipal Can Felipa, Pallars, 277, tel: (93) 308 6047. Two indoor pools in a stylishly renovated old factory, now a community centre in Poble Nou. Easy to reach by metro.
Piscina Municipal Montjuïc, Av. Miramar, 31, tel: (93) 443 0046. Two pools with a view. The Olympic diving events took place here, against the dramatic backdrop of the city.

TENNIS

Vall Parc, Ctra. de l'Arrabassada, 97, tel: (93) 212 6789. Courts open: 8am–midnight. Quite expensive.

Spectator Sports

Check the weekly entertainment guides or the daily sports magazines, *Sport* and *El Mundo Deportivo*, for a full calendar. The daily papers also have good sports coverage.
Most local fiestas have various sporting activities as part of their programme, notably the Barcelona fiesta of La Mercé at the end of September.

BASKETBALL

Basketball is gaining as ardent a following as football. The "Barça" basketball team is part of the Fùtbol Club and matches are played in the Palau Blaugrana, next to Nou Camp, tel: (93) 496 3600.

FOOTBALL

When the favourite local team "Barça" is playing you will know all about it: firstly from the traffic jams to get to the match or to the television, secondly because the town goes silent, and thirdly thanks to the explosion of fireworks, car horns and bugles following a victory.
Fútbol Club Barcelona, Carrer Arístides Maillol, tel: (93) 496 3600. The stadium, Nou Camp, is the second largest stadium in the world, and can be visited. See *Museums*. To attend a match, *see "More than Just Football"*.

MOTOR RACING

A new racing track, Catalunya Circuit, was opened in 1991 about 20 km from Barcelona in Montmeló. For information tel: (93) 571 9777.

TENNIS

The Conde de Godó trophy is an annual event at the Real Club de Tenis Barcelona, Carrer de Bosch i Gimpera, 5, tel: (93) 203 7852.

Language
Catalan

Castilian (Spanish) and Catalan are both official languages in Catalonia. In the wake of the repression of Catalan under Franco, when its use in public was forbidden, it is undergoing a resurgence encouraged by the administration, with the aim of fully implementing it in every aspect of daily life. It dominates public signs, street names, maps, leaflets and cultural information.
Catalan is a Romance language; with a knowledge of French and Spanish you should find it possible to read a little. It is spoken in Catalonia, Valencia, the Balearic Islands, Andorra, the Catalan region of Southern France and L'Alguer, a town in Sardinia.
In the rural regions outside Barcelona you may come across Catalans who cannot speak Castilian, but in the city even the most ardent Catalanista should readily respond if you communicate in Castilian, especially knowing you are a foreigner. Also many people you meet in bars, restaurants and public transport will be from other parts of Spain and so will be primarily Castilian speakers.
If you want to win a Catalan's heart, however, here are a few expressions in Catalan:
Good morning – *Bon dia*
Good afternoon/evening – *Bona tarda*
Good night – *Bona nit*
How are you? – *Com està vostè?*
Very well thank you, and you? – *Molt bé, gràcies i vostè?*
Goodbye, see you again – *Adéu, a reveure*
See you later – *Fins després*
See you tomorrow – *Fins demà*
What's your name? – *Com us diu*?
My name is... – *Em dic...*

Pleased to meet you – *Molt de gust*
Do you have any rooms? – *Per favor tenen habitacions lliures?*
I'd like an external/internal/double room – *Voldria una habitaci exterior/ interior/doble*
...for one/two persons – *...per a una persona/dues persones*
I want a room with a bath – *Vull una habitació amb bany*
I have a room reserved in the name of... – *Tinc reservada una habitació a nom de...*
How much is it? – *Quin és el preu?*
It's expensive – *Es car*
Could I see the room? – *Podria veure l'habitació?*
At what time do you serve? – *A quina hora es pot?*
Breakfast/lunch/dinner – *esmorzar/ dinar/sopar*
How do you say that in Catalan? – *Com es diu això en català?*
Speak a little more slowly, please – *Parleu una mica més a poc, si us plau*
How do I get to...? – *Per a anar a...?*
Is it very far/close? – *Es lluny/a prop?*
Where's the nearest motor mechanic? – *On és el pròxim taller de reparació?*
Can I change this traveller's cheque? – *Pot canviar-me aquest xec de viatge?*
Where can I find a dentist? – *On puc trobar un dentista?*
This tooth is hurting – *Em fa mal aquesta dent*
Don't take it out. If possible give me something for it until I get home – *No me l'extregui. Si és possible doni'm un remei fins que torni a casa*
Please call a doctor – *Cridi un metge, per favor*
Where does it hurt? – *On li fa mal?*
I have a bad cold – *Estic molt refredat*
I want to make a phone call to... – *Vull telefonar a...*
It's engaged – *La línea está ocupada*
I am... I'd like to speak to Mr... – *Sóc... voldria parlar amb el senyor...*
What time will he be back? – *A quina hora tornarà?*
Tell him to call me at this number – *Digui-li que truqui al número...*
I'll be in town until Saturday – *Seré a la ciutat fins dissabte*

Further Reading

Good Companions

Translated Catalan works of literature are few; they are difficult to find in Barcelona and are probably more available in languages other than English.
Barcelona, Robert Hughes, Penguin.
Barcelona: a thousand years of the city's past, by Felipe Fernandez-Armesto
Catalan Cuisine, Coleman Andrews, Headline
Forbidden Territory, by Juan Goytisolo, Quartet Books
Homage to Barcelona, by Colm Toíbín, Simon & Schuster
La Ciudad de los Prodigios, Eduardo Mendoza.

Other Insight Guides

The 190-title Insight Guides series includes eight books on Spain and its islands, all combining the exciting pictures and incisive text associated with this series.

Insight Guide: Spain is an award-winning title in the series, containing top photography and providing complete background reading to the country.

Insight Guide: Madrid provides an insider's view of a city with a history full of colourful characters. The writers and photographers show you how to make the most of this dynamic destination, where life is lived to the full.

Insight Guide: Catalonia provides provides comprehensive coverage of this alluring region, ranging from the excitements of Barcelona to the peace of timeless fishing villages, from Romanesque churches to rare wildlife.

Insight Pocket Guies

Madrid and *Barcelona* are both covered in the complementary 120-title Insight Pocket Guide series. These books, which are specifically written for short-stay visitors, provide a series of carefully timed itineraries designed to help you get the most out of a short visit. Other titles in this series include *Costa Brava*, *Costa Blanca* and *Costa del Sol*.

Insight Compact Guides

Compact Guide: Barcelona, one of the titles in Apa Publications' third series of books, is the ultimate "portable encyclopedia" to the city. Up-to-date and packed with facts and photographs, it is the ideal easy-reference book to keep in your pocket or handbag.

Index

A
B
C
D
E
F
G
H
J
a
b
c
d
e
g
h
i
j
k
l

The Insight Approach

The book you are holding is part of the world's largest range of guidebooks. Its purpose is to help you have the most valuable travel experience possible, and we try to achieve this by providing not only information about countries, regions and cities but also genuine insight into their history, culture, institutions and people.

Since the first Insight Guide – to Bali – was published in 1970, the series has been dedicated to the proposition that, with insight into a country's people and culture, visitors can both enhance their own experience and be accepted more easily by their hosts. Now, in a world where ethnic hostilities and nationalist conflicts are all too common, such attempts to increase understanding between peoples are more important than ever.

Insight Guides:
Essentials for understanding
Because a nation's past holds the key to its present, each Insight Guide kicks off with lively history chapters. These are followed by magazine-style essays on culture and daily life. This essential background information gives readers the necessary context for using the main Places section, with its comprehensive run-down on things worth seeing and doing. Finally, a listings section contains all the information you'll need on travel, hotels, restaurants and opening times.

As far as possible, we rely on local writers and specialists to ensure that the information is authoritative. The pictures, for which Insight Guides have become so celebrated, are just as important. Our photojournalistic approach aims not only to illustrate a destination but also to communicate visually and directly to readers life as it is lived by the locals.

Compact Guides
The "great little guides"
As invaluable as such background information is, it isn't always fun to carry an Insight Guide through a crowded souk or up a church tower. Could we, readers asked, distil the key reference material into a slim volume for on-the-spot use?

Our response was to design Compact Guides as an entirely new series, with original text carefully cross-referenced to detailed maps and more than 200 photographs. In essence, they're miniature encyclopedias, concise and comprehensive, displaying reliable and up-to-date information in an accessible way.

Pocket Guides:
A local host in book form
However wide-ranging the information in a book, human beings still value the personal touch. Our editors are often asked the same questions. Where do *you* go to eat? What do *you* think is the best beach? What would you recommend if I have only three days? We invited our local correspondents to act as "substitute hosts" by revealing their preferred walks and trips, listing the restaurants they go to and structuring a visit into a series of timed itineraries.

The result is our Pocket Guides, complete with full-size fold-out maps. These 100-plus titles help readers plan a trip precisely, particularly if their time is short.

Exploring with Insight:
A valuable travel experience
In conjunction with co-publishers all over the world, we print in up to 10 languages, from German to Chinese, from Danish to Russian. But our aim remains simple: to enhance your travel experience by combining our expertise in guidebook publishing with the on-the-spot knowledge of our correspondents.